Management for Professionals

The Springer series *Management for Professionals* comprises high-level business and management books for executives. The authors are experienced business professionals and renowned professors who combine scientific background, best practice, and entrepreneurial vision to provide powerful insights into how to achieve business excellence.

More information about this series at http://www.springer.com/series/10101

Stefan H. Vieweg

Editor

AI for the Good

Artificial Intelligence and Ethics

 Springer

Editor
Stefan H. Vieweg
Institute for Compliance and Corporate
Governance
RFH - University of Applied Sciences
Cologne
Cologne, Germany

ISSN 2192-8096   ISSN 2192-810X   (electronic)
Management for Professionals
ISBN 978-3-030-66912-6   ISBN 978-3-030-66913-3   (eBook)
https://doi.org/10.1007/978-3-030-66913-3

*For humans who dare to shape future
at its best.*

Preface

There is already a comprehensive amount of specific literature available on ethical issues of the world, as is on digitization and modern technologies such as artificial intelligence ("AI"). While this is true, we are at the crossroads of how factually uncontrollable technology can be used in a useful and societal comparable way. This leads directly to the fact that a society must find a reflective way of dealing with this technology and thus also has to relocate ethical standards, because AI has enormous potential—both in a socially good and destructive sense.

The following basic considerations can serve as orientation:

1. The human being is a social being and needs exchange; therefore, ethics are needed that summarize the social conventions, even if they differ in time and place, and provide orientation and support.
2. Digitization is currently changing our world massively, and with it the way we interact with each other. AI is one integral part and probably not obvious to everyone. Some applications such as service robots for people in need of help may quickly raise ethical issues—despite major technical AI insufficiencies (see 3. below)—such as the relationship of dependencies.
3. AI is a technology that has become enormously more powerful in technical terms (information processing speed and capacity) over the last few decades, thus opening new application possibilities. However, this progress is by no means at the cognitive level! Today's AI applications stagnate in fact in pattern recognition, i.e., all applications—even if they come along in different forms—can ultimately be traced back to pattern recognition, which either orientates itself on previous templates (e.g., speech recognition, facial recognition, text recognition, tracking of individuals, and chatbots) or tries to recognize new connections "unsupervised" (e.g., by specific deep learning ("DL") approaches). In this respect, AI can now recognize patterns and process information in repetitive processes much better than ever before and with impressive success: much better than humans could ever do (so-called weak AI). But AI has no soul, no desire, no emotions, and no values (for which it is worthwhile to use—out of—quite changeable—conviction) as we humans have. In this respect, a human-like so-called strong AI still seems to be a long way off from today's perspective.

4. General characteristics, which must be given, so that AI works well, are firstly suitable algorithms and secondly suitable data. Only in the combination of algorithm and data new insights can be gained. If one of the components is questionable, unsuitable, or even insufficient, the result can be disastrous, as real application examples have repeatedly shown (e.g., unintentional discrimination of applicants in an AI-based recruitment process (Amazon 2018) or AI-based photo categorization identifying a black person as a gorilla (Google 2015)).

5. AI—even if in a weak form—is already a fact today and it requires a reflective handling of this technology, since this technology has enormous innovative but also enormous destructive power. A sweeping demonization and rejection of this technology is just as out of place as a naive good faith that nothing negative will happen ("I have nothing to hide").

6. The social challenge that increasingly determines the way we live together in a globalized, fast-moving world that is also threatened by its own over-consumption of resources is that increasing complexity must remain manageable in a highly dynamic manner. Ethical understanding as a societal point of reference for "good" ("desirable") and "bad" ("intolerable") will certainly continue to adapt to digitization, as has always been the case. However, due to the acceleration in the digitized world, previous social-ethical correctives no longer work or work too late. What is needed is a new basic understanding of how to deal with the technical possibilities in society, and where the "no go areas" lie. A disinhibited exploitation of all technical possibilities will sooner or later lead to social and ecological collapse with hardly assessable and certainly mostly irreversible consequences. This new basic understanding should take into account the element of phenomenological evidence in order to support credibility and confidence in an AI-based decision that cannot be fully analyzed.

7. A competence is needed that enables the responsible use of the technology in order to make it usable in a socially positive sense.

8. Strengths and weaknesses of us humans and AI are complementary: where AI has very strong strengths (fast pattern recognition, detection of facts, and provision of evidence) humans tend to be limited. Here, AI can support humans in their inadequacies in order to help them make decisions that are sustainable for society. Used in a targeted manner, AI can be more of a blessing than a curse: in addition to technical optimizations, which ultimately all lead to efficient value creation and thus resource conservation. AI plays a special role in social and economic decision-making processes in order to keep the aforementioned complexity under control. In contrast to this, only humans in their great diversity are by far the only ones capable of making final decisions with their cognitive abilities, their socialization and permanent development and enormous adaptability (e.g., through the neuroplasticity of the brain), their curiosity, their sense of responsibility, and last but not least their soul.

9. AI can and should provide exactly the evidence necessary to strengthen confidence in human decisions.

10. It is up to us to shape the world in which we want to live.

The phenomenon of new technologies is by no means new. If we consider the Collingridge dilemma (which is discussed in more detail in Sect. 1.5.3), AI with its enormous (positive and negative) possibilities also represents a potential that we will only fully develop over time. However, in the case of an ethically and socially unreflective and "carefree" approach, the undesirable characteristics may already have manifested themselves as a reality in such a way that they cannot be revised or only at socially unwanted expense. Accordingly, now that AI "merely" refers to comparatively harmless applications around pattern recognition, it is high time to critically deal with the fundamental questions.

Therefore, this book addresses "big" topics across the board and wants to offer the readers an orientation in the sense of an introduction: Ethics—a fundamental topic that has always preoccupied people—been placed in the context necessary for AI. Pragmatic issues are especially considered. Digitization—already a very broad field in itself—is also presented in an overview, and approaches of AI with ethical questions are shown. Furthermore, concrete approaches to consider appropriate ethical principles in AI-based solutions are described and pragmatic though comprehensive roadmap for implementation is proposed.

This book brings together the complex question of how technology can be perceived as "good" in a cross-functional way, alternating between theory and practice. To reflect the concepts with "real life," concrete effects are illustrated with the overarching topic of 2020—the COVID-19 pandemic crisis. As disruption is anything but new, famous and relevant historical examples are used likewise. In this respect, academics, e.g., from humanities, business, or technical disciplines, will find this to be of added value in their respective fields, as well as practitioners who are looking for an introduction to the topic and orientation for concrete questions and assistance. The contributions in this book originate from authors covering a wide field of experiences from ethics to technology and business from different industries.

Part I gives a focused understanding of ethics and the relevant perspectives that allows decent assessment for business managers utilizing AI technologies in a sustainable manner. In particular, the shortcomings of each side, human and AI, is being addressed and an outlook of complementary approaches such as an "integral intelligence" is given.

Part II focuses on AI as enabler for sustainable management in a more than ever complex world. Specifically, immanent shortcomings of AI technology approaches are discussed and linked back to the ethical challenges and requirements of self-discipline in algorithm design and data analysis.

PART III showcases practical examples from different industries and functions such as financial industries, production, or human talent management and illustrates stimulating approaches of sustainable AI utilization. Finally, a concrete way forward on the required journey of ethical orientation, standards, and rule setting will be provided, based on legitimacy in business and candorship.

This book project took almost a year for full realization. At the end of 2019, my Institute for Compliance and Corporate Governance ("ICC") initiated and hosted a symposium on "Artificial Intelligence and Ethics" in Cologne, Germany, with major contributions from experts in the field. The fruitful discussions and challenging questions showed the need for capturing the wide aspects of using technology in a sensible manner in favor of society. I am very happy that thought leaders followed my invitation to contribute to the project. In particular, I would like to thank Susann Spinner, CEO of the CFA Society Germany; Matthias Müller-Wiegand, Vice president of the Rheinische Fachhochschule Köln; and Matthias Groß, TU Mittelhessen, for their contribution.Last but definitely not least, my thorough thanks are addressed to Corry for inspiration, continuous motivation, and infinite patience.

Cologne, Germany   Stefan H. Vieweg
October 2020

Contents

Part I Ethical Concepts and Business Virtues

1 Ethics for Non-philosophers: Basis of Ethics and Ethical Perspectives 3
Stefan H. Vieweg

2 Human Rationality and Morals 23
Stefan H. Vieweg

3 Business Ethics 39
Stefan H. Vieweg

4 Ethics in an International Context 55
Stefan H. Vieweg

5 Value-Based Corporate Management and Integral Intelligence 77
Matthias Müller-Wiegand

Part II AI and the Digital Age

6 Digitization: Learnings from Ancient Disruptions, AI and the Digital Trio's Functional Stage, and AI Superpowers Disrupting Us 95
Stefan H. Vieweg

7 AI and the Ethical Challenge 143
Stefan H. Vieweg

Part III Practical Examples

8 AI in the Financial Industries: Between Apathy and Hysteria 161
Susan Spinner

9 Ethical Best Practice Applying AI in a Socially Sensible Manner .. 177
Stefan H. Vieweg

**10 Yes, AI Can: The Artificial Intelligence Gold Rush Between
     Optimistic HR Software Providers, Skeptical HR Managers,
     and Corporate Ethical Virtues** 191
     Matthias Groß

11 Ethical AI Implementation 227
     Stefan H. Vieweg

Index 253

About the Editor and Contributors

About the Editor

Stefan H. Vieweg Prof. Dr.-Ing. Dr. rer. oec. Stefan Vieweg, CFA, is Director of the Institute for Compliance and Corporate Governance (ICC) at the Rheinische Fachhochschule Cologne, Germany. He has a professorship for international business management and heads an MBA international program. His background is in engineering and business administration. In his early career in aeronautics, he led awarded research on AI-based (ANN) integrity systems for safety-critical applications some 25 years ago and led ISO standardization work for encrypted telematics services. He has more than 20 years of management experience, including technical program lead, CFO, executive board, and supervisory board positions, mainly in the fast-paced agile ICT environment and manufacturing industries. As a Chartered Financial Analyst (CFA), he is committed to the world's highest compliance standard in the financial world and is the initiator of the Compliance on Board Index.

As a certified Systemic Change Manager, SAFe® SPC, and RTE trainer and coach, his consulting is on sustainable and agile organizational development, compliance, and operational transformations (process automation, BPO, etc.). Prof. Vieweg has more than 100 publications in the areas of agile management, AI, automation, business transformation, business ethics, compliance, controlling, data encryption, digitization, governance, leadership, and predictive analytics.

About the Contributors

Matthias Müller-Wiegand is vice-president (faculty economics and law) at the Rheinische Fachhochschule Cologne (RFH), Germany. After years of leadership experience particularly in the media and publishing industry, he joined RFH in 2004, where he teaches value management, controlling, and corporate accounting. In applied research and consulting as well as management education, he focuses on value-oriented leadership systems and sustainable corporate management (decision-making and transformation management).

Susan Spinner CFA, is Executive Chairman and founding member of the CFA Society Germany. She is also a lecturer at the Goethe Business School—Goethe University Frankfurt in the Master of Finance Class in Ethics. Prior to that, she worked for COMINVEST Asset Management GmbH as Senior Structured Financial Analyst, HSH Nordbank (Trader, Structured Products), and Bank of Montreal, Chicago, as Director Global Financial Products. She studied at the University of Michigan and is, of course, Chartered Financial Analyst Charterholder.

Matthias Groß is professor of business administration, in particular human resources management, at Technische Hochschule Mittelhessen, Germany. His research emphasis lies at the interface of business administration, psychology, and business informatics with a focus on "future of work." In consulting projects, Prof. Groß supports companies in the design of sustainable leadership and HR systems.

Part I

Ethical Concepts and Business Virtues

Ethics for Non-philosophers: Basis of Ethics and Ethical Perspectives

Stefan H. Vieweg

1.1 Learning Objectives

1. Differentiating between morals and ethics.
2. Structuring social norms.
3. Describing the concept of ethics from different dimensions, including the philosophical aspects.
4. Differentiating ethics and social norms.
5. Describing problems by means of ethical methodology and ethical perspectives.
6. Recognizing an ethical dilemma.
7. Identifying the causes of unethical behavior of managers.
8. Explaining how managers can incorporate ethical considerations into their decision-making.
9. Describing the importance of normative corporate governance as a framework for ethical behavior.
10. Differentiating the meaning of business ethical frameworks and elements.
11. Identifying specific ethical challenges in an international context and formulating possible solutions.

> *Example Corona Crisis 2020*: Due to the SARS-CoV-2 virus that spread across the globe since the end of 2019, the COVID-19 problem has the world fully under its control in the first months of 2020 and after a little relief that summer: after initial hesitation in the Western world to react to the

(continued)

S. H. Vieweg (✉)
Institute of Compliance and Corporate Governance, RFH - University of Applied Sciences Cologne, Cologne, Germany
e-mail: dr.vieweg@vieweg-beratung.de

avoidable "Chinese" problem, political decision-makers have taken radical measures, some of which were not very well coordinated, such as entry bans, exit bans, closure of stores, and setting up of frontiers between very close allies in the European Union under the Schengen concept. With devastating consequences—at least for the economy: for example, Germany got off relatively lightly during the first infection wave in the spring of 2020, but only if the number of cases of infection and associated mortality rate are considered. If instead of applying only a short-term view (immediate avoidance of infections), the collateral effects and societal damages are taken into consideration as well, the findings may be different: As the lockdown affected public life entirely and massively restricted private lives likewise, the effects on the society and economy are unparalleled. The economical livelihood of many companies of any size was endangered despite some governmental aid programs (that current and future taxpayers have to pay for) when work was suspended, and the entire public and private life came to a halt. This led to at least one lost term on social contacts, learning, and developing for children. For those just finished school, chances for apprenticeship jobs shrank, and left university students losing their sideline jobs for financing their studies, as demand collapsed.

Hence, the moral problem is to decide: Is it better to force entire populations into self-quarantine with massive economic and social collateral (long lasting) damage, or is it morally and socially better to isolate only a small group of vulnerable people to the detriment of a split society with different rights? Not a trivial question...

1.2 Morality

What is morality? Morality is by no means rigid, but it is rather fluid. Morality is what is considered good, desirable, relationally bad, and to be avoided in a society, in a certain culture, at a certain point in time by the vast majority of society members (Bak 2014, p. 2). Thus, these different dimensions have an effect and determine what is regarded and accepted as moral. Different social cultures have been studied extensively over the last few decades; certainly the most outstanding works are Hofstede (1991), Trompenaars (1993), and the GLOBE study (House et al. 2004). Here, societies are differentiated from one another on the basis of several dimensions, whereby a society does not necessarily have to be linked to a state or nation. What is decisive is that one and the same fact can be interpreted in completely different ways, which can lead to considerable problems between societies. In the economic context, this also leads to considerable challenges, not least regarding compliance issues. To illustrate this, here are a few examples:

1. An Asian "yes" is not an agreement: Saving face, you will not hear a direct "no" in various Asian countries, but you need to interpret what is actually meant by complex, multilayered (non-verbal) signals.
2. Relying on your own (family) network for decisions (as is typical in India) instead of (supposedly) independent expertise.
3. Prudery in North America: e.g., sauna visits only in swim suits, whereas this is unthinkable in (Northern) Europe.

Morals also changes over time and across generations. Generational conflicts are therefore precisely due to evolution. What today's generations in many societies regard as opportune was often unacceptable in previous generations. Children are socialized (and thus learn what is good or bad, what is right or wrong), especially through their parents, in the family and at school. By means of explicit rules and prohibitions as well as implicitly through behavior, children are provoked to behave in a way that is considered desirable. Nevertheless, children in their developmental phases (e.g., from Rubicon (9th–10th year of life) via puberty to solidary growing up) challenge the previous value system. The conflicts at generation transitions lead in the long run to adjustments of the moral conceptions. This is to be understood as a clear indication of the social evolution and saves chances of the advancement as well as risks (of the "moral decline"). This is true both on a small scale within families and in societies as a whole. One example of this in the political arena is climate protection efforts.

Although the initiatives have been running for decades, it was not before

1. The World Climate Conference in Paris in 2015,
2. The ever more noticeable consequences of real climate change, and
3. The subsequent initiatives such as the "Fridays for Future" demonstrations, which were extended as a mass phenomenon in 2019 in particular, that the topic has been very much present in the public.

Consequently, companies are also gearing up for the issue of climate change and environmental protection: from "green investment" to corporate environmental protection measures, this issue has now found its way into various sectors of the economy.

It should be noted that moral values and actions in society are by no means congruent.

Example: At least in various high(er)-developed Western countries there is a noticeable "veggie" trend to do completely without meat products and to change over vegetarian/vegan nutrition, clothing, etc. The motivation: Be a good citizen, stay healthy, and act consciously for the environment—so basically: to save the planet. But to bring nevertheless their children by gasoline guzzling SUV daily to school before one feeds oneself in the eco-supermarket with (allegedly) ecologically cultivated soya and palm oil products from far-off countries.

Thus, morality is changeable and culture-dependent and expresses socially desirable behavior. But even if morality is changeable, it is by no means arbitrary, especially since the change process itself takes a relatively long time (measured in years rather than weeks). This is also because a social value framework—and thus morality—provides an important orientation function: Since time immemorial, people have been thinking about moral issues and dealing with them. This makes it clear that consistent values, norms, and moral concepts always play a major role when people organize themselves in social communities. Ultimately, this also results in answers to questions of justice, solidarity, and care as well as the distribution of goods and resources.

Morality acts here as the common lowest denominator for a given society. The advantage is based on the fact that the values underlying morality convey a socially accepted basic understanding and provide orientation in concrete decision-making situations. This makes morality functional and efficient for social groups: In order to be accepted in a community, the individual will strive not to act against this community. Conversely, this means that the behavior of the individual and the social group is ultimately predictable. As a result, uncertainty about behavior is reduced and trust is built up.

However, morality is changing because both the individual and her or his preferences are changing, as is the context in which she or he lives.

However, there is, so to speak, a minimal consensus of basic values that have proven themselves for the coexistence of people and which therefore remain untouched. This basis of human rights can be found worldwide, for example in the Universal Declaration of Human Rights (UN 1948) or in the first articles of the Basic Law of the Federal Republic of Germany (BMJ 1949).

1.3   Ethos

While morality describes the value system of a certain social group at a certain point in time, there is still little said about the individual values and convictions of the individual members of this society. Here, the terminus ethos plays an important role, since it describes the attitude of the individual. However, this does not automatically ensure that individual attitudes and social consensus are compatible. A concrete example was shown in the Corona crisis in 2020: despite the politically prescribed separation and compulsory masking in many countries, not everyone was convinced of the measures required to prevent the spread of the virus. As a result, individuals did not take seriously the requirement to maintain minimum distances and curfews, etc., and even deliberately—almost to the point of sabotage—took countermeasures such as "corona parties." This results in constellations in which social ideas (morality) and individual convictions (ethos) are antinomic. Table 1.1 shows this discrepancy:

Social norms provide a society with orientation and trust for what is right and what is wrong. Social norms are accepted in a society, are universally valid, and concern both cognitive and emotional abilities on the one hand, and concrete behavior on the other.

Table 1.1 Field of tension between society and the individual (own presentation).

		Individual	Individual
		Consent	**Denial**
Society	**Consent**	✓ Internalized morality of the individual is consistent with society	✗ Internalized morality of the individual is in conflict with the social consensus
	Denial	✗ Personal conviction is contrary to social opinion	✓ Internalized moral rejection of the individual is consistent with social consensus

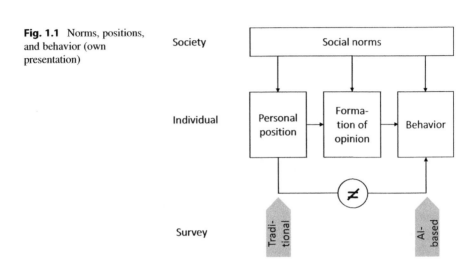

Fig. 1.1 Norms, positions, and behavior (own presentation)

Behavior is not necessarily congruent to thinking and feeling, as the examples discussed above show. Here, it is to be considered the possibilities of artificial intelligence (which will be discussed in Chap. 6 in detail) relating to the collection of preferences of a society—e.g., by questioning a sample of the society—only the personal attitudes could be seized, but not the actual behavior. This is becoming increasingly possible with the possibilities of artificial intelligence (see Fig. 1.1).

These social norms of a society can be presented formally or explicitly (e.g., fixed in writing) or informally or implicitly (quasi as "unwritten law"). They thus form the framework for a social sense of justice.

The binding nature of these social norms can be divided into optional, desired, and mandatory norms (Bak 2014, p. 6):

- Optional norms:
  They represent desired behaviors, which are not forced by society. Example: Greeting in personal and written contact, offering needy people their own seat on public transport, etc.
- Target norms:

Fig. 1.2 Relationship between social norms and laws (own presentation)

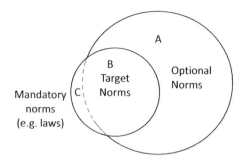

They set limits on behavior, i.e., setting individual members of society beyond these legal limits leads to public disapproval. Example: Noise pollution, e.g., through lawn mowing during lunchtime.

- Mandatory norms:
  Concrete (legal or company) rules specify correct behavior/omissions. Example: Smoking only in explicitly designated zones.

Although the first two categories do not lead to legal action, non-governmental authorities such as religious communities exert pressure to comply with the commandments and impose sanctions for violations.

Often these social norms are vague, non-binding, fuzzy, and open to interpretation. This ultimately leads to uncertainty as to what happens in the event of violations of precisely these norms and what sanctions are to be imposed. The change in social norms also has the effect that moral concepts (can and should norms) change significantly over time. The mandatory norm, as a legal anchor and reflected in the jurisdiction, is mostly lagging and reflects the changed context, sometimes only after years. Ultimately, laws cover only a part of the societal norms (see Fig. 1.2).

> *Examples of subsequent legislation* are the discussions (and demonstrations) around the complex issue of abortion. The only thing that is emphasized here is the anachronism that until 1953 the death penalty for foreign abortion was still specified in the wording of §218 of the Criminal Code of the Federal Republic of Germany (StGB), although the death penalty was abolished immediately after World War II by Military Government Law No. 1 (Article IV No. 8) (BGBL 1956) and in 1949 by the entry into force of the Basic Law (Grundgesetz)) (BMJ 1949, 1957). In the course of the liberalization of 1968 with social changes in Germany and the wave of emancipation, passionate demonstrations took place in West Germany (e.g., the striking demand for the abolition of §218 of the Criminal Code StGB, "My belly belongs to me"), which were just as vehemently rejected by religious representatives, especially

(continued)

those of the churches. Finally, after various attempts, a new version of §218 was only published in 1976.

Consequently, inconsistent regulations on this topic in Europe led to "abortion tourism," in which affected pregnant women had the abortion performed in countries with a more liberal interpretation. An example of this was Great Britain with a social-medicine-induced indication regulation, the Abortion Act from 1967 (UKGov 1967), where a liberal practice developed that complied with the corresponding time limit regulation. Only with further liberalized legislation in the countries of origin did this "abortion tourism" decline.

In the fall of 2020, this topic is high on the agenda in Poland, where the conservative government influenced the Constitutional Tribunal to tighten the already strictest rules in Europe on abortion. Tens of thousands of people protested (Ptak and McDonald 2020).

A completely different example, in which the legal basis is only subsequently adapted to the changing social norms, can be seen in the Internet economy. Here often the problem of a "law-free area" arises, since e.g. minimal requirements of social interaction are not reflected in laws. One example is that until 2018, the topic of data protection was only rudimentarily anchored in Europe and only then, with the introduction of the General Data Protection Regulation (GDPR) (EU 2016), were more restrictive practices regulated, even if these do not directly meet with social consensus. In the USA likewise initiatives emerged since 2018 to protect consumers from exploitation of Internet companies, in particular the "Big Tech" GAFAM[1]: the California Consumer Privacy Act's ("CCPA") (Mactaggert 2019) intent is to counter the ever-increasing exploitation of consumers' behavior and preferences using AI technologies by providing indiscriminating possibilities of consumers' self-determination.

Similarly, there are discrepancies between the binding nature of email and electronic media and typical practice. On the basis of the eIDAS (EU 2014) regulation issued by the European Union as early as 2014, the German Trust Services Act (VDG) (BMJ 2017) did not come into force in Germany until 2018 to guarantee a qualified signature (by so-called trust service providers, who in turn act under the supervision of the federal network agency "Bundesnetzagentur") for electronic business transactions.

In addition to the phenomenon that societal norms (Section A in Fig. 1.2) are reflected in legislation to a limited extent only afterward (Section B in Fig. 1.2), there is also the case that there is a general consensus in society, but ultimately no congruent behavior among the individual members of society. This corresponds to the situation shown in Table 1.1 "Society Approval/Individual Rejection" in the

---

[1]GAFAM: acronym for Google, Amazon, Facebook, Apple, and Microsoft.

upper right corner. Here, laws can enforce congruence (Section C in Fig. 1.2). One example of such a situation is the issue of equality: Despite various appeals over the years, there has been no balanced representation of the genders in leadership positions in Germany. Accordingly, a new law FüPoG[2] (BMFSFJ 2015) was introduced in 2015 to promote this balance.

1.4 Ethics

Ethics is the philosophical discipline that deals with the question of the criteria of good and bad actions. This question of what is "good" and what is "bad" is not at all trivial, because it is to be seen in the context in which it is located. A social "good" is not easy to answer simply because a society consists of different people in different phases of life with different needs. A generalization in the sense of "one size fits all" is naturally forbidden. Accordingly, solutions for concrete social questions are difficult to find and, in purely practical terms, tend to be concerned with the search for the least evil.

Ethics as a science and theory of lived morality can help to derive models for concrete action. Although models—no matter whether of technical systems, social coexistence, or individual ways of thinking and acting—are always only a (sometimes strongly) simplified image of reality, they help to cope with concrete questions, because they

- Enable a projection of different options for action.
- Represent the starting point of critical reflection of one's own actions.
- Facilitate decision-making in concrete individual cases.
- Provide legitimacy for their own decisions.
- Enable traceability of your own actions.

Ethics also forms the starting point for

- Applied ethics, which deals with concrete questions and problems from technical areas such as technologies and media.
- Individual ethics, which is the (ethical) requirements for individual persons.
- Forming a society's or community's specific ethics.

In later chapters, the applied ethics in terms of the use of artificial intelligence will be explained.

The ethical theories can be distinguished for this purpose according to two essential aspects:

---

[2]In order to increase the proportion of women in management positions in Germany, a gender quota of 30 percent has been in force since 2016 for new supervisory board positions to be filled in about 100 large companies.

1. Descriptive ethics—"What is considered good?" This question shows the descriptive (lat. *Describere*—to write down) approach, which does not evaluate the connections. Accordingly, this scientific approach only involves observation and explanation but no positioning of the content.
2. Normative ethics—"What should be good?" This question shows the target state (lat. *Norma*—rule, regulation) and is in this respect directly evaluative and thus contrary to descriptive ethics. The aim is to formulate binding, generally valid rules, on the basis of which individual actions can be morally evaluated and thus make it easier to make a decision.

Two—contrary—approaches are of practical relevance in the field of normative ethics.

1.4.1 Deontological Approach

A morally good action is given exactly when the actor decides for this action due to his normative obligation. An essential representative of this line of thought is Immanuel Kant (1724–1804), who decisively influenced deontology (greek *deon* = duty): Categorical imperative "*Act only according to that maxim by which you can simultaneously want it to become a general law*" (Weischedel 1977) (or "What you do not want to be done to you, do not do to others.") But then, under certain circumstances, this leads to the acceptance of negative consequences in order to do justice to his maxims. The direct consequence of this is that negative consequences may be accepted in order to remain true to one's own—normative—principles ("whatever the cost"). The dilemma arises in the determination of when the consequences count more than the fundamental adherence to certain commandments. This is a difficult task, is quite controversial, and must be decided anew from case to case.

> *Example COVID-19*: The Corona crisis of 2020 (CoV19) is a good example: If the comprehensible social norm prohibits the evaluation of individual persons as "valuable/less valuable," i.e., no multi-class society is considered normatively correct, this ultimately means that the same rules should apply to all members of society. Accordingly, the (forced) quarantine of risk groups such as elderly people is prohibited. Finally, the consequence is that the entire population is massively restricted from contact with the delayed spread of the SARS-CoV19 (WHO 2020) virus. Consequently, all quasi-public institutions, stores, restaurants, etc. were closed, passenger traffic was stopped/restricted, and massive impairment in the manufacturing industry and massive restriction of the freedom of movement in many places resulted. At least the economic collateral damage is extraordinary, despite a

(continued)

comparatively harmless sickness rate: as an example, during the first wave of COVID-19 spread in the spring of 2020, in Germany more than 700,000 companies with short-time work and massively increased insolvencies to an extent unknown in Germany. When has the limit been crossed in which deviation from the principle of equal treatment of the members of society is to be made in order not to further increase the collateral damage of this political decision? According to the ifo Institute, more than 50% of all companies from Germany surveyed cannot survive for more than 6 months if the sanctions continue for longer (ifo 2020).

1.4.2 Utilitarianism or Consequentialism

Utilitarianism (lat. *Utilitas* for benefit, advantage) points out that an action is good if it has the best social consequences or if there is no better action at the present time under the present conditions. In this ethical approach it is distinguished between

1. *Hedonistic utilitarianism* (from Greek *hedone* for joy, pleasure, lust): here, right action is everything that maximizes happiness in the world. One of the most famous representatives is John Stuart Mill (1806–1873).
2. *Preferential utilitarianism*:
   Satisfaction of rational preferences serves as a yardstick to judge an action and its effects. The fulfillment of preferences must be *maximized*. Preference in this context means all rational and emotional interests. The problem with this approach, however, is that there is uncertainty about an action at the time of the decision. To mean well is typically not enough: "Well meant does not equal well done!"

A typical ethical problem (model) in this context is the so-called *trolley problem*, which leads to an ethical dilemma in such a way that an uncomfortable decision is forced if there are no compatible options. This problem, formulated as early as 1967 by philosopher Philippa Foot, allows only two negative options: either to move a streetcar switch so that five workers are saved but another worker is run over on the siding, or not to move the switch and risk five lives. As various studies show, a clear majority of respondents are in favor of changing the switch—making five lives more valuable than one. In some variations, this ethical problem shows the psychological component: In the modified scenario, there is only one track, a disconnected streetcar car rolls unbraked toward the five workers. However, there is a bridge on which a large man stands. If this man is pushed off the bridge (and dies), he would stop the car and be the five workers—at the price of one human life. Here, it can be seen that the vast majority of the test persons do not actively want to cause the death of a human being. The fifth commandment of Christians ("You shall not kill" [Exodus 20:13]) seems to be internalized. It also turned out in neuro-psychological researches that when the death of a person is directly induced, a significantly higher level of activity in the emotional brain center was observed. So, the perception of "right" and "wrong" is not just a purely logical weighing up of the two. Such models have been repeatedly criticized for being too simplistic. However, the reference to reality becomes quickly clear when, for example, following the discussion after 9/11 terrorist attacks of September 11, 2001, in the USA the subject of induced aircraft shooting when there is a terrorist threat is taken into consideration: In the aftermath of the terrorist attacks, a political discussion flared up about the precautionary shooting down (as a "quasi-defense case") of a passenger plane to save a large number of lives in various countries. In Germany, audience surveys on a fictional TV court drama (Welt 2016) from 2016 show that the vast majority (>80%) of viewers interviewed in the DACH[3] region pleaded for the acquittal of an air force major who shot down a passenger plane hijacked by terrorists with 164 people on board to prevent an attack on a soccer stadium with 70,000 people. The dimension of the ethical dilemma becomes obvious when the alternative outcome (i.e., a guilty verdict) is considered on the basis of the judicial grounds: The judge argues that the defendant disregarded the basic values of the constitution. The airplane passengers were defenselessly handed over not only to the terrorists, but also to the air force major, and "their dignity, their inalienable rights, their entire humanity was disregarded. People are not objects. Their lives cannot be measured in numbers. They are not subject to the laws of a market." (Welt 2016).

The dilemmas can also be seen in the concrete, real world, for example in the form of the refugee crises in the Mediterranean since 2016 and the blockade of the European Union members to grant a humane reception to the refugees who landed in Greece/Italy.

Another real example are the alleged decisions in France (Alsace) in March/April 2020 in the context of the Corona pandemic on the non-treatment of patients over 80 years of age (Zeit 2020a), which are tantamount to triage.

In the transition to artificial intelligence, the following problem is already apparent from an ethical point of view: since machines and automats have no needs like humans, the further development of AI to "strong AI"poses very big problems (Hüther 2018). Accordingly, the ethical interpretation becomes difficult. Take, for example, autonomous driving: the ethically correct decision as to who is affected by a collision and who is to be protected—the playing child or the pensioner—is by no means easier.

Individual behavior reveals the ethical dilemma of how to motivate individuals to behave morally correct. For this purpose, the continuation of the classic prisoner problem according to Robert Axelrod (2006) is often used, which also contains a basic consideration of game theory: depending on the behavior (cooperate or deny) of the individual players, this leads to different penalties, depending on the behavior of the other player (see Fig. 1.3). With the help of these models, decision behavior can be described that provokes optimal decisions under defined (= simplified) conditions. It has been shown that the best strategy

---

[3]DACH—Germany (Deutschland), Austria, Switzerland.

Fig. 1.3 Prisoner dilemma—
possible prison sentences in
years (own presentation after
(Axelrad 2006))

		Player B	
		Co-operative	denial
Player A	Co-operative	3/3	0/5
		Prison Term A/B	
	denial	5/0	1/1

- In a unique situation and from an individual perspective the best option is cooperation. From a group perspective, however, the best option is when both deny.
- This changes with several moves: according to Axelrod, the "tit for tat" strategy is recommended from the third round onward, i.e., behaving as the opponent did in the previous round (Axelrad 2006).

1.5   Specific Ethical Perspectives

1.5.1   Ethics of Attitude

Ethics of attitude considers the motives for behavior and actions of individuals. Every single (humane) person has individual needs, preferences, and convictions or an inner disposition which ultimately leads to subjective will and from which action is taken. Here the problem arises when, according to Table 1.1, the case of "society denial/individual consent," there is a discrepancy between individual conviction and socially accepted norm: Is a noble disposition, which—if it has to be—has to oppose the prevailing norm (and, if necessary, the law) in order to address injustice, ethically correct? Concrete examples are resistance and underground movements against authoritarian unjust regimes up to assassinations against the authoritarian leadership.

Example Venezuela: A more recent example is the situation in South American Venezuela (Zeit 2020b), in which since 2018 riots with mass protests with many dead against the former president Nicolás Maduro, who in the view of many people wrongly declared himself the winner of the elections, took place. Juan Guaidó, then president of the parliament, appointed himself interim president and was internationally recognized as such by the EU and USA, among others. His opposition has, for example, received aid from abroad for the impoverished population (Venezuela is one of the most oil-rich countries

(continued)

in the world, but suffers massively due to the drop in oil prices and the mismanagement at home: according to the IMF, the GDP has been predicted from its peak in 2011 to drop to 19% (i.e., a reduction of 89%!) for 2020.[4]

From an ethical point of view, it is problematic that in principle any action could be justified by the reference to the attitude ("attitude offender"). Consequently, generally accepted rules are necessary, which stand above the individual attitude. Without these, each individual could refer to his or her conviction and thus evade moral evaluation by others.

1.5.2 Ethics of Duties

Duty is in Kant's sense an action, which is done out of attachment to the valid morals and norms. Ethics of duty thus defines actions that are required or prohibited (see Sect. 1.4.1). According to Kant, however, the observance of duties is only an expression of morality if the inner driving force for good is given, i.e., if an ethos is the basis. On the other hand, the observance of rules and the fulfillment of duties out of the motivation of avoiding punishment (fear of punishment) would be reprehensible.

The ethics of duties has a decisive advantage of efficiency for the individual: The individual receives clear instructions and orientation points for his or her own actions. The decision what is good and what is bad is not up to the individual. This means that the individual is freed and relieved from the individual decision.

1.5.3 Ethics of the Consequences

Here the consequences of the action are placed in the foreground. Thus, it is morally correct to behave in such a way that the good is achieved or to act in such a way that the consequences become maximally good. In other words: the action is evaluated from the point of view of the consequences. This means that moral perception is congruent, where behavior ultimately does not lead to negative consequences.

The problem with this approach is that the inherent prerequisite is a very good understanding of the possible consequences. However, this is rarely given in advance (ex ante), especially in the case of new types of questions such as technology issues. One might think here, for example, of the dilettantish way in which nuclear energy has been handled since the 1950s, when the great dangers and issues

---

[4]Own evaluation based on data from the IMF (October 11, 2019). Venezuela: Gross Domestic Product (GDP) in current prices from 1980 to 2018 and forecasts to 2021 (in billions of US dollars) [Graph]. In Statista. Accessed on 05 May 2020, from https://de.statista.com/statistik/daten/studie/321115/umfrage/bruttoinlandsprodukt-bip-von-venezuela/

of the final storage of nuclear waste were effectively ignored. Likewise, the side effects of the "miracle fiber" asbestos (weight, strength, insulation, fire protection, etc.), which was massively used as a building material and basic material in various products (up to baby powder (ORF 2018)), were for a long time ignored.

Another example is the dependency (addiction) on smartphones/mobile apps (with the disclosure of considerable personal information) or the currently still difficult to assess impact (suspected macular degeneration) by pulsed radiation from LED light sources (NDR 2018) as a replacement for incandescent bulbs or energy-saving lamps. From an environmental point of view certainly praiseworthy and well comprehensible, the political directive of the European Union, however, does not consider the harmful side effects of a conversion of the lighting to LED.

Another well-known phenomenon is the so-called free-rider problem: Here, the effect of the non-compliant actions of one individual is negligible if all others follow exactly these rules. In contrast, the effect of good, rule-compliant action by one individual is virtually ineffective if all others break exactly these rules. Thus, the factual consequence cannot be directly attributed to a single person. The problem known as Hardin's "Tragedy of the Commons" (Hardin 1968), that a common good is overexploited because of the supposed free availability for everyone, has also had its meaning for 50 years. This can be seen, for example, in the short-term economic optimization of processes and products without considering the long-term environmental consequences.

A further problem from the ethics of consequences is that an intrinsically motivated person, who initially does the right thing out of conviction, becomes quasi demotivated if all others do not follow the rules. This process, known as "carving out," must of course be prevented, as otherwise the role model function is completely abandoned and ultimately the right action is not considered desirable.

A further challenge in technology assessment is that in many areas the state of technology is now so high that these technologies are easily capable of destroying individual people and the whole of humanity. This double-bind dilemma described by David Collingridge (Collingridge 1982; Genus and Stirling 2018) requires great discipline and rational action: the problem lies in the fact that at the beginning of the implementation of a new technology, only little is known about the potential consequences thereof; later, once the technology has established itself, it is basically too late to stop or revert it due to an overwhelming control problem.

1.5.4 Monological Ethics

In monological ethics, it is left to the individual to find out by his own reflection which actions are moral. Thus, this approach is in some ways contrary to mandatory ethics (see Sect. 1.5.2). On the other hand, widespread rules provide orientation. The "golden rule" is found in many religions and says that one should treat others as one would like to be treated by them. This is also articulated in the proverb "Do not do to others what you do not want them to do to you."

Certainly here Kant's imperative can offer orientation: "Act in such a way that you need humanity, both in your own person and in the person of every other one, at any time at the same time as an end, never merely as a means" (Kant, I.).

In the case of great uncertainty in decision-making, it can be helpful to ask oneself whether one would publicly acknowledge the rules of one's actions (this idea is also taken up again in Chap. 4 in the international context in the discussion of the moral compass).

Ultimately, these ethical approaches require competence or knowledge to assess the negative consequences of one's own actions.

1.5.5 Ethics of Discourse

In contrast to monological ethics, discourse ethics is based on the search for a social consensus. Thus, it is a common search for "right" and "wrong" and a weighing up of the different points of view of the persons involved in the discourse. In Sect. 11.3, we will come back to this topic when considering different initiatives for the ethical evaluation of artificial intelligence. For example, ethical guidebooks are one way for politicians to conduct precisely this discourse.

The disadvantage of this approach is that consensus and thus compromise can quickly be used as an excuse for not reaching an acceptable (ideal) state, i.e., in the end a "lazy" compromise or a "well meant is not equally well done".

The "Harvard approach"from the Harvard Program on Negotiations by Roger Fisher et al. (2009) shows a proven path to "win-win situations" that avoids an unfavorable compromise: This approach separates the personal and the factual level by implementing four essential rules of negotiation:

1. Treat people and problems separately.
2. Focus on interests, not on positions.
3. Develop decision possibilities (options) to your mutual advantage.
4. Insist on the application of neutral assessment criteria.

1.5.6 Justice as a Moral Theme

Justice is one of the central principles by which a community can orient itself and shape the community (see also UN Human Rights (UN 1948)). In the final analysis, justice is a matter of comparison. Fundamentally influencing work in a business ethics sense is John Rawls' Theory of Justice (Rawls 1971): his concept is based on two fundamental positions:

1. *"Original position"*: this is deemed to be a theoretical (not reflecting reality)

Table 1.2 Different aspects of justice (own presentation)

Justice	Focus
Retributive	Retaliation, sanctions and penalties
Distributive	Fair distribution of goods, rights, access to resources
Processive	Fair procedures
Restorative	Remedy and reparation

stage of rational people finding (contractual) arrangements of fair distribution of resources.

2. *"Veil of ignorance"*: Intendedly ignoring characteristics of the opposite party (such as gender, ethnicity, appearance, financial wealth, and education) helps to achieve unbiased assessments and with that to promote fairness.

He suggests a set of elements to be implemented before lifting the veil of ignorance (i.e., in this stage the parties do not know their counterparts yet): (1) setting up of a contractual arrangement, (2) unanimous acceptance of the contract, (3) ensuring that fundamental minimum social standards such as freedom of speech are included in the contract, (4) maximizing the welfare of the most disadvantaged parties, and (5) provisions to ensure the execution of the contract. With these measures a system of justice toward fairness is hoped to be possible.

A distinction is made between the following types of justice (Table 1.2):

Diverse problems of justice can be derived, such as

- Social justice: (distributive)
  How can a discrimination of the weak and multiple burden on the service provider be avoided or minimized—even if the privileged members of the society need to (voluntarily?) sacrifice share of their wealth?
- Wage justice: (distributive)
  Is it just if gender differences in salaries and wages still occur?
- Generational justice:
  Is it just that—at the expense of the younger generation—elderly are specifically protected (see the example on the discussion on COVID-19), or the other way around?
- Equal opportunities/equal rights: (processive)
  The principle of equality, the principle of need.
- The principle of performance (processive)
  How to ensure justice in comparison of different parties' performance if there are comparability problems as the equivalence of different services is hard to assess?
- The random principle: (processive)
  Applying a random selection leads to a special form of the principle of equality.

While the concept of fairness by using the "veil of ignorance" as proposed by John Rawls (1971) resonates with many academics, it needs to critically reflect its implications in a context of AI and machine learning: the essence of AI technologies such as deep learning is based on thriving for an unlimited access to and usage of data, in order to optimize the target function (however, this is defined). That is whereas according to the veil of ignorance, specific criteria shall be disregarded, exactly the opposite idea can be found in today's AI implementations. In Chap. 7, this issue will be picked up and discussed in a broader context.

1.6   Finish Line Quiz

1.01	Are social cultures unique and can they be differentiated by their own preferences on morals?	
	1	Yes, as there is a static characteristic of each society that does not change over time.
	2	No, as there are a multitude of characteristics that change over time.
	3	Yes, though there are multiple dimensions and the interpretation is complex.
	4	No, because the interpretation of the characteristics is impossible, and it changes over time.
1.02	Morals deteriorate in the age of digitization. This is a unique phenomenon.	
	1	No, morality has always changed. Morality is a common denominator of a society and its members' preferences and values change over time.
	2	Yes, societies used to have comparatively stable moralities that are unique. With digitization, the common denominator diminishes.
	3	No, for individuals to be an accepted member of the society they strive to comply with all rules. Hence, there is no clear tendency of deterioration due to digitization.
	4	Yes, with the digitization and the so-called digital natives, they are basically ignoring social rules entirely.
1.03	A team member resists to join the WhatsApp group, as she is seriously concerned about data protection issues. She does not want to support business models exploiting consumers' personal data. In this case, ...	
	1	... the internalized individual's ethos is in line with social consensus.
	2	... the social consensus is not (yet?) consistent with individual's ethos.
	3	... the individual mistakenly ignores the social consensus.
	4	... the individual must convince the group to follow her conviction.
1.04	A standards technique to provide evidence of societies' preferences includes surveys. With AI, better evidence is available because ...	
	1	... In traditional surveys, only individuals' preferences could be asked without seeing the true link to individuals' behavior.
	2	... AI measures individuals' preferences without the need to see the actual behavior.
	3	... traditional surveys provide evidence of personal positions and actual behavior.
	4	... traditional surveys provide evidence of actual behavior, though fail to identify personal preferences.
1.05	Ethics act as a guardrail for a society, because ...	
	1	... constitute the end of a personal reflection of actions.
	2	... applied ethics give general advise for "good" behavior.
	3	... it is more important than personal ethos.
	4	... ethics comprises a model for concrete decisions.
1.06	According to the (preferential) utilitarian approach, a morally good action is given exactly when ...	

(continued)

	1	. . . people act only according to that maxim that they want it to become a general law.
	2	. . . it minimizes happiness in the world.
	3	. . . it maximizes happiness in the world.
	4	. . .the fulfillment of preferences is focused.
1.07		Which statement is correct on the specific ethical perspectives?
	1	According to ethics of duty, moral perception is congruent where behavior ultimately does not lead to negative consequences.
	2	Ethics of consequences has the advantage of efficiency for the individual.
	3	Following the ethics of consequences, moral perception is congruent where behavior leads to best results.
	4	According to ethics of consequences, positive results can be achieved as a very good understanding of the possible consequences is always given.
1.08		Generational justice is a specific form of ...
	1	. . . retributive justice.
	2	. . . distributive justice.
	3	. . . processive justice.
	4	. . . restorative justice.

Correct answers can be found at www.vieweg-beratung.de/downloads

References

Axelrod, R. M. (2006). *The evolution of cooperation*. New York: Basic Books.

Bak, P.M. (2014). *Wirtschafts- und Unternehmensethik - Eine Einführung*. S. 2.

BGBL. (1956). *Militärregierungsgesetz Nr. 1 (Art. IV Nr. 8)*. Retrieved May 4, 2020, from https://www.bgbl.de/xaver/bgbl/start.xav?start=//*%5B@attr_id=%27bgbl156s0437.pdf%27%5D#__bgbl__%2F%2F*%5B%40attr_id%3D%27bgbl156s0437.pdf%27%5D__1603961501707

BMFSFJ. (2015). *Gesetz für die gleichberechtigte Teilhabe von Frauen und Männern an Führungspositionen. FüPG*. Retrieved May 4, 2020, from https://www.bmfsfj.de/bmfsfj/themen/gleichstellung/frauen-und-arbeitswelt/quote-privatwitschaft/quote-fuer-mehr-frauen-in-fuehrungspositionen%2D%2Dprivatwirtschaft/78562?view=DEFAULT

BMJ. (1949). *Grundgesetz für die Bundesrepublik Deutschland in der im Bundesgesetzblatt Teil III, Gliederungsnummer 100-1, veröffentlichten bereinigten Fassung, das zuletzt durch Artikel 1 u. 2 Satz 2 des Gesetzes vom 29. September 2020 (BGBl. I S. 2048) geändert worden ist, Article 102*. Retrieved October 22, 2020, from https://www.gesetze-im-internet.de/gg/BJNR000010949.html

BMJ. (1957). *Strafrechtsänderungsgesetz (1953): Bundesgesetzblatt Nr. 1953/44*.

BMJ. (2017). Vertrauensdienstegesetz vom 18. Juli 2017 (BGBl. I S. 2745), das durch Artikel 2 des Gesetzes vom 18. Juli 2017 (BGBl. I S. 2745) geändert worden ist. Bundesamt der Justiz und für Verbraucherschutz, Bundesamt der Justiz. Retrieved October 22, 2020, from https://www.gesetze-im-internet.de/vdg/BJNR274510017.html

Collingridge, D. (1982). *The social control of technology*. New York: St. Martin's Press.

EU. (2014). *Verordnung (EU) Nr. 910/2014 des Europäischen Parlaments und des Rates vom 23. Juli 2014 über elektronische Identifizierung und Vertrauensdienste für elektronische Transaktionen im Binnenmarkt und zur Aufhebung der Richtlinie 1999/93/EG*. Retrieved May 4, 2020, from http://data.europa.eu/eli/reg/2014/910/oj

EU. (2016). *Regulation (EU) 2016/679 of the European Parliament and of the Council of 27 April 2016 on the protection of natural persons with regard to the processing of personal data and on the free movement of such data, and repealing Directive 95/46/EC (General Data Protection Regulation)*. Retrieved May 4, 2020, from https://eur-lex.europa.eu/legal-content/EN/TXT/PDF/?uri=CELEX:32016R0679

Fisher, R., Ury, W., & Patton, B. (2009). *Das Harvard-Konzept – Der Klassiker der Verhandlungstechnik* (3rd ed.). Frankfurt: Campus-Verlag.

Genus, A., & Stirling, A. (2018). Collingridge and the dilemma of control: Towards responsible and accountable innovation. *Research Policy, 47*, 61–69. https://doi.org/10.1016/j.respol.2017.09.012.

Hardin, G. (1968). The tragedy of the commons. *Science, 168*, 1243–1248.

Hofstede, G. (1991). *Cultures and organizations. Software of the mind. Intercultural cooperation and its importance for survival*. New York: McGraw Hill.

House, R. J., Hanges, P. J., Javidan, M., Dorfman, P. W., & Gupta, V. (Eds.). (2004). *Culture, leadership, and organizations: The GLOBE study of 62 societies*. Thousand Oaks, CA: Sage.

Hüther, G. (2018). *Würde – Was uns stark macht*. New York: Random House.

Ifo Institute. (2020). Wie lange schätzen Sie, könnte Ihr Unternehmen überleben, wenn die Einschränkungen aufgrund der Corona-Pandemie noch für längere Zeit aufrechterhalten werden? (29. April, 2020) [Graph]. In *Statista*. Retrieved May 4, 2020, from https://de.statista.com/statistik/daten/studie/1113650/umfrage/corona-krise-umfrage-unter-unternehmen-zur-ueberlebensdauer/

Mactaggert, A. (2019). *The California Privacy Rights and Enforcement Act of 2020*. Retrieved October 21, 2020, from https://oag.ca.gov/system/files/initiatives/pdfs/19-0019%20%28Consumer%20Privacy%20-%20Version%202%29.pdf

NDR. (2018). *LED-Lampen: Schädliches Licht für die Augen*. Retrieved May 5, 2020, from https://www.ndr.de/ratgeber/gesundheit/LED-Lampen-foerdern-Makuladegeneration,led266.html

ORF. (2018). *Aktien von Johnson & Johnson stürzen nach Asbestskandal ab*. Retrieved May 5, 2020, from https://orf.at//stories/3104362/

Ptak A., & McDonald, L. (2020). *Thousands protest across Poland against curbs on abortion access*. Retrieved October 23, 2020, from https://www.reuters.com/article/us-poland-abortion-idUSKBN2780UK

Rawls, J. (1971). *A theory of justice*. Cambridge, MA: Harvard University Press.

Trompenaars, F. (1993). *Riding the waves of culture: Understanding cultural diversity in business*. New York: Random House Business Books.

UKGov. (1967). *An Act to amend and clarify the law relating to termination of pregnancy by registered medical practitioners; the law came into force half a year later*. Retrieved May 4, 2020, from http://www.legislation.gov.uk/ukpga/1967/87/contents/enacted

UN. (1948). *Universal Declaration of Human Rights*. Retrieved April 24, 2020, from https://www.un.org/en/universal-declaration-human-rights/index.html

Weischedel, W. (Hg.) (1977). *Immanuel Kant – Werkausgabe* (Band VII, 3. Auflage). Frankfurt: Suhrkamp Verlag.

Welt. (2016). *Das ist die Begründung für schuldig, die nicht in der ARD lief*. Retrieved May 4, 2020, from https://www.welt.de/kultur/article158845701/Das-ist-die-Begruendung-fuer-schuldig-die-nicht-in-der-ARD-lief.html

WHO. (2020). *Coronavirus disease (COVID-19)*. Retrieved May 4, 2020, from https://www.who.int/news-room/q-a-detail/q-a-coronaviruses

Zeit. (2020a). *Coronavirus: Was hat Frankreich mit den Alten gemacht? Sediert statt gerettet: In Frankreich mehren sich die Indizien dafür, dass Patienten auf dem Höhepunkt der Pandemie nach Alter selektiert wurden*. Retrieved May 4, 2020, from https://www.zeit.de/wissen/gesundheit/2020-04/coronavirus-frankreich-triage-altenheime-todesfaelle

Zeit. (2020b). *Kommt es zum Umsturz?* Retrieved April 5, 2020, from https://www.zeit.de/thema/venezuela

Human Rationality and Morals

2

Stefan H. Vieweg

2.1 Learning Objectives

1. Identify the importance of a rationality-based view in economic models and approaches.
2. Assess the limitations of this one-sided approach in both economic and ethical terms.
3. Explain and justify deficiencies such as irrationality and cognitive biases and establish a moral distance to them.
4. Recognize the ethical consequences of a misinterpretation or misunderstanding of data sets.
5. Reflect recent trends in the convergence of morals and economics and critically identify the motivation behind them.
6. Realize the additional ethical challenge AI technologies imposes on decision-making, as psychological distance increases.

2.2 The Concept of Rationality

From the discussion of preference utilitarianism (see Sect. 1.4.2), it can be deduced that even in difficult situations (e.g., the "trolley" problem) the best (mini-mired negative or maximum positive) result for the respective context can be achieved by rational decision. This functional rationalism is inherent in many models of the economy. It assumes that the human being acts in each case in a way that maximizes the benefit and thus is purpose-oriented. This logically founded ideal type, called "homo oeconomicus," is not at all to be found in reality, since man is not only

S. H. Vieweg (✉)
Institute of Compliance and Corporate Governance, RFH - University of Applied Sciences Cologne, Cologne, Germany
e-mail: dr.vieweg@vieweg-beratung.de

23

rational but also characterized by emotion. In this respect, a purely economic view is not enough. Therefore, findings of psychology are increasingly taken into account. Examples of this are behavioral finance (i.e., the "psychology of investors" and the study of shareholder behavior) or behavioral risk management (Shefrin 2016) (i.e., the "pathology" of organizations in dealing with risks).

The cognitive limitations of individuals and also of groups can lead to misjudgments and thus often to worse results than a rational decision would promise.

Ultimately, another problem area is that the motivation of individuals is not necessarily congruent with the company's goals (see as well Sect. 1.3 where the discrepancy between individual's and society's perception was dealt with).

In the following, the different problem areas are briefly discussed.

2.3 Rationality as an Explanatory Pattern

Most management approaches are still based on the assumption of rational behavior. Economic models, which are still influential today, are based on the assumption of a "homo oeconomicus," although this is known to be an inadequate description of actual actions. An example from the financial market should illustrate this: The basis of many of the models used today, such as the still predominant capital market theories, is Markowitz's portfolio theory from the 1960s (Brealey et al. 2016), as well as the Nobel Prize-winning "Capital Asset Pricing Models" ("CAPM") based on it, after W.F. Sharpe and others. Without going into detail, the factual positive correlation between expected return and risk ("no risk—no fun") is certainly rationally obvious. But that the markets act highly irrationally can always be seen, especially when the company's share price falls despite good real results or vice versa. It is therefore not surprising if a model that is not designed for prediction (but is nevertheless used for it) only provides limited coverage with reality.

> *Example of market irrationality* in the context of COVID-19: Take the example of the share price development in Germany under the spell of the COVID-19 crisis: The business newspaper Handelsblatt of 11.05.2020 headlines in its morning briefing "Economy paradox: The worse the economic data and the profit expectations of the companies, the stronger the share prices currently rise" (Jakobs 2020).

The reason why such one-dimensional rational attempts of explanation are common despite the well-known limitation may be the logical and thus understandable derivation of the relations. This creates confidence and orientation. Irrational—thus not deducible behavior—would not be understandable in explanations and thus hardly acceptable.

In addition, a purely rational approach offers a convenient "escape pattern": instead of critically weighing up the most diverse qualitative and quantitative aspects and making this process of knowledge transparent, traditional statistics are used—

sometimes very unreflectively—to justify ethically difficult decisions. This can have fatal consequences in extreme situations, where good decisions are more important than ever, because the starting point is not right. Bent Flyvbjerg sums it up with his approach "regression to the tail" when he outlines that in extreme situations such as natural disasters, terrorist attacks, and pandemics, the risk of a disaster is very high. "Prudent decision makers will not count on luck—or on conventional Gaussian risk management, which is worse than counting on luck, because it gives a false sense of security—when faced with risks that follow the law of regression to the tail" (Flyvbjerg 2020).

Example COVID-19—Statistics: The unreflective handling of statistical findings can be demonstrated again very well with the example of COVID-19: In particular in the media, three characteristic numbers are represented and serve as argumentations and justifications for political decisions; without their force of expression, inaccuracies and restrictions are critically examined:

- Infection rate (the number of new infections per day)
- Mortality rate (the number of deaths related to COVID-19)
- Reproduction rate R: the (statistical) number of newly infected persons during the current so-called generational period (mean period from the infection of a person to the infection of the subsequent cases infected by him/her, in Germany in April 2020 within 4 days) in relation to the sum of new infections of the previous generational period. A reproduction number $R = 2$ corresponds to a doubling within the generation time, $R = 1$ to a linear and $R = 0.5$ to a halving of new infections (Gigerenzer et al. 2020).

Table 2.1 shows the individual outstanding problem areas in the (statistical) data.

In general, the process chain should be viewed from a rational point of view. The questions shown in Fig. 2.1 can help in this regard. Very often, problems arise in sampling, evaluation, and proper communication.

With regard to an ethical context in connection with artificial intelligence, the following can be said about rational behavior, which holds both opportunities and risks:

1. Due to its complexity (social morality vs. individual ethos, socialization and cultural dependencies, generational conflicts, variability, etc.) ethics is already a challenge that cannot be clearly described by rationality. This is expressed, among other things, in the different philosophical ethical approaches (see Chap. 1).
2. (Human) Persons who have to make decisions in ethically relevant questions combine different roles at the same time: A manager is not only a business person with the obligation to protect the interests of the company, but at the same time an individual who brings her or his entire personality from emotionally charged

Table 2.1 Example COVID-19 Identification of key parameter, evaluation of the data of the Robert-Koch-Institute ("RKI") in April 2020 (own presentation, data based on [an der Heiden and Hamouda (2020)])

Value	Infection rate	Mortality rate	Reproduction rate
Outstanding problem area	is based on the positive test results without knowledge of the actually infected persons, i.e. it is associated with an unknown number of unreported cases	no distinction whether the persons died "of" or "with" the virus	1. The generation time is only estimated (in April 2020 in Germany by the Robert Koch Institute with 4 days) and represents the first significant uncertainty factor; the shorter, the stronger would be an exponential increase. 2. Reports of new infections are not determined by representative panel samples, for example, but are estimated on the basis of complex (and delayed) reporting processes (so-called "nowcasting"), which in turn is subject to statistical uncertainty 3. A prediction interval of 95% is used (a rather mediocre level in statistics as a compromise between fast information from few measured data and quality). This means that the statistical statements can vary widely, as for example the data for April 9, 2020 show: estimated new cases in DE: between 2085 and 4175, i.e. a range of 2100 cases, i.e. more than 100% of the baseline!

    experience / skills / knowledge / needs and social / family role into the decision-making process.

3. Non-human AI-supported automation or bots, on the other hand, are one-dimensionally trained for their functional role and the tasks involved. They lack the complexity of human life. Even if it should ever be possible to come close to human empathy (Bak 2016), authentic empathy is not recognizable for the foreseeable future due to the lack of (human) desiderata[1] (Hüther 2018).

---

[1]See Sect. 1.4.2.

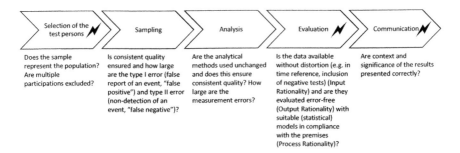

Fig. 2.1 Appropriate (decision-useful) consideration of data, which are particularly important in times of crisis (own presentation)

From this it can be deduced that a mature AI in a society with clear ethical preferences (e.g., deontological approaches or utilitarianism) could make ethically more consistent decisions than humans, precisely because of its one-dimensionality (see Trolley Problem in Sect. 1.4.2). However, this chance is also opposed by the significant risk that due to this limitation of the AI emotionless and thus in the true sense of the word "inhuman" seeming decisions are made.

2.4   Irrationality and Cognitive Biases

Irrational decisions are often caused by cognitive distortions. In the wide field of behavioral economics, there are now a wide variety of conspicuities that promote irrational decisions. Some aspects important for the ethical dimension are listed below, without claiming to be complete. Particularly problematic are a number of biases, which are manifested in various forms. Examples are

- *Overconfidence bias*: The phenomenon also known as hybris, where the more difficult the task is, the greater the overconfidence. This is particularly noticeable in management circles when decisions are made without a self-critical assessment of the probability of success of a risky venture.
- Overestimating one's own importance (*egocentric bias*): This is expressed, for example, by unrealistically overestimating one's own contribution to a joint success result and marginalizing the contribution of others.
- Tendency to attach and maintain known false beliefs (*confirmation bias*): This is also articulated as the so-called *anchor* effect. An example of this is the phenomenon that when a project is first assessed, a quantification that is not reliable at this point in time, such as "we can save an estimated X million euros with this", is repeatedly used as a reference in the further course of the project, even though in the meantime much better findings have been obtained, perhaps a much smaller number than the first-mentioned figure.

- *Base rate fallacy*: The problem is the correct interpretation of probabilities, which refer as percentage value to a base rate. This misinterpretation is widespread, as the experiment at Harvard Medical School shows (Hoffrage et al. 2000):
  If a test to detect an infection with a prevalence of 1/1000 (i.e., one person actually infected per 1000 persons) has a false-positive rate of 5% (i.e., 5% of the tested persons test positive due to measuring/testing errors of the first type, even though in reality there is no infection), what is the probability that a person tested positive is actually infected (assuming that nothing is known about the symptoms or signs of illness of the tested person)? In the classic Harvard case, 27 out of 60 respondents (experts, employees, and students) answered with 95%—almost half of the respondents. But now the correct answer is of a completely different order! If Bayes' theorem had been correctly applied, one would not have succumbed to the "false-positive"paradox.[2]

> **Example of Base Rate Fallacy in COVID-19 Infection Testing in Germany**
> If a test for COVID-19 infection with a prevalence of 1/1000 (i.e., one person actually infected per 1000 people) has a false-positive rate of 5 percent (i.e., Type I error due to measuring/testing errors), the test is considered to be false positive (i.e., 5% of the tested persons are tested positive, even if there is no actual infection). What is the probability that a person tested positive is actually infected—assuming that they know nothing about the symptoms or signs of the person (e.g., the scenario of a comprehensive nation-wide COVID-19 test)? The following data and applying Bayes' formula show a probability of 0.6%!

(continued)

---

[2]The correct answer in the classic Harvard case is 2%.

Statistics (Input)		Remarks
Population (2018)	82,927,922	https://data.worldbank.org/country/g ermany?view=chart, (access 13.05.2020)
Total cases (May 2020)	173,171	https://coronavirus.jhu.edu/map.html, (access 13.05.2020)
Recovered (May 2020)	147,200	https://coronavirus.jhu.edu/map.html, (access 13.05.2020)
Active (May 2020)	25,971	https://coronavirus.jhu.edu/map.html, (access 13.05.2020)
Active/Population	**0.3‰**	
Death (May 2020)	7,738	https://coronavirus.jhu.edu/map.html, (access 13.05.2020)
Bayes formula		
$p(D) = p(D|\text{infected})\, p(\text{infected}) + p(D|\text{not infected})\, p(\text{not infected})$		
$p(\text{infected}|D) = \dfrac{p(D|\text{infected})\, p(\text{infected})}{p(D)}$		
Calculation		
p(D|infected)	1.0000	
p(D|nicht infected)	0.0500	
p(infected)	0.0003	
p(not infected)	0.9997	
p(D)	0.0503	
p(infected|D)	**0.6%**	

- Distortions due to *emotional influences* (e.g., put on rose-colored glasses): this problem, which is also related to the *halo* effect, results from the fact that it is easy to lose the overall context and the critical view ("wishful thinking") if a characteristic outshines other circumstances. This can be observed very well in the climate protection debate and environmentally friendly technologies. For example, one positive aspect of the introduction of electric vehicles is certainly the reduction in the amount of climate-damaging exhaust gases in city centers. However, if one considers that the necessary electrical energy is not necessarily generated in an environmentally friendly way, that the raw materials for the necessary energy storage in the vehicle are extracted under ethically questionable conditions, and that the batteries have considerable power losses, the advantage of higher engine efficiency is quickly put into perspective. A comprehensive consideration of efficiency and life cycle assessment (Life cycle assessment ("LCA")) would be appropriate for a realistic assessment.

Another problem with cognitive bias is the sequence of decisions. Often these decisions are made in isolation one after the other (sequentially), so that major problems can arise here: Instead of anticipating dependencies and only making decisions at the latest possible point in time,[3] individual decisions are made in an early phase, which cannot be revised without loss. This loss can manifest itself both materially in the form of additional costs and emotionally in the form of admitting a wrong decision. Especially the latter is often more difficult to cope with.

Finally, another cognitive problem—*group-think*—needs to be addressed: In an effort to reach a consensus, groups may make decisions that ignore individual critical voices. In addition, groups are more willing to take a higher risk than any individual of that group. This can be explained by the collective responsibility, which does not hold the individual accountable in case the decision turns out to be wrong. Attempts to explain this can be found in the egocentric distortion (see above) or in the prospect theory (Kahneman and Tversky 1979), which describes risk-seeking behavior in the loss range but risk-averse behavior in the profit range.

The unfavorable combination of group-think, excessive optimism, and overconfidence bias led, for example, in the financial crisis of 2008 to the crash of major US financial institutions Fannie Mae, Freddie Mac, AIG (Shefrin 2016).

2.5   Moral Distance to Irrational Behavior

A significant effect in the context of behavioral economics, especially in the ethical context of relevance, is the so-called Fudge factor (Ariely 2012): Small, everyday inaccuracies are often dealt with without a guilty conscience or accompanied by justifications such as "others do it too" or "nobody notices." The decision to cheat is not rational, but nevertheless very common—with fatal consequences (see below). Behavioral economist and psychologist Dan Ariely demonstrates this clearly in his experiments (Ariely 2012).

Example of identifying the "fudge factor": Ariely influenced groups of subjects who were to take a simple written arithmetic test by giving the participants designer sunglasses in advance: one group was told that these sunglasses were authentic, the second group was told that they were fake, and the third control group was not told anything at all. Each group had the opportunity to deceive during the test. In the control group, 42% had cheated. In the authentic group, the deception rate decreased to 30%. In the interpretation, the participants' self-image was strengthened by the advantageous deal. But in the group with the allegedly fake glasses the fraud rate was 74%! This leads to the conclusion that deliberate dishonesty—no matter how small— increases the probability for others to do the same.

---

[3]As this practice is used successfully by agile methods such as the scaledagileframework.com (SAFe®) (SAFe 2020), that assumes variability and preserve options (Vieweg 2020a).

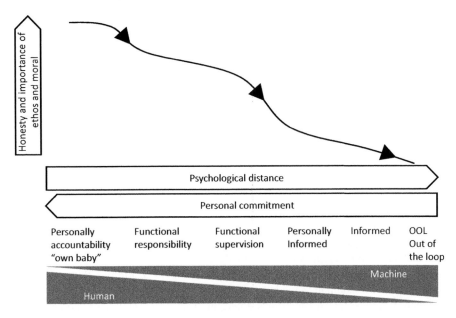

Fig. 2.2 Principle relationship between honesty and commitment level (own presentation)

The probability of cheating also increases with the psychologic distance to the crime. This is an important aspect especially in the environment of digitization (and artificial intelligence). "The more cashless our society becomes, the more our moral compass slips" (Dan Ariely).

With the further spread of AI, the psychological distance will inevitably increase massively. Figure 2.2 shows the principle relationship of honesty and care.

2.6   Morals and Economics

Morality and economy are in conflict with each other. What a society advocates (morality) is only, in exceptional cases, congruent with the interests of economically active decision-makers, who ultimately perform a fiduciary task for the company's equity investors.

In this respect, the approach of the economist Adam Smith (1723–1790) offers only one facet, which does not comprehensively reflect reality. In essence, Smith's approach says that through the "invisible hand of the market"—i.e., through self-regulation from supply and demand—the respective maximization of property ultimately also increases the prosperity of the general public. However, the reality is much more complex: For example, entrepreneurial economic success (profit in particular) does not automatically lead to an increase in employees' wages and salaries or the creation of more jobs. Far away from Smith's ideal, there is rather an exploitation of market power up to monopolistic structures. One example of this is the tax avoidance of the large GAFA[4] Internet groups, which have been systematically shifting their profits (legally) through licenses for years in such a way that they did not pay any taxes in the important sales market of Europe (where in fact no development took place). The participation of the European national economies has failed to materialize. On the contrary, their market power leads (even if not originally intended) to the fact that these companies exert considerable influence on the respective national politics (Beutelsbacher et al. 2016), as the examples of Amazon and Luxembourg or Apple and Ireland have shown: in 2017, official politics opposed the political initiative of the European Commission to eliminate the tax loopholes through a digital tax. The trend over the last decade shows that these four mega-corporations together have already reached a market capitalization equivalent to 1/3 of the entire EU 27 (excluding the UK, which left the EU on January 31, 2020)[5] and Apple's market capitalization exceeded the magic $2 trillion mark on August 19, 2020, almost reaching the GDP of the third largest EU economy, Italy. Such monopolistic structures effectively cancel out the laws of a free and fair market with a socially legitimized political force. Even in stakeholder economies, in which a socially more acceptable variant of the liberal market economy is represented, there are considerable distortions due to market asymmetries, for example in the labor market.

Interestingly, some change is now emerging from the entrepreneurial perspective and a—certainly profit-driven interest—in taking into account the trend toward sustainability in social and ecological terms. Inclusive capitalism will be explained below as an example.

2.6.1   Inclusive Capitalism: Example of an Initiative to Consider the Sustainability Aspect—Not Only for Ethical Reasons

Today's standard financial reporting—certified by auditors—no longer does justice to the increasing complexity of sustainable corporate management and reporting to its stakeholders: funds from the last century are still being used, which do not at all capture the essential components that characterize the value of a company. This is due in particular to the backward-looking focus on financial indicators (ex post) and thus the neglect of long-term—leading—indicators that characterize the internal value of a company and its impact on the corporate environment. Some studies show that in 2018 only 20% of the company's value will be recorded in the balance sheet, compared to over 80% in the mid-1970s (Brand Finance 2018).

More or less suitable indicators and modern management methods are available in abundance—nevertheless, the comprehensive implementation of such methods in

---

[4]GAFA—referred to Google, Apple, Facebook, and Amazon. Sometimes quoted as GAFAM including Microsoft: in August 2020 the five US-tech giants had a market cap of >$ 7.4 TN, which is c. 45% of the entire EU 27 BIP (2019).

[5]Own analysis based on ec.europa.eu/eurostat "European Union: Gross domestic product (GDP) in the member states in current prices in 2019." and (Janson 2020).

the broad mass of organizations is mostly to be considered a failure: the reasons are to be found in the one-sidedness of the content, the complexity, and the actual motivation (mostly focused on one's own profile or business advantage) of those responsible for implementation. Well-known examples are the "Shareholder Value"e.g. with the "Economic Value Add—EVA" or the "Balanced Score Card."

The monitoring structure of compliance is no longer up to date, as both the process-bound internal and the avoidance of independent external (but paid for before the organization to be reviewed) review by auditors do not meet the highly competitive pressure. Due to

1. Lack of standardization in comprehensive reporting (which in turn is due to mostly manual or max. Semi-automated processes)
2. Latent and/or concrete dependencies (e.g., in some cases substantial economic and financial losses)

there is neither a reliable transparency nor reliability of the audit certificates itself. A good example is the comparison of the Wirecard scandal in 2020—the now insolvent tech company, which barely 2 years earlier had been included in the renowned DAX 30, Germany's "most valuable" 30 companies, and whose balance sheet forgeries were recognized far too late on a large scale. The similarity to the US scandal about Enron about 20 years earlier is astonishing and sobering: despite tighter regulations and progress in digitization, it is frightening to have to state that obviously nothing has been learned. In both cases, auditors have a special role to play, since the expectation of stakeholders (and thus shareholders in the narrower sense) is that reporting is reliable. However, this was not achieved in the abovementioned cases and led to considerable damage to the company's reputation, which, at least in the Enron case, led to the dissolution of the auditing company.[6]

Various initiatives that were already concerned with changing or expanding the reporting system were only able to establish themselves to a limited extent. The reasons for this are in two areas:

1. Complexity:
   There is too much reporting complexity and therefore not operationalizable for many (e.g., GRI—Group Reporting Initiative—an extremely comprehensive set of rules and regulations with regard to sustainable management, which at best large companies with a high level of resources can only implement to some extent[7])

---

[6]Arthur Anderson was at that time one of the world's "Big Four" accounting firms and was dissolved in the wake of the Enron scandal; the consulting business was renamed "Accenture." The EY involved in the Wirecard case currently has to fear corresponding damage to its reputation; see (FT 2020).

[7]The main manual alone comprises more than 400 pages!

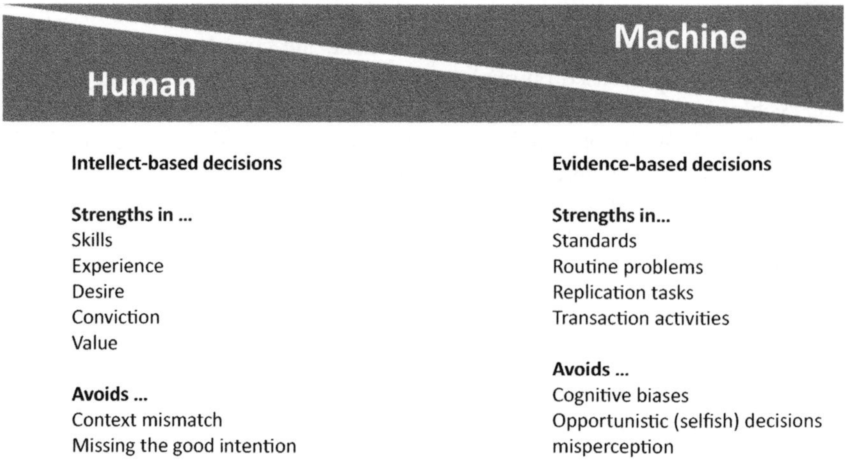

Intellect-based decisions	Evidence-based decisions
Strengths in ...	**Strengths in...**
Skills	Standards
Experience	Routine problems
Desire	Replication tasks
Conviction	Transaction activities
Value	
	Avoids ...
Avoids ...	Cognitive biases
Context mismatch	Opportunistic (selfish) decisions
Missing the good intention	misperception

Fig. 2.3 Human–machine interaction (own illustration)

2. Sloping toward auditing firms:

   Drivers of the initiative are obviously biased toward accounting auditors (presumably primarily on generating new business) and not consensus-oriented, so that neither the companies that generate primary value added (e.g., manufacturing companies) were sufficiently involved, nor were the competitors of these drivers visible in the initiative, which could have ensured broader acceptance. An example is the initiative "Coalition for Inclusive Capitalism" (EY 2018), which of its 31 members only involved nine(!) companies worldwide with primary value creation and all others only from the field of asset management (asset owners[8]). In addition, this project was dominated by an auditing and consulting firm.[9]

Despite this sobering summary, it should be pointed out that a "keep it up" with single-sided pure short-term economic focus seems as unsuccessful as some current initiatives that are characterized by exuberating complexity (Vieweg 2020b). Finding a practicable, purposeful, and pragmatic middle way that includes those actually affected is a concrete challenge. Here it quickly becomes apparent that the use of artificial intelligence can help in the sense of information processing for evidence-based decisions and to avoid cognitive (human) bias. On the other hand, skills, beliefs, and values of individuals are crucial to find the "right" decision in a changed context (see Fig. 2.3). In this respect, a complementary approach seems to be promising. This can be seen in the case of extended reporting outlined above: Key upstream and downstream key performance indicators—uniformly defined, recorded in a standardized way, and automatically processed in compliance with good

---

[8]This term is misleadingly used in the "Embarkment Project for Inclusive Capitalism," since insurance companies and pension funds also manage assets.

[9]16 of the 19 members come from the consultancy and auditing firm EY (2018).

business practice ("Machine") can lead to a pragmatically sustainable and decision-useful supply of information to stakeholders, taking into account the individual situation of what is feasible in a meaningful way ("Human").

2.6.2 Stewardship as an Approach to Sustainable and Ethically-Morally "Good" Corporate Governance

The field of tension between the motivation of corporate decision-makers and their monitoring is sufficiently described in theoretical considerations ranging from principal-agent theorem to stewardship (Davis et al. 1997) theory and illustrates the agents' framework for action.

The starting point for each of these theories is a different conception of man, assumed motivation, and thus congruently derived focus of action of the principal (owner and his representative, e.g., supervisory board) and the agent acting on behalf of the principal (manager, e.g., board of directors). The stewardship theory complements the principal–agent theory in a context-dependent manner and thus offers further explanations for the respective behavior of the actors.

The principal–agent theory assumes a fundamental conflict of goals between the two actors, which results from the human image of selfish opportunism. The motivation assumed for the agent is extrinsic; i.e., the manager is not primarily interested in the well-being of the company. Accordingly, the principal distrusts the agent, and the principal's primary framework for action will lie in monitoring the agent.

In contrast to this, the stewardship theory sees a fundamental congruence of goals between the two actors, which is based on the idea of a manager who is primarily concerned with the well-being of society and the company, i.e., who is intrinsically motivated and puts personal interests second. Accordingly, the principal trusts the agent and the principal's primary scope of action will be to advise the agent.

For the company, there are considerable differences in efficiency, provided that the assumed basic assumptions correspond to reality in each case: thus, with the principal–agent approach, costs (damage) can be minimized (see Fig. 2.4: Agent/Agent), whereas with the stewardship approach, corporate performance is maximized accordingly (see Fig. 2.4: Steward/Steward).

If the ethical and moral dimension is now added to the stewardship approach, it becomes clear that the social contribution is also maximized beyond the corporate framework.

In order to remain within the picture of the extended stewardship theory, the challenge of sustainable and ethically-morally "good" corporate governance is therefore to minimize the risk of constellations that do not lie on the main diagonal of Fig. 2.3 ("red fields"), which should be evidence-based.

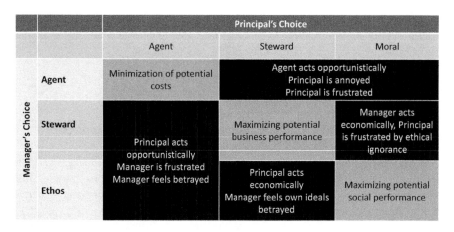

Fig. 2.4 Extended stewardship theorem (own extended presentation, based on Davis et al. (1997))

2.7   Finish Line Quiz

2.01		The model of the "homo oeconomicus" is…
	1	… is a proven and comprehensive approach to reflect reality.
	2	… is a concept introduced in times when the psychological dimension of business decision was not reflected at all.
	3	… fully reflects the behavioral aspects of human decision-making.
	4	… is not used anymore.
2.02		Comparing humans and AI regarding rational decision-making process in business, …
	1	… humans combine with their personality different roles at the same time, which influences the decision.
	2	… humans combine with their personality different roles, though they focus their decision on the business side.
	3	… AI mirrors various aspects of human perspectives in the decision-making.
	4	… AI does not take decisions; humans do.
2.03		Given a prevalence of 1/1000 on a virus test with a false-positive rate of 1.0%, what is the probability that a person tested positive is actually infected (assuming that they know nothing about the symptoms of the person)?
	1	99.0%
	2	95.0%
	3	9.1%
	4	1.0%
2.04		What is to be expected if people act in an environment of fake?
	1	They stick to their principles and ethos.
	2	Large fraud cases with significant damage are to be expected, as all people act fraudulently.
	3	Given possibilities of conceiving "short cuts" people tend to cheat "a little."
	4	People always cheat at the same intensity, independent of the environment.

(continued)

2.05	How are personal commitment and psychological distance related to each other?
1	Importance of ethos is highest if functional supervision is given.
2	Psychological distance is higher in functional responsibility than in personal accountability.
3	Psychological distance is lower in functional responsibility than in functional supervision.
4	Importance of ethos is low if personally informed.
2.06	Adam Smith's theory of the "invisible hand" is ...
1	... flawed, because compensation rise of executives is not directly mirrored in payment stagnation to staff.
2	... flawed, because compensation rise of executives is directly mirrored in payment stagnation to staff.
3	... flawed, because compensation rise of executives is not directly mirrored in payment rise to staff.
4	... fits, because compensation rise of executives is directly mirrored in payment rise to staff.
2.07	Extending the valuation of a business beyond traditional (financial) reporting such as the balance sheet (aka statement of financial position) is ...
1	... adequate, as the minority of the company's value is recorded on the balance sheet.
2	... likely to produce additional complexity that is motivated by auditing firms, financial advisory, rating firms, and financial information brokers to extend their business opportunities. Comprehensive technology assessment is not envisaged.
3	... likely to reduce additional complexity although a comprehensive technology assessment is envisaged.
4	... inadequate, as the minority of the company's value is not recorded on the balance sheet.
2.08	Humans and machines are complementary in such regard that ...
1	... humans are better in context mismatch prevention.
2	... machines have a higher degree of misperception.
3	... humans are better in avoiding misperception.
4	... machines are better in context mismatch prevention.
2.09	Stewardship theory sees the following critical constellations between the actors:
1	When the principal correctly expects the manager to apply stewardship.
2	When the principal falsely expects the manager to act as agent.
3	When the principal acts economically, as the manager does.
4	When the principal acts short term economically and the manager pursues high ethical standards.

Correct answers can be found in www.vieweg-beratung.de/downloads

References

an der Heiden, M., & Hamouda, O. (2020). Schätzung der aktuellen Entwicklung der SARS-CoV-2-Epidemie in Deutschland – Nowcasting. *Epidemiologisches Bulletin, 17*, 10–16. https://doi.org/10.25646/6692.4.

Ariely, D. (2012). *The honest truth about dishonesty: How we lie to everyone - especially ourselves.* New York: HarperCollins.

Bak, P. (2016). Maschinelle Empathie. In *Zu Gast in Deiner Wirklichkeit.* Berlin, Heidelberg: Springer Spektrum.

Beutelsbacher, S., Sommerfeldt, N., & Zschäpitz, H. (2016). *Die gefährliche Dominanz der großen Vier.* Retrieved May 11, 2020, from https://www.welt.de/finanzen/article150809163/Die-gefaehrliche-Dominanz-der-grossen-Vier.html

Brand Finance. (2018). *Global Intangible Finance Tracker (GIFTTM) 2018—An annual review of the world's intangible value.* Retrieved from http://brandfinance.com/images/upload/gift.pdf

Brealey, R., Myers, S. C., & Allen, F. (2016). *Principles of corporate finance* (12th ed.). New York: McGraw-Hill.

Davis, J. H., Schoorman, F. D., & Donaldson, L. (1997). Toward a stewardship theory of management. *The Academy of Management Review, 22*(1), 20–47.

EU. (2019). *European Union: Gross domestic product (GDP) in the member states in current prices in 2019.* Retrieved May 13, 2020, from ec.europa.eu/eurostat

EY. (2018). *EPIC – Embarkment Project for Inclusive Capitalism.* Retrieved May 13, 2020, from https://www.epic-value.com/

Flyvbjerg, B. (2020). *The law of regression to the tail: How to mitigate pandemics, climate change, and other deep disasters.* Retrieved November 1, 2020, from https://www.sciencedirect.com/science/article/pii/S1462901120308637?via%3Dihub

FT. (2020). *EY fights fires on three audit cases that threaten its global reputation,* FT June 8, 2020. Retrieved June 20, 2020, from https://www.ft.com/content/576e4c7f-93e5-4e8a-b5ba-5e1161533c5a

Gigerenzer, G., Krämer, W., Schüller, K., & Bauer, T. K. (2020). *Corona-Pandemie: Die Reproduktionszahl und ihre Tücken.* Retrieved May 11, 2020, from https://www.rwi-essen.de/unstatistik/102/

Hoffrage, U., et al. (2000). Communicating statistical information. *Science.* https://doi.org/10.1126/science.290.5500.2261.

Hüther, G. (2018). *Würde – Was uns stark macht.* New York: Random House.

Jakobs, H.-J. (2020). *Schlachthöfe, der neue Hotspot.* Retrieved May 11, 2020, from https://www.handelsblatt.com/meinung/morningbriefing/morning-briefing-schlachthoefe-der-neue-hotspot/25817868.html

Janson, M. (2020). *Jahrzehnt des Wachstums für US-Techriesen [Digitales Bild].* Retrieved May 11, 2020, from https://de.statista.com/infografik/20417/marktkapitalisierung-von-gafam/

Kahneman, D., & Tversky, A. (1979). Prospect theory: An analysis of decision under risk. *Econometrica, 47*(2), 263. https://doi.org/10.2307/1914185.

SAFe. (2020). Retrieved May 11, 2020, from www.scaledagileframework.com

Shefrin, H. (2016). *Behavioral risk management: Managing the psychology that drives decisions and influences operational risk.* New York: Palgrave.

Vieweg, S. (2020a). *The art of unleashing full SAFe potential – results from an independent empirical research amongst SAFe experts.* Retrieved October 02, 2020, from https://youtu.be/Ck7Nh54Il38

Vieweg, S. (2020b). *Response for the consultation paper on the development of the CFA Institute ESG Disclosure Standards for Investment Products.* Retrieved October 02, 2020, from https://www.cfainstitute.org/-/media/documents/code/esg-standards/esg-consultation-paper-comment-stefan-vieweg.ashx?la=en&hash=AB522D11420C85A288361897A6170F49B4ED9BDE

Business Ethics

Stefan H. Vieweg

3.1 Learning Objectives

1. Identify a business's relevant stakeholders and influencing groups that take a specific ethical responsibility.
2. Elaborate on the responsibility of consumers toward ethical standards, as they are driving the supply by their demand.
3. Analyze major dimensions of the producer ethics.
4. Illustrate the challenges and practical approaches to ensure a well-functioning whistle-blowing system.
5. Identify employees' obligations to their employers with regard to loyalty, but also to counteract any encouragement of unethical behavior by superiors.
6. Discuss the extended reach of investors' obligations to act in an ethical manner and assess the usefulness and limitations of current initiatives to include non-economic data in companies' reporting.
7. Identify elements of an ethical framework for businesses.

3.2 Ethical Stakeholders

Business decisions are not limited to the management. In fact, all stakeholders of an organization will participate in economic decisions, either directly or indirectly. Stakeholders can be classified into influence and stakeholder groups (see Fig. 3.1).

S. H. Vieweg (✉)
Institute of Compliance and Corporate Governance, RFH - University of Applied Sciences Cologne, Cologne, Germany
e-mail: dr.vieweg@vieweg-beratung.de

© The Author(s), under exclusive license to Springer Nature Switzerland AG 2021
S. H. Vieweg (ed.), *AI for the Good*, Management for Professionals,
https://doi.org/10.1007/978-3-030-66913-3_3

Fig. 3.1 Influence and stakeholder groups of companies, own presentation based on Dillerup and Stoi (2012)

From an ethical perspective, it is irrelevant whether or not there is a permanent contractual obligation to the company.

Of these stakeholders, customers and end consumers, managers as representatives of the companies, employees, and investors play a special role from a business ethics perspective. This is examined in more detail in the following sections.

3.3 Consumers' Ethics

In a buyer's market—and this situation is undoubtedly present in most markets in the course of globalization and digitization—consumers play the most important role.

"There is only one boss. The customer. And he can fire everybody in the company from the chairman on down, simply by spending his money somewhere else" (Sam Walton Quotes n.d.). This quote, made by the Walmart founder Sam Walton and already somewhat old, has not lost any of its topicality. Against the background of the almost unlimited supply of information via the Internet, consumers today are more competent than ever (or at least they could be). Customer preferences change with the spirit of the times, so that, for example, needs established over generations are changing. This becomes clear if the importance for concrete consumer and investment products is looked at: for example, the passenger car has lost its (prestige) appeal in many cases among the younger generation, and other substitutes of the "sharing economy" made possible by digitization have overtaken the car.

Other needs, e.g., more conscious nutrition, also lead to distortions of previous market dynamics. However, there are inconsistencies everywhere, when evidence and claims diverge considerably. This is briefly demonstrated by a small example of organically produced meat for Germany using available statistical data:

Table 3.1 Organic meat demand and supply in Germany (own presentation)

Statistics (Germany—DE)	2018	Remarks
Per capita total meat consumption	60.2 kg	Heinrich, Ph. (2020): Ethischer Konsum—Statista Dossierplus zum ökologischen und sozialen Konsumverhalten, S. 22
Population	83 Mio	https://data.worldbank.org/country/germany?view=chart. Accessed: 13.5.2020
Calculated total consumption	**4,992,261 t**	
Total organic production actually in DE	**118,130 t**	DBV—Situationsbericht 2019/20, Seite 45, https://www.bauernverband.de/situationsbericht. (access 08.08.2020)
Organic food sales	12.0 Mrd El	Ökologische Landwirtschaft—Branchenreport 2020, Seite 25, in Statista ID 4109
Total share of organic food sales	5.5%	Ökologisahe Landwirtschaft—Branchenreport 2020, Seite 17, in Statista ID 378372
Assumption: Organic meat share same as total share of organic food sales		
→ Organic meat demand	274,574 t	
Share actual organic meat production (in country) covering demand	**43.0 %**	assuming no organic meat export surplus (very conservative view, as actually there at least for all meat categories an export surplus, see below)
Meat import to DE (inbound)	8,829 MEUR	Genesis-Online Datenbank—51000-0005, in Statista ID 459309
Meat export from DE (outbound)	10,514 MEUR	Genesis-Online Datenbank—51000-0005, in Statista ID 459319
Meat export surplus	16%	
Assumption: Organic meat trade on pro rata basis as total meat trade, export surplus		
Share actual organic meat production (in country) covering demand	**36.1%**	assuming that the organic meat export surplus on a pro rate basis being the same as the total meat export

Example organic meat—demand and supply inconsistencies. Based on statistical data available from official governmental statistics and farmers' associations, the following calculations show significant discrepancies between the (much higher) demand for organic meat and the supply (see Table 3.1):

Best case, only 43% in Germany is produced of what is consumed under very conservative assumptions (reflecting Germany's meat export surplus, it is only 36%).[1] The solution can only be then:

(continued)

---

[1]Own analysis based on Statista data on organic food consumption, total meat consumption, and organic meat production. In 2018, the share of organic food was 5.5%. Due to the primary justification to buy organic for the benefit of animal welfare, the actual organic consumption share is likely to be much higher.

1. More than half of the organic meat consumed in the leading European economic nation Germany is imported: Here the question arises immediately, how is this to succeed, if a highly developed country like Germany, which is a net exporter of meat (with a 16% meat export surplus), is not able to cover its own organic meat demand? - OR -
2. Not everything that is sold as "organic" is actually "organic."

The interpretation is left to the reader. This example shows that evidence-based (machine-based) analysis can quickly expose such discrepancies. Further AI technology can help to identify mismatches early and to prevent misrepresentation, as the challenge is not in actually doing the calculation, but rather pulling together various data and analyzing it toward the proof point.

In general, consumer behavior is of central—also ethical—importance, since purchasing behavior has a considerable influence on the business strategy of producers and production conditions. Thus, the demand for cheap(est) products has a direct impact on the business strategy of companies that want to be successful in this market: They will strive for price and thus cost leadership and hence optimize their value-added chain in one go, without taking other goals into account. This customer behavior is then also often used to explain their own corporate (non-) responsibility. One example is the textile discounter KiK of the Tengelmann Group:

Example Customers' Responsible on the Supply Chain
It is argued that the customer is primarily interested in the price (Böcking et al. 2015) and thus not for the conditions under which the products are manufactured. Auditing in accordance with demanding occupational safety standards is also often used as a relieving argument (here: Social Accountability International SAI SA8000® (SAI 2020)), but these certificates are not meaningful if they are bought on the de facto black market (Böcking et al. 2015). The German textile discounter KiK was recently involved in two disasters involving its suppliers in Asia: In September 2012, a devastating fire at the Ali Enterprises textile factory in Karachi (Pakistan) claimed 258 lives and injured 32 people. Two months before the disaster, Ali Enterprises was certified as SA8000 compliant, but this did not correspond to the reality at the time of the catastrophe, as there were no emergency exits, sprinkler systems, or usable escape routes and the employees were effectively trapped in a deadly trap by barred windows (Haufe 2019). KiK had purchased about 75% of the production and was therefore the dominant customer for whom it would have been easy to demand humane working conditions and minimum safety standards (ECCHR 2019). Relatives and survivors sued KiK

(continued)

for appropriate damages in a liability lawsuit initiated by ECCHR in German courts. Although the case was decided against the plaintiffs on formal (statute of limitations) grounds, there is no decision on the merits of the case itself. In the jurisdiction the understanding seems to broaden that the implementation of minimum standards belongs to the fundamental care obligations of the management of enterprises starting from a certain size, so that with neglect quite legal liability consequences can follow (BGH, judgement of 17.9.2009, 5 StR 394/08). A uniform international legal regulation on the duties of care in the entire supply chain—as also demanded by the ECCHR—is the basis for legal security of companies and for the avoidance of distortions of competition.

In a buyer's market—and this situation is undoubtedly present in most markets in the course of globalization and digitization—consumers play the most important role. However, despite excessive information, consumers are typically hardly able to understand the complexity of production conditions and supply chains and use them as decision support for their purchase.

The behavior of individual consumers has a direct impact on the individual, but in the medium term, similar behavior will also have an impact on society. It is well known that unhealthy nutrition and lack of exercise leads to obesity and serious health problems for the individual. But in the medium term, the entire society is also affected by this, with considerable economic consequences in the form of drastically rising health costs and reduced performance. In 2017, for example, over 52% of adults in Germany were overweight, an increase of about 8% compared to 20 years earlier (DSTATIS 2017). In the same period, healthcare costs have increased by 91%[2]; the cost of obesity, a "widespread disease," is already estimated to account for 5%–15% of total healthcare expenditure in Western industrialized countries (DSTATIS 2017).

A further example of the ethical implications of consumer behavior is shown by a non-material consumption—the media consumption. The negative correlations have now been sufficiently substantiated in scientific studies. For example, the study shows that children and adolescents have developmental disorders (concentration, language, hyperactivity) when they consume media on a daily basis, already over 30 min (Büsching and Riedel 2017). This raises the question of ethical parenting responsibility if guardians do not (or cannot) meet their responsibility toward their children.

---

[2]Own evaluation based on data according to (BMG 2020).

3.4   Producers' Ethics

Based on the considerations made in the previous section, producer ethics is seamlessly linked to consumer ethics. Producers are basically responsible for all corporate processes, although the definition of the value/(supply) chain is partly disputed; see examples in Sect. 3.3. In a buyers' market with comparatively high competitive pressure, the ethical demands on producers can be derived directly from consumer expectations as follows:

- Quality:
  - The product or service corresponds to the published or advertised characteristics (so no cheating like relabeling occurs, which is very often seen in food production).
  - The company is liable for quality losses to an appropriate extent and meets its guarantee, warranty, and liability obligations. From an economic point of view, it can be shown that it typically pays off to provide additional ex gratia agreements and services—more than just the bare minimum requirement. The reason is in the fact that acquiring a new customer in a competitive market may be in the order of 10 times the costs than keeping an existing customer (and developing the relationship with that customer in the form of upselling and increasing the share of wallet[3] with that customer).
- Environmental compatibility:
  - Environmentally friendly production with minimum consumption of resources is guaranteed. This requirement in principle aligns with economic (profit maximization) objectives, though only in the long run, as for reducing resources typically means upfront investments into new procedures, new production means such as machines, new suppliers (that need to be qualified), etc. So, the key challenge for the producer is to apply a long-term sustainable view.
  - Nature and animal protection are considered in an appropriate manner. Though the definition of "appropriate" is a complex topic in its own rights (see example MSC).

Example sustainable-certified fishery according to MSC: Sustainable quality standards such as the Marine Stewardship Council ("MSC") came into massive critique due to too lax standards, e.g., by allowing vessels in one fishing trip to follow the sustainable-certified standards for parts of the

(continued)

---

[3]Share of wallet is the amount of annual spend of a particular customer for a specific group of products or services. A low share of wallet a producer A has with customer B, e.g., 10%, would suggest that the producer A has still a high potential to increase the future spent of customer B with A, instead of spending the funds with another supplier.

catch, and to ignore it for the rest (White 2018). Only after protest from a worldwide advocacy group of different part of the societies, including marine conservation activists, food retailers, and politicians (White 2017), the MSC board changed this particular rule. Though it needs to be reflected that the certification requirements are based on self-disclosure procedures (e.g., every fishery can define its target stocks, management areas, fishing gear, and vessels, known as its unit of assessment ("UoA") (White 2018)), and with that there is no proof that a particular fishery is truly reflecting the needs of sustainability.

- Social compatibility
  - Fair wages are paid for all parties in the supply chain, especially the original producers (small farmers, workers).
  - Renouncement of child labor, which comprises not only own direct workforce, but as well in the entire supply chain all along upstream to the initial raw producer (see Sect. 4.3).
  - No discrimination, which comprises all sorts of inadequate differentiation criteria such as gender, ethnicity, and appearance.
  - No morbid working conditions.
- Governance
  - Conformity to regulations and full respect of the minimum legal requirements.
  - Fair competitive behavior. The producer ethics are subject to various influencing factors. For example, strategic decisions have a direct impact on the structural and process organization and thus on the various stakeholders (see Fig. 3.1). Furthermore, the personnel and management policy is decisive for the anchoring and operationalization of corporate ethics. In this respect, managers in particular bear far-reaching moral responsibility for anchoring the basic under-standing, values, and concretely set rules in the company.

The reason for this is that managers make personnel-related decisions and act as role models for employees and other stakeholders. Qua function, they have a knowledge advantage over other stakeholders and thus managers are given respon-sibility. They have a responsibility to their employees, who are bound to loyalty by their employment contract, to refrain from committing any immoral acts themselves and to immediately prevent individual employees from taking advantage of immoral behavior. Otherwise, tolerating immoral actions would undermine their own credi-bility and cause lasting damage.

For managers, this means to reflect critically on their own activities against the background of potentially ethically offensive behavior: Even if a manager's actions are within the legal framework, they may need to be questioned from an ethical point of view, as they may appear unethical to stakeholders and thus undermine the credibility of the manager. Accordingly, it is the task of the manager to reflect on

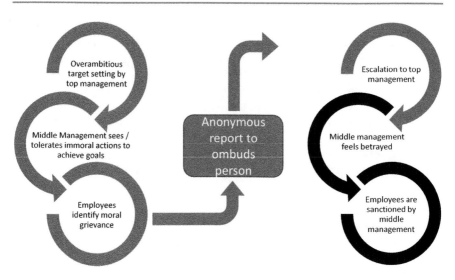

Fig. 3.2 Whistle-blowing challenge (own presentation)

this perspective. The moral compass, for example, which will be examined in more detail later on, helps to do this.

On the one hand, managers should remind their employees of their obligation to behave loyally and morally impeccably. On the other hand, managers should also ask their employees to point out justified grievances if immoral behavior is expected of them. Due to the dependency situation of the employees on the employer, the problem arises here that the employees must not suffer any disadvantage from this so-called whistle-blowing. The employer can contain this problem by creating structures that strengthen trust in the whistle-blowing system. If this is not taken into account, the whistle-blowing system quickly becomes a pro forma institution, but it does not contribute to the improvement process of the company (see Fig. 3.2).

It is recommended to consider at least the following:

- Establishing an absolutely independent trustworthy authority outside the company as an anonymous contact point for employees. It is completely irrelevant whether or not a completely adequate level of protection of the person making the report can be achieved technically and operationally, for example, through internal company data protection measures. The mere fact that, for example, a company internal telephone number or e-mail address is given as contact leads to a considerable loss of confidence in the system by the employees.
- It must be ensured that repression and sanctions by management against individual (supposedly reporting) employees or entire groups are rigorously prevented: due to the often very specific knowledge, even in larger organizations in the reporting chain, there is a subliminal risk of discrimination.
- The system may not permit a distinction between different persons—a VIP bonus or inviolability of the executive committee would be fatal for the reliability.

- The effectiveness of the system should be made transparent (in the sense of consolidation and further confidence building) and mistakes should be dealt with openly. Causes for rule violations should be on the factual level ("Why could it come to this, what was missing/what went wrong/what can we improve in the process to prevent this grievance in advance in the future?") and not on the personal level ("Whom to blame?").

3.5 Jobholders' Ethics

Jobholders' ethics deals with the responsibility and duties that workers and employees in companies must fulfill. Examples here are:

- Work performance to the full extent and as contractually agreed. In some settings of knowledge work, it is anticipated that jobholders utilize their full capabilities on the job. The famous proverb from Steve Jobs illustrates this: "It doesn't make sense to hire smart people and then tell them what to do. We hire smart people so they can tell us what to do" (Jobs 2011). This expectation is directly linked to the principal–agent theorem (see Sect. 2.6.2): likewise the explanation given there, it can be transferred to functional staff as well as they have the operational knowledge and details that may be used in a way of optimizing the employer's results (e.g., through staff that is intrinsically motivated) or—alternatively—just doing the minimum workload in order to optimize their own personal welfare.
- Jobholders need to apply full loyalty to the employer; in particular, this results in a non-competition clause and the requirement that the employer avert damage.
- Obligation to save the company resources, which is typically as well a contribution to sustainability, needs to be encountered.
- Health care of their own and colleagues is a basic requirement, in order not to endanger anyone associated with the employer and its stakeholders. In particular in times of specific crisis like the 2020 COVID-19 crisis, acting without excuse in line with the rules (face mask, disinfection, social distancing) is paramount. In general, this includes as well competent decision on whether or not staying (physically) away from the employer's premises and stakeholders in case of an infection.
- Act in a trustworthy reliable way by not giving false information to stakeholders.
- Jobholders are supposed to fully meet their tax obligations. In particular settings this may be a nontrivial topic such as in labor leasing arrangements that involve fictitious self-employment:

> *Example labor leasing:* For many companies (the lessee or client), worker leasing is an attractive alternative instead of hiring permanent staff. The benefits include higher flexibility, less administrational effort, and spot-on

(continued)

skills as required. The provider of such services, the worker leasing company or professional employer organization ("PEO"), though, will recruit individuals and assign those persons to work at and for the client. In contrast to temporary staffing, worker leasing constitutes a permanent employment between the PEO and the worker, but it is the client that assigns specific tasks to the worker.

Fictitious self-employment arose when employers wanted to avoid social security contributions for their employees (and thus maximize their profits) by dismissing them and then re-integrating them as self-employed. A self-employed is responsible for her/his own social security, receives no sick pay, and must take care of the acquisition of orders her/himself.

Some jurisdictions handle fictitious self-employment in such a manner that it is not "just" linked to the person but to the specifics of a contract. That is in Germany it can happen that the self-employed person can be both self-employed and pseudo-independent in different job situations at the same time! The status may be audited by the pension insurance agency and lead to consequences for all involved parties, the PEO on obligation to contribute to the social insurance, the self-employed on social pension contributions, and the client on permanent employment contract. (Weidner 2018).

Employees are thus required to behave loyally and morally without objection, but at the same time they should refuse to obey if immoral behavior is demanded of them and if necessary even report this (publicly) (see also Sect. 3.3).

3.6   Investors' Ethics

Investor ethics focuses on the responsibility and duties of investors for companies. By deciding in which type of companies they invest their own capital ("asset owners") or that of their clients ("asset managers"), they also bear corporate responsibility. Equity capital providers belong to the stakeholder groups; lenders at least still belong to the influence groups of companies (see Fig. 3.1). As already shown in Sect. 2.6.1, there is a certain awareness for the topic and different approaches. These initiatives try to capture value regarding environmental, social, and governance ("ESG") impact of business activities. So far, the initiatives have rather restrained success—are represented in the investment market. This is mainly due to the conflict of goals between (short-term) profitability and (medium to long-term) sustainability (Caseau and Grolleau 2020). A comparison of (still dominant) traditional investment strategy and sustainable investment (so-called impact investment) shows the tension and the increase in the complexity of impact investment (Table 3.2).

Table 3.2 Comparison of traditional investment and impact investment (own presentation based on Caseau and Grolleau (2020))

	Traditional investment	Impact investment
Objective	(Short-term monetary) wealth maximization of equity providers	(Short-term) monetary prosperity maximization AND non-monetary social prosperity
Main selection criteria	Risk-adjusted return	Risk-adjusted return AND non-monetary social value contribution
ESG aspects (Environmental, Social, Governance)	Incidental, not in focus	Intended

With impact investment, there are various exclusion criteria that prevent the granting of credit or investment. Examples are Bak (2014):

- Production or distribution of military weapons
- Ownership or distribution of nuclear power plants
- Processing genetically manipulated plant or seed
- Allowing child labor
- Introducing animal testing for cosmetics
- Speculation with raw materials and food
- Present blatant cases of bribery and corruption
- Commit blatant violations of human rights
- ...

Even if overall impact investment does not yet dominate the market by a long way (e.g., in Germany the share in 2018 was just once 0.5%[4]), a considerable increase over the past years is to be registered nevertheless [5], as awareness increases and especially exclusion criteria push investors into sustainable investment(s).

Against the background of (AI-supported) automation in the investment process by so-called robo-advisors, there will be a considerable challenge in the future to map automated investment decisions in an ethically correct manner. Even though the market penetration is still very manageable (for Germany, the network rate in 2018 was 0.9%, but in 2020 already 2.5%), the managed investment volume will increase by a factor of 16 by 2024 compared to 2018[6].

---

[4]Own calculation based on (BVI 2020).

[5]According to FNG (2019), there is an increase from 2014 to 2018 of 3.5 times.

[6]https://de.statista.com/outlook/337/137/robo-advisors/deutschland (accessed 07.08.2020).

3.7   Ethical Frameworks for Businesses

Normative corporate governance is the permanent foundation of a company and thus sets the framework for the basic orientation of the company and the actions of its stakeholders (see Fig. 3.1). Thus, normative management determines the self-image of a company, creates identity and meaning, and ultimately gives the company legitimacy and the right to exist.

A distinction is made between five elements (see Fig. 3.3), of which the corporate values, as a meaningful basis, determine the ethical orientation of a company. The corporate philosophy forms the starting point and determines standards as a benchmark for the actions of the management, describes values, and defines the ethical standards of the company.

Ultimately, the company values are based on the ethical convictions, education, and experience of the people who shape the company and its society. In Schein's organizational culture model (Schein 1985), this corresponds to the deepest level below the surface—the "basic assumptions." These are formative for the company and by far outlast the period of effect of the persons who initially form it. This becomes visible, for example, in corporate succession when the core of the company (the ultimate reason for existence or the "raison d'être") is preserved and the established behavior patterns are continued as tradition.

The ethics of a company are the result of the ethical, moral, and social attitudes and values of the actors in a company. These are often documented as a code of ethics and communicated internally and externally.

Meaningful and ethical corporate values, which offer stakeholders a strong opportunity to identify with the company and are authentically communicated by top management, not only promote corporate culture but also economic added value. This has been comprehensively proven in a study conducted by the Great Place To Work® Institute, for example, in an employee survey of 1000 US companies (Guiso et al. 2013): Particularly when employees perceive their top management to be

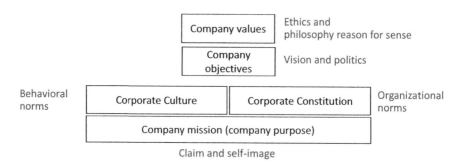

Fig. 3.3 Normative corporate governance—terms (own presentation)

ethical and trustworthy, an overvaluation of the market (Tobin's Q[7]) and thus added value for shareholders can be detected.

In order for ethical business convictions to be anchored in business operations, an ethical business framework is required that applies equally to all players. For example, the fair design of economic processes requires binding regulations at both national and global level. Otherwise, two effects become obvious: First, a distortion of competition in favor of the unethically acting (and ethics cost-saving) company, and second, a dilution of the position of the ethically acting company, since the latter can hardly bear the suffered competitive disadvantage in the long run and can hardly defend it against its own stakeholders.

Even though legal regulations are usually implemented reactively, government intervention via laws and regulations is important to safeguard principles such as justice, freedom, and responsibility or environmental protection concerns. Imbalances between countries lead to different development perspectives of the countries concerned: For example, the strong export power of a highly developed country (such as Germany) is one reason why the development of precisely these competencies in the importing country is severely limited because they are not economically viable.

3.8   Finish Line Quiz

3.01	The inner stakeholder group comprises of ...	
	1	... managers, competitors, customers, suppliers.
	2	... managers, customers, suppliers, owners.
	3	... managers, consumers, employees, owners.
	4	... managers, partners, customers, suppliers.
3.02	Consumers' role on ethical business standards ...	
	1	... is often overstated, as it is the producing companies' customers (business to business, "B2B") that drive the demand.
	2	... cannot be overestimated because finally it is the end consumer's demand that drives the production and ethical conditions.
	3	... is indifferent, as the consumers themselves are non-rational, hence acting without and ethical agenda.
	4	... is a non-issue in highly developed countries as broadly consumers demand for highest ethical production standards.
3.03	How can AI help in fostering ethical standards?	
	1	Early identification of mismatches and discrepancies between claims and facts.
	2	Providing a comprehensive analysis on consistency.
	3	Guide consumers to decipher misrepresentations.
	4	All the above.

(continued)

[7]Tobin's Q is a financial ratio that indicates if a corporation or even an entire market is under-(0–1) or overpriced (>1): basically calculated as the total market value divided by the total asset (or replacement value) of a specific corporation or even markets.

3.04	The ethical dimensions of customers' demand toward producers are …	
	1	… quality aspects.
	2	… environmental aspects.
	3	… social and governance aspects.
	4	… all the above.
3.05	The whistle-blowing challenge can be met by the following considerations:	
	1	Use an internal Ombud person as single point of contact.
	2	Extra preventive measures against discrimination even in larger organizations.
	3	Larger organizations do not have issues, as whistle-blowing will be done anonymously.
	4	The system shall differentiate between different persons and their status, in order to ensure a tailor-made dealing with allegations.
3.06	An employee of the investors relations (IR) department is asked by an investor to explain the supposed massive loss in running last quarter (no public report yet).	
	1	The IR person shall provide full details in order to act in a trustworthy reliable way by giving all information to stakeholders.
	2	The IR person shall deny that any losses occurred; this is the loyalty obligation toward the employer.
	3	The IR person shall not disclose full details in order to act ethically correct.
	4	The IR person can disclose the information as it is the obligation of any member of the IR department to disclose stakeholder relevant information.
3.07	Impact investment reflects …	
	1	… exclusion of genetically manipulated plant or seed, animal testing for cosmetics, and speculation with raw materials.
	2	… the output of businesses ("impact"), disregarding how this is being achieved (utilitarian approach).
	3	… the allowance of ownership or distribution of nuclear power plants, child labor, speculation with food.
	4	… only the effects ("impact") of business activities regarding environmental and social aspects, disregarding economic performance.
3.08	Major elements of normative corporate governance are as follows:	
	1	Company's objectives reflect the vision and philosophical reason for sense.
	2	Company's purpose reflects its claim.
	3	Corporate culture is defined by organizational norms.
	4	Vision and politics are reflected in the company's values.

Correct answers can be found in www.vieweg-beratung.de/downloads

References

Bak, P. M. (2014). *Wirtschafts- und Unternehmensethik - Eine Einführung.*

BGH, judgement of 17.9. (2009), 5 StR 394/08.

BMG. (2020). Gesundheitsberichterstattung. gbe-bund.de. In *Statista ID 5463.* Retrieved May 13, 2020.

Böcking, D., Kazim, H., & Klawitter, N. (2015). *Umstrittener Textildiscounter So biegt sich der Kik-Chef die Fakten zurecht. Kik-Chef Heinz Speet verteidigt die Strategie des Textildiscounters*

- *Verantwortung für die Unglücke an den Billigstandorten weist er von sich. Doch viele seiner Argumente sind so nicht richtig. Ein Faktencheck.* Retrieved August 7, 2020, from https://www. spiegel.de/wirtschaft/unternehmen/kik-chef-des-textildiscounters-verteidigt-billig-strategie-a-1034311.html

Büsching, U., & Riedel, R. (2017). *BLIKK-Medien: Kinder und Jugendliche im Umgang mit elektronischen Medien.* Abschlussricht. Retrieved August 7, 2020, from https://www. bundesgesundheitsministerium.de/fileadmin/Dateien/5_Publikationen/Praevention/Berichte/ Abschlussbericht_BLIKK_Medien.pdf

BVI – Jahrbuch. (2020). Seite 93. In *Statista ID 12460.* Retrieved May 13, 2020.

Caseau, C., & Grolleau, G. (2020). Impact investing: Killing two birds with one stone? *Financial Analysts Journal,* https://doi.org/10.1080/0015198X.2020.1779561. Retrieved August 08, 2020.

Dillerup, R., & Stoi, R. (2012). *Fallstudien zur Unternehmensführung* (2nd ed., p. 19). Wiesbaden: Vahlen.

ECCHR. (2019). Retrieved August 7, 2020, from https://www.ecchr.eu/fall/kik-der-preis-der-arbeitsbedingungen-in-der-textilindustrie-suedasiens/

DSTATIS. (2017). *Mikrozensus - Körpermaße der Bevölkerung 2017,* Seite 11. Retrieved May 13, 2020, from https://www.destatis.de/DE/Themen/Gesellschaft-Umwelt/Gesundheit/ Gesundheitszustand-Relevantes-Verhalten/Publikationen/Downloads-Gesundheitszustand/ koerpermasse-5239003179004.pdf?__blob=publicationFile&v=4

FNG. (2019). Retrieved February 13, 2020, from https://www.forum-ng.org/images/stories/ Publikationen/fng-marktbericht_2019.pdf, p. 13f.

Guiso, L., Sapienza, P., & Zingales, L. (2013). *The value of corporate culture.* Retrieved August 7, 2020, from http://economics.mit.edu/files/9721

Haufe. (2019). *Hoffnungen der Opfer des Brandes in Pakistan auf Schadensersatz von KiK sind geplatzt.* Retrieved August 7, 2020, from https://www.haufe.de/compliance/recht-politik/ haftungsprozess-wegen-brand-in-pakistan-gegen-kik_230132_479196.html

Heinrich, P. (2020). *Ethischer Konsum - Statista Dossierplus zum ökologischen und sozialen Konsumverhalten,* p. 22.

Jobs, S. (2011). *Steve Jobs: His own words and wisdom.* Cupertino: Cupertino Silicon Valley Press.

SAI. (2020). Retrieved August 7, 2020, from https://sa-intl.org/programs/sa8000/

Sam Walton Quotes. (n.d.). BrainyQuote.com. Retrieved August 6, 2020, from BrainyQuote.com Web site: https://www.brainyquote.com/quotes/sam_walton_146810

Schein, E. H. (1985). *Organizational culture and leadership. A dynamic view.* San Francisco, CA: Jossey-Bas.

Weidner, C. (2018). *Scheinselbstständigkeit, verdeckte Arbeitnehmerüberlassung & Co.* endlich richtig verstehen. Retrieved May 13, 2020, from https://www.vgsd.de/scheinselbststaendigkeit-verdeckte-arbeitnehmerueberlassung-co-endlich-richtig-verstehen/

White, C. (2017). *"On the Hook" advocacy group formed to challenge MSC tuna certification.* Retrieved May 13, 2020, from https://www.seafoodsource.com/on-the-hook-advocacy-group-formed-to-challenge-msc-tuna-certification

White, C. (2018). *MSC changes policy after intense criticism.* Retrieved May 13, 2020, from https:// www.seafoodsource.com/news/environment-sustainability/msc-changes-policy-after-intense-criticism

World Bank. (2020). *Germany.* Retrieved May 13, 2020, from https://data.worldbank.org/country/ germany?view=chart

Ethics in an International Context

4

Stefan H. Vieweg

4.1 Learning Objectives

1. Raising awareness of the problem of acting ethically in an international context.
2. Illustrating that there is no "one-size-fits-all" ethical solution to international business.
3. Reflecting the common denominator of minimum international standards derived from the UN Convention on Human Rights and the potential discrimination in the use of AI technologies.
4. Utilizing the Fragile State Index (FSI) and the example of the AI superpower China, elaborate on the 12 different dimensions of index and the countries' performance considering key political events.
5. Identifying current issues where the effects of the "Tragedy of the Commons" can be seen, e.g., the wide spread of the SARS-CoV2 virus that caused COVID-19 pandemic crisis in 2020.
6. Analyzing the CPI as indicator for corruption and basic international agreement to fight against corruption such as UNCAC and OECD's Convention against Bribery of Foreign Public Officials.
7. Defining an ethical dilemma.
8. Elaborating on the factors that enable ethical management in an international context using the ethical compass.

S. H. Vieweg (✉)
Institute of Compliance and Corporate Governance, RFH - University of Applied Sciences Cologne, Cologne, Germany
e-mail: dr.vieweg@vieweg-beratung.de

Table 4.1 Example of applicable working conditions standards abroad (own presentation)

Working conditions in host country are worse than in home country	in the home country (head-quarters)	in host country (production sites)	Possible positive economic implications	Possible negative economic implications
Applicable standards of the …	Home country	Home country	Reputation as "good citizen", fulfillment of stakeholder expectations regarding sustainability	Cost and thus competitive disadvantage
	Home country	Above those of the host country, but below those of the home country	Minimization of reputational damage	Damage to reputation, legal consequences
	Home country	Host country	Short-term maintaining of competitiveness	Damage to reputation, legal consequences of non-compliance with other applicable (e.g. international) standards

4.2 Applicable Ethics

In the previous chapters, the complexity and multifaceted nature of ethical questions and possible approaches have already been explained. An additional dimension, which is particularly important in the globalized world, is internationality. Societal norms and rules that give expression to the respective ethics depend on the respective culture as well as on the (mostly economic) environment in which they operate. Accordingly, standards of Western industrial nations cannot simply be projected onto countries with little economic development. On the other hand, simply applying the usually lower standard of a developing country to the more restrictive home country leads to considerable inconsistency, at least in terms of reputation problems and even legal disputes (e.g., see once again the example of the textile discounter KiK, Sect. 3.3). In other words, the moral obligation of multinational companies or companies with suppliers in less ethically restrictive countries requires a targeted approach and goalsetting: which standards are to be used as appropriate. Example (Table 4.1):

However, setting minimum acceptable standards of compliance with fundamental workers' rights is not enough: effective and regular monitoring is needed to ensure that standards are actually met. Companies based in countries with high CSR requirements are faced with the great challenge of ensuring the effectiveness of the review. To illustrate the issue, the KIK example from Sect. 3.3 is referred to once more: even official audits are to be questioned very carefully, since this service is also in part in strong competition and then unethical courtesy reports seem to be quite common.

Example: the auditing dilemma: Even renowned certifiers are not immune (if one thinks of the devastating dam burst in Vale, Brazil in 2019): Under the leadership of ECCHR, a complaint was filed against the auditor TÜV Süd, since obvious structural defects did not lead to the responsible engineer (in Germany) refusing to issue the certificate (Maus 2019). Even if in this particular case the problem seems to be extended to the fact that in the highly developed home country of the auditor the deficiency was known, the overall conclusion is that foreign subsidiaries and subcontractors are regularly audited to ensure that they will meet the standards and take corrective action if necessary (Hill 2014).

AI provides significant support for ethical decision-making, in particular in an international context. For example, the current practice of identifying and selecting local suppliers (typically in low-cost countries), the process of a strategic purchasing manager will be quite manual. Search is basically performed via the Internet incumbent search engines (that have their own dynamics in terms of search engine optimization ("SEO") and AI-based consumer analysis (see Sect. 6.5). Hence, AI can help in structuring the search for potential supplier identification and later on in the qualification as well as onboarding process. Based on ethical minimum standards, the selection process can be optimized.

4.3   UN Declaration of Human Rights as Minimum

The basis for an international understanding of basic human rights is the resolution of the General Assembly of the United Nations of December 10, 1948 (UN 1948)—the Universal Declaration of Human Rights. The most important of the following human rights conventions have developed from this (DIM 2020):

1. Civil pact (ICCPR)
   International Covenant on Civil and Political Rights (ICCPR):
   This pact covers protection against torture, slavery, and a general ban on discrimination; the protection of private life, minorities; freedom rights of expression, religion, assembly; as well as the right to vote and stand for election.

2. Social pact (ICESCR)

   The International Covenant on Economic, Social and Cultural Rights (ICESCR) originating from 1966 (together with ICCPR) states that economic, social, and cultural rights form an indivisible unit together with civil and political rights.

3. Anti-racial convention (ICERD)

   The International Convention on the Elimination of All Forms of Racial Discrimination (ICERD) intends to ensure that people are protected in law and in fact from racial discrimination.

4. Women's rights convention (CEDAW)

   The Convention on the Elimination of All Forms of Discrimination against Women is the most important international human rights treaty for women. The signatory states commit to the legal and factual equality of women in all areas of life, including the private sphere.

5. Children's rights convention (CRC)

   The center of this convention is the recognition of children as human rights holders. Its principles include the right to non-discrimination, the right to life and development of the child, the right to have the best interests of the child a primary consideration, and the right to be heard and to have the views of the child taken into account. Extensions include prevention of participation of children in armed conflicts, sale of children, child prostitution, and child pornography.

6. All migrant workers convention (ICRMW)

   The International Convention on the Protection of the Rights of All Migrant Workers and Members of their Families protects migrant workers and their family members regardless of their residence status. The protection extends to the entire migration process, from leaving the country of origin to their stay and return.

7. Disability Rights Convention (ICRPD)

   The Convention on the Rights of Persons with Disabilities

   The Disability Rights Convention concretizes the universal human rights for people with disabilities such as autonomy and self-determination as well as inclusion, i.e., the equal coexistence of people with and without disabilities.

8. Anti-torture convention (CAT)

   The Convention against Torture and Other Cruel, Inhuman or Degrading Treatment or Punishment is one of the few human rights norms that claim legal validity without exception and also apply in emergency situations. Each state party to the Convention undertakes to take effective legislative, administrative, judicial, or other measures to prevent torture and inhuman treatment. Extradition or deportation of persons to States where they are at risk of torture is prohibited.

9. Convention against disappearances (CPED)

   The International Convention for the Protection of All Persons from Enforced Disappearance requires state parties to undertake to define and punish enforced disappearances as a criminal offense.

   Disappearances are often accompanied by other human rights violations such as torture or extrajudicial executions.

The first seven conventions comprise a set of potential ethical issues if AI technologies are applied in a way that would lead to discrimination. Deliberately or not, as will be shown in Chaps. 6 and 8, there is a realistic chance that due to the approach taken to set up algorithms and to train them, a discrimination potential toward various groups is given.

Basic human rights are a matter of course in developed countries, but by no means in developing countries. This raises the question of the responsibility of companies that have activities in or with countries where basic human rights are not respected: Is it ethically permissible for companies to do business with countries with repressive regimes? It would be naive to retreat to the position of not doing any business there. Arguments against this are that, on the one hand, the company might close significant markets to itself (if such a renunciation can be identified at all), because its place in globalized competition will certainly be taken quickly by one of its competitors and, on the other hand, that economic exchange between countries with high standards and countries with lower standards will lead to an increase in low standards in the medium term.

4.4 Countries' Perception Regarding Their Ethical Orientation

Do multinational business activities really help to bring about change in these countries and ultimately improve citizens' rights?

This is a non-trivial question. Reflecting analysis findings such as the Fragile State Index (FSI) of the Fund for Peace (FFP 2020), which indicates the stability of a state, it becomes clear that 105 out of 178 countries are considered by a warning or alert, the minority considered stable or even sustainable. The Fund for Peace is a non-profit organization based in the USA and has a history of over 60 years. According to its own information, the Fragile State Index has been measuring the social, economic, and political pressure that 178 countries around the world have been exposed to since 2005. The index is composed of 12 primary indicators (normalized to maximum of 10, reflecting worst situation) in the four dimensions of cohesion, economic, political, and social, and uses a triangulated methodology that combines content analysis of millions of documents from more than 10,000 sources around the world with quantitative datasets and qualitative review. The index and its indicators are based on a social science framework that has been used by practitioners in the field of conflict early warning for over two decades (Fig. 4.1).

China is a case in point: according to the FSI, the overall situation in China has substantially improved (in 2020 69.9 on a scale with highest alert at 120, which corresponds to the 86th rank; see Fig. 4.2).

For example, the expectation that major international events such as the Olympic Games (2008) would bring about further opening and improve the situation in the long term was certainly given. However, in 2008 massive food scandal (see Sect. 7.4, where this event will be analyzed in the context of AI-based total surveillance) led to a massive drawback, followed by a steep improvement thereafter. Another

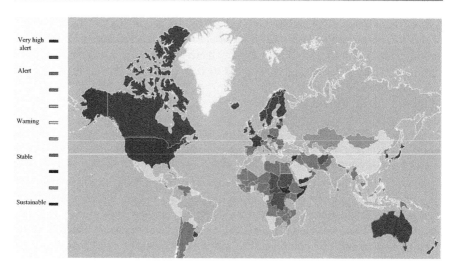

Fig. 4.1 Total ranking FSI 2020 (own presentation, data based on FFP (2020), 53 out of 178 countries are considered as alert)

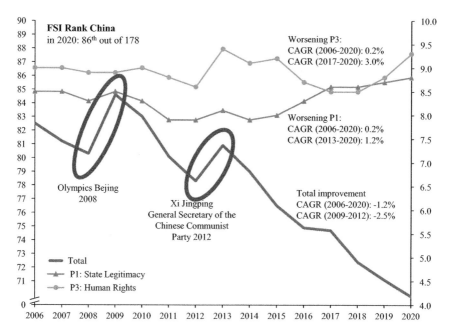

Fig. 4.2 Development of the FSI Index for China and major events (own presentation, data based on (FFP 2020))

setback followed after Xi Jinping took power in China in 2012. While the majority of indicators (see Table 4.2) improved, there are specific parameters that worsened significantly even further from a high level: P1-State Legitimacy reflects the citizens'

Table 4.2 FSI Indicators (own presentation based on FFP (2020))

Cohesion	Economic	Political	Social	Comprehensive
C1: Security Apparatus	E1: Economic Decline	P1: State Legitimacy	S1: Demographic Pressures	X1: External Intervention
C2: Factionalized Elites	E2: Uneven Economic Development	P2: Public Services	S2: Refugees and IDPs	
C3: Group Grievance	E3: Human Flight and Brain Drain	P3: Human Rights and Rule of Law		

confidence in political processes, political opposition, transparency, and fairness in the political process; P3 Human Rights and Rule of Law reflects whether fundamental human rights and freedoms are protected and respected and if there is a widespread abuse of legal, political, and social rights (FFP 2020). Hence, ethical relevant aspects lag behind. The widespread use of AI technologies, in particularly regarding population surveillance, control, and sanctions (see "social credit system" in Sect. 7.4), shows the pervasive nature of the ethical question.

4.5 Tragedy of the Commons

In addition to the social issues, which are articulated as a minimum in the protection of human rights, the ecological dimension represents a further, very great challenge with far-reaching effects. This is especially the case in those areas where the environment is a public good, i.e., where there is no (private) owner. Here the question is to what extent exploitation is justified if it degrades the environment. This problem is aggravated if the environmental regulations in the host country are worse than in the home country. Is a multinational company allowed to pollute the environment in developing countries just because there are no local regulations against it?

Here the local legal standard is clearly lower than the ethical standards in the home country.

The model of the "tragedy of the common language" (Hardin 1968) describes the dilemma in which a freely available but limited resource is not used in a socially efficient manner, thus threatening overuse that ultimately leads to social damage. As soon as a resource is unrestrictedly available, everyone will try to use this resource to maximize their own profit. As soon as too many users exploit this resource and it cannot regenerate, this not inexhaustible resource will inevitably degenerate and society will have to bear the costs of this degeneration, ultimately damaging the resource and, in the medium term, society. While adequate returns are still possible for the individual in the short term, the increased costs for the individual only become visible in the medium term.

The example of fishing and overfishing makes this obvious: if the limited resource of free-living fish in the waters is overfished, a collapse is imminent, as was the case with cod in the Baltic Sea in 2015 (Schröder 2020). However, regulation as practiced in the European Union is a controversial under-catch, because although there is an understanding of the need for catch quotas, the detailed assessment is usually very controversial, since a very restrictive catch quota can endanger the existence of fishermen in the short term and the scientific findings that are incorporated into the political decision-making process are usually still a considerable obstacle to the development of a sustainable fisheries policy. In the Brexit situation, the confrontation between Great Britain and the EU escalated exactly at the point of the catch quotas.

Example Brazil: A further example in South America is the overexploitation of the Brazilian rainforest, which has increased massively since the election of the controversial Jair Bolsonaro in 2018. Most of the time, large companies profit from the clearing and conversion into arable and pastureland, displace small farmers, and are devastating for the climate. The extent to which Brazil's (local) economic development should take precedence over a global commitment to climate protection is the subject of intense international debate. To what extent it is justifiable to involve, for example, German companies such as Bayer and BASF as suppliers of agricultural products, or SAP as a technology (software) supplier for digital agriculture, in which fertilizer and water requirements are determined automatically, cannot be answered trivially: On the one hand, such companies ultimately help to implement more effective agriculture with their products, and on the other hand, such activities promote controversial deforestation.

4.6   Extensive Land Use as a Social Hazard, e.g., SARS-CoV-2

The conversion of natural habitat into agricultural land or urban areas has another effect worthy of consideration, which must also be ethically located from the perspective of international business management: according to recent scientific findings, in addition to environmental problems, the conversion into usable land leads to a worrying change in the animal world. It is not only that the diversity of species is threatened enormously, but also that those animal species that could become dangerous for humans in the short term are best adapted to the new conditions: Zoonoses, i.e., diseases that are transmitted from animals to humans (and vice versa), are becoming more prevalent. The typically small host animals such as mice, rats, bats, or sparrow species serve as host species for corona-, henipa-, arena-, and flaviviruses or bacterial pathogens such as Borrelia and Leptospira (Gibb et al. 2020).

The SARS-CoV-2 virus, which first triggered the respiratory disease COVID-19 in Wuhan, China, at the end of 2019 and was classified as a pandemic by the World

Fig. 4.3 Global crisis effects on GDP development (own presentation, data based on IMF Global Outlook 2020 (IMF 2020))

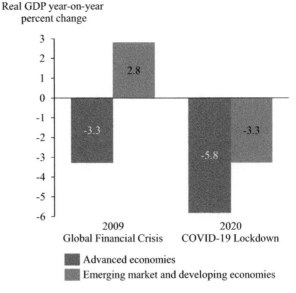

Real GDP year-on-year percent change

Health Organization (WHO) on March 11, 2020, due to its rapid spread, shows that this danger and the losses it causes—both in terms of human suffering and economic losses—are real. According to a forecast by the International Monetary Fund (IMF), the economic consequences imposed in many countries in the spring of 2020 as a result of lockdowns led to the biggest economic downturn worldwide since the Great Depression in the 1920s (Gopinath 2020) (Fig. 4.3).

This example shows that with increased exploitation of natural resources the likelihood of social and economic detrimental impact increases.

4.7   Corruption in an International Context

An important task in the economic context is the prevention of corruption. Although this can also be a compliance problem in the host country, business activities in the host country with low ethical standards present a particular challenge. Due to the mostly weak legal systems, the concentration of power without an effective corrective (e.g., through democratic structures with an effective opposition or media), this problem is perhaps even the greatest problem in the age of digitalization, in which a high degree of transparency and thus fewer chances of maladministration are generally attributed.

Corruption ultimately means the detour of resources intended for a certain community to (corrupt) individuals for sole, short-term, and selfish advantage. As can be seen in Fig. 4.4, the issue of corruption (at least in 2019) is still a global problem. Even the least corruption-prone countries (rank 1 in the Corruption Perception Index CPI) show a 5% increase since 2014. The CPI is a meta-index based

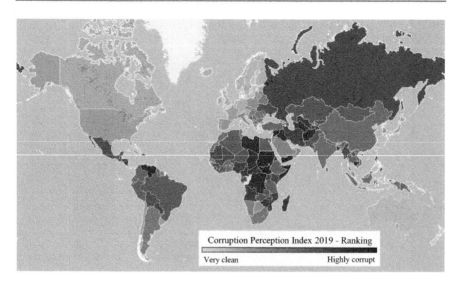

Fig. 4.4 Ranking according to the Corruption Perception Index 2019 (own presentation, data based on Transparency International (2020))

on scoring 13 sources (including African Development Bank, Bertelsmann Foundation Indices, Economist Intelligence, Freedom House, IMD, Varieties of Democracy Project, World Bank, World Justice Project Rule of Law Index, and others). The CPI has a maximum of 100 points; in 2019, the top-ranked countries New Zealand and Denmark had a CPI of 87, compared with 92 in 2014 DK (Transparency International 2020).

There are corresponding agreements at the international level, such as the conventions on combating bribery, for example:

- The United Nations Convention against Corruption (UNCAC) is the only legally binding universal instrument for fighting corruption. The convention covers many different forms of corruption, including bribery and abuse of office. Of particular importance is the restitution of assets, which aims to return assets to their rightful owners, including the countries from which they were unlawfully stolen.
- OECD's The Convention against Bribery of Foreign Public Officials in International Business Transactions requires member states to criminalize bribery of foreign public officials.

First, it is obviously ethically imperative not to allow corruption. But if in a country with an underdeveloped or inefficient administration, permits take years instead of days, is it acceptable for multinational companies to pay government officials to facilitate projects if it will create local income and jobs faster?

Ultimately, it comes down to the question whether it is not legitimate (not necessarily legal) to do a little evil to achieve a greater good.

4.8 Ethical Obligations of Internationally Active Companies

The orientation for internationally active companies in the decision-making process should be to assume social and ecological responsibility. This means that the social and ecological consequences of economic actions must be taken into account. This promotes decisions that have both good economic and good social consequences. The companies can position themselves as "good citizens," so to speak. In particular the idea of "noblesse oblige" comes into play here. Even if, in the figurative sense, the privileged are generally concerned (power, money, education), the promotion of the community and stabilization of the society in which the companies generate their value creation through social commitment is also a relevant component of entrepreneurial decisions that can pay off in the medium term. Proponents argue that companies need to give something back to the societies that have made their success possible. One example is the promotion of society in developing countries, where not only (short-term) production takes place, but also new sales markets can be opened up in the medium term. This strategy can be found, for example, with car manufacturers such as Volkswagen in China.

4.9 Ethical Dilemma

There are many situations in business life, but especially in an international context, in which none of the available alternatives seem ethically acceptable. This is because decisions in the real world are complex, the problem is often difficult to formulate, and the consequences are very difficult—if at all—to quantify. Here again, the example of overfishing and fishing quotas should be recalled (see Sect. 4.5).

> Example: An international construction group with headquarters in Europe, which regularly carries out projects for FIFA, is also active for the 2022 FIFA World Cup in Qatar. During an on-site visit by a group manager, he discovers that the working conditions of the temporary workers from Bangladesh hired by the local subcontractor contracted by the group are in violation of both the group's specifications and official FIFA guidelines. He instructs the local manager to demand the working conditions to the required level with the subcontractor or otherwise to terminate the contractual relationship immediately...

However, this decision, which may be desirable from an ethical point of view, is completely unrealistic: the employer support system "Kafala System" in Qatar, which gives employers extensive rights over workers and prevents them, for example, from changing jobs or leaving the country without the consent of their previous employer, is far from being a non-discriminatory form of employment, despite massive international protests and some reform efforts (Amnesty International

2019). To this extent, immediate termination of the assignment leads to the loss of jobs for the guest workers, who are mostly indebted to the employer due to advance support services provided by the employer (such as visas, residence permits, accommodation), so that their economic existence is ruined. Demanding better working conditions from the subcontractor, on the other hand, leads at best to the project becoming so expensive that it is no longer competitive or is not economically viable for the contracting construction company.

Typical dimensions of an ethical dilemma include

- Priority of the interests of the community or of a single person
- Trust in loyalty
- Short-term versus long-term
- Justice or forbearance

In a dilemma, correct action is not always clearly recognizable. An ethical framework or "ethical compass" is required here, which allows a structured weighing of the alternatives for a decision. Although the ethical compass is not only relevant in an international context, the additional complexity of societal differences makes it more difficult to find ethically justifiable decisions.

4.10 Factors of Unethical Behavior in an International Context

Figure 4.5 summarizes the main factors that promote unethical behavior. Specifically, in the international context it should be emphasized that it is particularly difficult to maintain personal ethics (or ethos) during an assignment abroad (ex-pat) if, for example, a significantly different standard is in place in the host country. As an example we can mention waste separation: while in the home country it may be a matter of course to separate waste and this may be done out of conviction (and the corresponding infrastructure such as separate garbage cans, etc., is available everywhere), abroad, where waste separation is not established, it may be very difficult to follow one's own convictions and, at the expense of additional effort (e.g., finding suitable collection points).

Social determinants, such as those found in Hofstede's taxonomy (Hofstede 1991) for the delimitation of social cultures, can also provide indications of potentially unethical behavior:

- Individualism and uncertainty avoidance: ethical behavior likely
- Masculinity and power distance: unethical behavior likely

If the organizational culture is geared toward short-term profit and less socially and ecologically sustainable action, it will be correspondingly difficult for individuals to manage their own affairs at a very high ethical level.

If role models are missing, if ethical considerations are at best lip service and published in Code of Conducts on websites, and—if necessary—still trained, but by

Fig. 4.5 Factors of unethical behavior, especially in an international context (own presentation, after (Hill 2014))

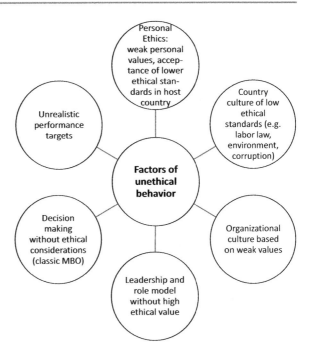

no means integrated into everyday life, than unethical behavior is quickly obvious. On the other hand, strong role models, which clearly demonstrate to the entire organization the importance of ethically correct behavior through one's own actions and, if necessary, by assuming responsibility and taking drastic measures in case of noncompliance, minimize the danger of unethical behavior in the organization.

Managers have a decisive role in setting appropriate goals. If ethical considerations are not taken into account in the decision-making process, which ultimately leads to the formulation of concrete objectives, unethical behavior is encouraged, since it is not relevant to the achievement of objectives. The classic, short-term oriented management method management-by-objective ("MBO") illustrates this, since here only the profit focus is set ("whatever it takes"). Of course, it is not a management method in itself that promotes or prevents ethical behavior; it is essentially the design of the parameters that counts, for example, the more modern variant—the objectives-key-results ("OKR")[1]—a management system in which the ethical dimension can be very well represented by formulating economic and ethically relevant goals (e.g., in social and ecological aspects).

Ultimately, however, the target level is just as decisive. If it is set too ambitiously and unrealistically, unethical behavior may result from the fact that (ethically questionable) ways to achieve the goal are sought. The consequences of this can

---

[1]This method is based on MBO and the SMART objective and has received a lot of attention due to its long-term use at Google.

be seen very clearly in the example of the Volkswagen diesel scandal surrounding exhaust gas manipulation, which became public in 2015.

4.11   Ethical Compass: A Guide to Ethical Conduct

Clear positions as blanket solutions are usually not conducive to an ethically based decision-making process. They are extreme positions that push the limits to impracticability. Some approaches to illustrate these extreme positions are discussed below using so-called strawmen models:

4.11.1 Righteous Moralist

The approach of applying the higher standards of the home country as well in the host country, with its low ethical standards, must be critically questioned with regard to its practicability: Ultimately, higher standards mean higher economic resource consumption (and thus higher costs), so that there is a very high risk that the entire undertaking cannot be presented in a commercially viable manner and may not be undertaken at all. The consequence is then, however, possibly even worse than if a small economic contribution is made in the host country while tolerating lower ethical standards.

One example is production in the textile, clothing, and shoe industry in Southeast Asian emerging or developing countries with lower occupational safety standards than in the (Western developed) home country: The demand for the same working conditions (working hours, vacations, wages, etc.) as in the home country will quickly lead to a migration of the workforce to other countries with wage advantages due to the high price and competitive pressure. Digitization in this sector is more likely to optimize customer orientation than to strive for further cost reductions, but by no means to improve working conditions.

4.11.2 Cultural Relativism

In contrast to universalism, which assumes a general and universally valid ethics, cultural relativism assumes that ethics is culturally determined. Accordingly, behavior is to be understood in the respective cultural context and is not to be evaluated from the perspective of another culture. Correspondingly, entrepreneurial decisions made in a social context of a host country with low social or ecological standards would then have to be evaluated on the basis of these norms established there and not on the basis of the stricter norms of the home country. Here as well, obviously universal norms such as human rights, for example, are not ethically represented by such an approach.

4.11.3 Naive Immoralist

Similar to local customs (see Sect. 4.11.2), the "naive immoralist" is: here the question arises whether it is opportune, for example, to tolerate illegal behavior in the host country with low legal standards, which is intolerable in the home country (with an effective legal system). As a classic example, protection money from warlords is used to protect the host country's employees and production facilities from attacks. Retreating into the belief that this is the lesser evil than exposing one's own local workers to the risk of attack is just as unsatisfactory as the prospect of not investing in the country and thus depriving the local society of benefits such as jobs, income, economic development, and prospects (Hill 2014).

4.11.4 Friedman Doctrine

For example, the doctrine of shareholder theory formulated by the influential Nobel Prize winner Milton Friedman (1970) states that shareholders must be given priority over all other stakeholders of a company, since they alone make economic activities possible in the first place. This means that a company (or its management, which was implemented by the shareholders) is only (socially) responsible to the shareholders. The shareholders as principals should then decide for themselves (and not the management appointed by the shareholders as their agents) which (social) corporate orientation is to be pursued within the framework of normative corporate governance. Ultimately, this leads to the conclusion that it is enough for a company to comply with the minimum legal requirements. This view, which is influenced by Adam Smith's "invisible hand"—the eighteenth-century understanding of capitalism (Bassiry and Jones 1993)—has received much criticism, particularly because the one-sided approach of shareholder value does not in reality help society, but rather, through massive concentration of economic resources in the hands of a minority, leads to alienation between rich and poor, which in turn threatens society itself in the medium term. We will reflect this further in Sect. 7.5 when reflecting on the effects of "Big Tech" and AI on the societies.

4.11.5 Determinants of Ethical Decisions (in an International Context)

The ethical compass is intended to provide orientation in difficult decision-making situations—even in the situation of an ethical dilemma. Figure 4.6 shows such an orientation aid, which considers both the organization (vertically), within which individuals make decisions, and the individuals themselves (horizontally).

Ethical consistency checks, for example:

3-Steps: Decision alternative is …
1. …within accepted standards
2. …communicable to all stakeholders
3. …advocated by colleagues/peers

4-Test:
1. Legal: Are there any legal concerns?
2. Frontpage: Would it be OK if the media reported about it prominently?
3. Mom Test: What will a person who is very close to you say about it?
4. Stench Test: Does the decision have "tastes" and appearance of non-compliance?

5-Steps Approach:
1. Identifying potentially affected persons
2. Identifying possible violations of fundamental rights
3. Moral intention
4. Engaging in moral behavior
5. Review / audit of decisions from an ethical perspective

Decision-making processes under consideration of ethical dimensions

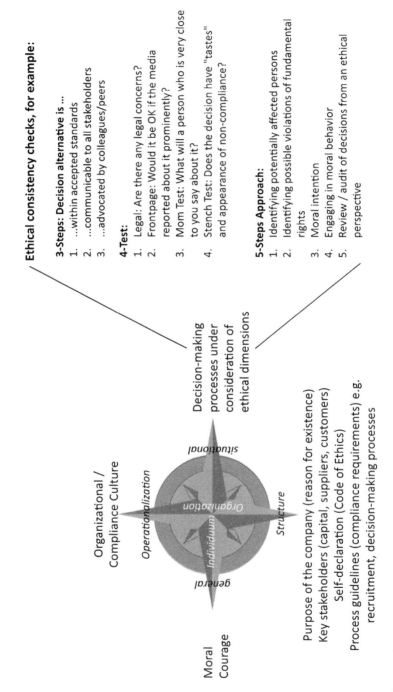

Organizational / Compliance Culture

Operationalization

situational

Organization

Structure

Individuum

general

Moral Courage

Purpose of the company (reason for existence)
Key stakeholders (capital, suppliers, customers)
Self-declaration (Code of Ethics)
Process guidelines (compliance requirements) e.g. recruitment, decision-making processes

Fig. 4.6 Ethical compass (own presentation, for tests cf. (Hill 2014), (Hedge 2019))

Dimension of the organization: The dimension of the organization sets the framework within which decisions are made (and this decision-making process can either be entirely human/individual or supported by an appropriate AI).

The organizational structure (structural organization) is the basis for the actual operationalization (process organization):

Of course, it is obvious to look first at the statements of an organization, e.g., in the form of a Code of Ethics.

Typical further questions of the ethically relevant structure are

- What is the self-declared purpose of the organization?
- Why does it exist at all, what is the intention?
- What is the importance of ethical aspects? What is the focus of the Code of Ethics or Code of Conduct?
- In what kind of business is the company active: who are the main stakeholders: especially shareholders, other investors, suppliers, customers? In which geography and (ethical) surrounding is the organization active?
- How are products manufactured and services provided: by whom and under what conditions? How do these conditions fit to the best or usual market conditions?
- How are the products and services actually used and by whom?
- How is ethical behavior rewarded/how is unethical behavior sanctioned?

Operationalization is ultimately about the question of how the structural guidelines are effectively lived out. For example, it is necessary to formulate and communicate a Code of Ethics or Code of Conduct. However, this does not mean that these guidelines can automatically be observed.

Concrete measures are necessary to ensure that these ethical principles are firmly established in the organization and are actually lived. These include

- Information and training:
  As a starting point it is important that the ethical objectives are made transparent and communicated at all. Training of the workforce can maximize the effect of the Code of Ethics on employees' "knowledge."
  But "knowledge" does not equal "understanding."
- Bonding:
  It is not enough to publish the Code of Conduct on the website without a reference to day-to-day business. How-to features in everyday processes with concrete artifacts help to make the ethical principles tangible.

Examples:

- "Green banking": typical lending decisions are made against the background of the ecological consequences; the bank's own environmental impact (consumption of resources) is at least partially offset in the form of compensation payments (environmental fund).
- Legitimacy before legality: if business transactions are legally impeccable, but not tolerable because of ethical convictions, companies for whom ethical orientation is really important will not do such business.
- For example, a company that requires special raw materials such as cobalt for its products (e.g., for the production of lithium-ion batteries as electrical energy storage devices) may decide not to cooperate with suppliers who use child labor under the worst conditions in the Congo. Although the Congo, which is one of the poorest countries in the world, devastated by civil war, has an important position in the raw materials market with over 60% of the world's cobalt deposits. As a company, you can structure your supply chain differently and, like Volkswagen for example, use other sources of supply (Australia, Russia, China) for your own electromobility products. According to your own statements, you can focus on reducing the amount of cobalt in your products on the one hand and on sustainability initiatives such as the Responsible Minerals Initiative ("RMI") (Volkswagen 2019) on the other. The tech giants Apple, Microsoft, Tesla, and Dell, for example, have not done so, and their sources of supply are in the Congo (Shapshak 2019). In December 2019, a prominent prosecution of these same corporations was made by the US organization "International Rights Advocates" in Washington DC, USA, which focuses on human rights.

- Recruitment and promotion:
  Only persons with a clear ethical attitude and conduct will be recruited; unethical persons will not be promoted regardless of their contribution to the economic success of the company.
- Role model function of managers:
  Leaders should emphasize the importance of ethics, both verbally and through their decision-making and authentic feedback. It should also be the task of managers to motivate their own employees to get involved in ethical issues, for example by making constructive contributions to improvement and maintaining a critical view in the sense of continuous, process-based monitoring. As an ultima ratio, whistle-blowing should also be included as an option. On the question of how a good whistle-blowing system can function, refer once again to Sect. 3.4.
- Dimension individual
  A culture is shaped and carried by people. Even if the framework is basically given, it is the individual person who pursues the purpose of the organization and contributes to achieving it through their congruent actions. In general, it requires

the courage of each individual to take action for improvement and, if necessary, to forego any amenities of their own "for the sake of the cause." This intrinsic motivation means to address any uncomfortable issues, to initiate and pursue extra activities (which do not occur when looking away), and, if necessary, to take a stand against one's own managers or even top management.

Despite a suitable, organizational environment, it takes a certain amount of courage to actually address this inconvenience.

For a concrete situation, it is advisable to have a checklist of guidelines at hand, so to speak, in order to be able to evaluate the ethical implications of a decision for yourself. Figure 4.6 shows three different checklists, each of which provides an orientation and a reflected evaluation of your own actions.

4.12   Finish Line Quiz

4.01		Applying the home country's ethical standard abroad when working conditions in the host country are worse leads to . . .
	1	. . . minimization of the reputational damage and a cost advantage.
	2	. . . reputation as "good citizen" and a competitive (cost) disadvantage.
	3	. . . short-term maintaining of competitiveness
	4	. . . sanctions as such unethical approach is inacceptable.
4.02		Which information can be derived from the FSI?
	1	The level of corruption in a specific country.
	2	A country's progress toward five different categories (cohesion, economic, political, social, environmental)
	3	A country's progress toward various categories including cohesion, economic, political, social.
	4	Only the level of economic performance in a country.
4.03		An emerging country exploits its limited natural resources (burn down rainforest for generating farmland) with the help of AI technology from developed countries. What is the ethical position for such company?
	1	The company does not have to bother about the use of its technology as long as it stays within the customers' own country legal rules.
	2	The company does exactly right, as its advanced technology will help the destination country to prosper benefiting from newest technology and therewith most likely minimum resources.
	3	The company shall not sell any products or any other support to such a country.
	4	The position is very difficult and shall not be answered in general. A detailed assessment from ethical perspective is required.
4.04		Why is the fight against corruption—despite of all anti-corruption codes and standards—so difficult?
	1	Disregarding individuals' fraudulent motivations, for a business there may be the consideration of "doing a little evil to achieve a greater (quicker) outcome (e.g., by bribing local officials to accelerate the process)".
	2	Corruption is a problem of the past. There is hardly any corruption anymore, as with AI, full transparency is given.

(continued)

	3	Short-terminism and narrow (egocentric) view undermine the fight against corruption.
	4	Answer 1 and 3.
4.05		Which dimensions are typically seen in an ethical dilemma?
	1	Individual priority vs. interest of the group
	2	Justice and trust
	3	Answer 1 and 2.
	4	None of the above.
4.06		What are strawmen proposal good for?
	1	They show a simplified, though extreme position such as "stick to the high standards of the home country."
	2	They are not used anymore.
	3	They illustrate potential, practicable behavior such as applying local (low) host country's ethical standards under consideration of the fundamental basic rights.
	4	The "naive immoralist" provides a clear stance to focus on shareholders only, because they ultimately fund the company.
4.07		What are the dimensions of the suggested ethical compass?
	1	Operational/strategy/tactics/structure
	2	Structural/operational/general/situative
	3	Strategic/operational/situative/global
	4	Strategic/operational/tactical/global
4.08		Which key considerations shall be made in a specific situation, using the ethical compass?
	1	If it is legal, it is OK.
	2	Is there any appearance of noncompliance?
	3	Disregarding affected persons, the decision shall be taken under the "veil of ignorance."
	4	Ethic-critical questions are always subject to the individual and shall not be shared with peers, as they will have their own view.

Correct answers can be found in www.vieweg-beratung.de/downloads

References

Amnesty International. (2019). *Migrant workers rights with four years to the Qatar 2022 World Cup*. Retrieved August 10, 2020, from https://www.amnesty.org/en/latest/campaigns/2019/02/reality-check-migrant-workers-rights-with-four-years-to-qatar-2022-world-cup/

Bassiry, G. R., & Jones, M. (1993). Adam Smith and the ethics of contemporary capitalism. *Journal of Business Ethics,* (1026):621–627. Retrieved August 10, 2020.

DIM. (2020). *Menschenrechtsabkommen*. Retrieved October 30, 2020, from https://www.institut-fuer-menschenrechte.de/menschenrechtsschutz/deutschland-im-menschenrechtsschutzsystem/vereinte-nationen/vereinte-nationen-menschenrechtsabkommen

Friedman, M. (1970). *A Friedman Doctrine: The social responsibility of business is to increase its profits*. Retrieved August 10, 2020, from https://www.nytimes.com/1970/09/13/archives/a-friedman-doctrine-the-social-responsibility-of-business-is-to.html

FFP. (2020). *Fragile and conflict affected states*. Retrieved August 10, 2020, from https://fundforpeace.org/

Gibb, R., Redding, D. W., & Chin, K.Q. et al. (2020). Zoonotic host diversity increases in human-dominated ecosystems. *Nature.* https://doi.org/10.1038/s41586-020-2562-8. Retrieved August 10, 2020.

Gopinath, G. (2020). The great lockdown: Worst economic downturn since the great depression. *IMF.* Retrieved August 10, 2020, from https://blogs.imf.org/2020/04/14/the-great-lockdown-worst-economic-downturn-since-the-great-depression/

Hardin, G. (1968). The tragedy of the commons. *Science, 162,* 1243–1248.

Hedge, S. (2019). *What is an ethical dilemma?* Retrieved August 10, 2020, from https://www.scienceabc.com/social-science/what-is-an-ethical-dilemma-definition-examples-real-life.html

Hofstede, G. (1991). *Cultures and organizations. Software of the mind. Intercultural cooperation and its importance for survival.* New York: McGraw Hill.

Hill, C. W. (2014). *International business: Competing in the global marketplace.* Maidenhead: McGraw Hill.

IMF. (2020). *World Economic Outlook Database.* Retrieved November 5, 2020, from https://www.imf.org/en/Publications/WEO/weo-database/2020/October/download-entire-database

Maus, A. (2019). *Strafanzeige gegen TÜV-Süd-Manager.* Retrieved August 10, 2020, from https://www.tagesschau.de/investigativ/monitor/dammbruch-brasilien-tuev-sued-anzeige-101.html

Schröder, T. (2020). *Fangquoten in der Ostsee ausgefischt?* Retrieved August 10, 2020, from https://www.deutschlandfunk.de/fangquoten-in-der-ostsee-ausgefischt.740.de.html?dram:article_id=477838

Shapshak, T. (2019). Cobalt lawsuit against tech giants over child labour A 'Global Flashpoint of Corporate Social Responsibility'. *Forbes.* Retrieved August 10, 2020, from https://www.forbes.com/sites/tobyshapshak/2019/12/18/cobalt-lawsuit-against-tech-giants-over-child-labour-a-global-flashpoint-of-corporate-social-responsibility/

Transparency International. (2020). *CPI Corruption Perception Index 2019.* Retrieved August 10, 2020, from https://www.transparency.org/en/cpi/2019/results

UN. (1948). *Universal Declaration of Human Rights.* Retrieved August 10, 2020, from https://www.un.org/en/universal-declaration-human-rights/index.html

Volkswagen. (2019). *C is for Cobalt.* Retrieved August 10, 2020, from https://www.volkswagen-newsroom.com/en/c-is-for-cobalt-4949

Value-Based Corporate Management and Integral Intelligence

5

Matthias Müller-Wiegand

5.1 Learning Objectives

1. Describe the basic concepts of value-based management, surplus sense, and spiral dynamics.
2. Outline the concept of integral philosophy.
3. Reflect on the components and effects of a complementary set of intelligence forms: human-artificial and integrated.
4. Reflect on the laws of form and its effects on integral intelligence.
5. Characterize AI-based applications for decision-making.
6. Characterize and reflect on the efficiency of the concept of Syntegration.
7. Identify how co-creativity can be generated through collective intelligence and intuition.

5.2 Conceptual Framework

5.2.1 Value-Based Corporate Management

Companies create value for customers, employees, suppliers, society, and investors in a multidimensional manner. This requires integral corporate management, which includes value-oriented corporate management characterized by integrity, reliability, trust, and mutual recognition.

A company is a social system that creates values through cooperation. Each individual understands that the purposes he/she pursues are at the same time a condition for realizing the purposes of the other. And it is the people in the company and their participation that are thus able to generate values and future cash flows.

M. Müller-Wiegand (✉)
Rheinische Fachhochschule Cologne gGmbH, Cologne, Germany
e-mail: Matthias.Mueller-Wiegand@rfh-koeln.de

© The Author(s), under exclusive license to Springer Nature Switzerland AG 2021
S. H. Vieweg (ed.), *AI for the Good*, Management for Professionals,
https://doi.org/10.1007/978-3-030-66913-3_5

5.2.2   Theorem of Surplus Sense

Luhmann has proposed to observe societies with the theorem of surplus sense (Luhmann 1997 p. 409) under the aspect of the dominant distribution media of communication. Surplus sense is therefore a driver of social development. From the beginning, societies were characterized by their mediality, beginning with language (being able to talk about things that are not there now) and tribal society, then came writing, which goes beyond the constraints of the time horizon and the society of antiquity, later came printing with a surplus of criticism (everything can be criticized by anyone (Baecker 2016b, pp. 4–5)) and modern society, and now digitalization with the electronic media and the "Next Society"(Next Society after Peter Drucker (2002)) with an excess of control (Baecker 2018, pp. 54, 75), because electronic media and algorithms operate quasi instantaneously and have a quasi-infinite memory and depth of analytical focus (with big data analytics), which cannot be directly processed by humans in this granularity, but which become accessible through interaction. In addition, there are connectivity spaces with a multitude of connection possibilities. This leads to the social structural form of the network, and the evolutionary concept of spiral dynamics can build on this.

5.2.3   Spiral Dynamics

The starting point is the Graves value system, which Beck and Cowan further developed into spiral dynamics (Beck and Cowan 2014) (Fig. 5.1). Spiral dynamics is a model of successive evolutionary stages of human consciousness with corresponding value concepts and thought patterns (so-called Value Memes) of the history of mankind, which are also reflected in the individual maturity of the human being and can therefore be determined in relation to age. "Value Memes" define, as it were, a cultural genetic code that determines the values of a certain society and is passed on through social interaction. This evolution also shows a change of individual and collective emphasis in value and thought patterns. From the integral evolutionary stage onward, the second-order level is reached, transcending and integrating the underlying developmental stages.

Spiral dynamics also determines the understanding of leadership and the evolution of human forms of organization in companies. Effective leadership in a network society can therefore be achieved with an integral and collective perspective that embraces the human being and the possibilities of digital algorithms and artificial intelligence in a holistic way, hence basing leadership on an integral and holistic value system.

From the perspective of the second-order level, the positive aspects of the previous levels can be integrally considered. From an archaic perspective, for example, it is about securing the existence of a company; from a magical perspective, it is about a "family" identity; from a mythical perspective, it is about the power to think or do value-creating things that would otherwise not be realized; from an absolutist perspective, it is about security and compliance; from a rational

Fig. 5.1 Spiral dynamics (own presentation based on mack.partners (mack partners 2020) and based on Beck/Cowan)

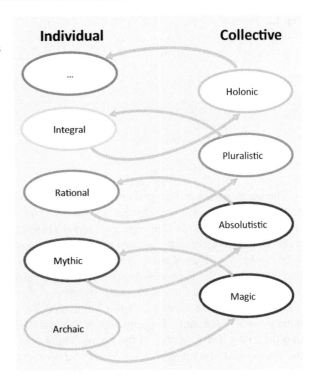

perspective, it is about success thinking, performance, and effectiveness; and from a pluralistic perspective, it is about appreciation and equality and teamwork.

5.2.4 Human Intelligence

Human intelligence is, among other things, the ability to think, solve problems, understand the environment, plan, learn, and figure out what to do and includes emotional and social intelligence (Malone 2018, pp. 23–24; Gottfredson 1997).

Emotional intelligence can be characterized by the abilities of emotional self-perception and self-regulation, the ability to self-motivate and reward postponement, and empathy. Social intelligence includes, for example, the ability to organize groups, decide what is done in the group, and thereby enforce decisions and transfer confidence of feasibility and enthusiasm to others (Goleman and Griese 2015).

5.2.5 Integral Philosophy

Value-based management is integral management, and its key is an integral philosophy.

Fig. 5.2 Four sense elements
(Heinrichs 2016, S. 26)

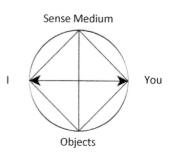

The starting point of integral reflection is the ego as both a sensory element in conscious activity and an element in the structure of several other elements (Heinrichs 2016, p. 25). The ego [as second sense element] stands opposite the world of the physical, of nature, and of objects. Dialogical thinking does not stop at subject–object dualism. Rather, the [subjective] ego is confronted by another "objective" ego, a you (third sense element). Thereby, the other (the you) is not understood as negatively limiting, but as liberating (Heinrichs 2016) (Fig. 5.2).

The fourth sense element, "spirit," the medium of meaning, represents the transpersonal dimension. Participating in this dimension turns the human being into the living being capable of the Logos. This Logos represents the epitome and the "condition of possibility" of all human communication media, primarily for the language that mediates between I and you (Heinrichs 2003, p. 3). The more, and the more powerfully, the true I or self can live this structure of self-reference-through-alterity and be individualized as a result, the more capable of participating in the supra-individual or infinite it will be (Heinrichs 2016, p. 34). Man is not only individually capable of the unconditional or the infinite, but also, in this individual capacity, participates in the shared infinite. It is precisely this participation (as opposed to being a part) that is the key to an integral understanding (Heinrichs 2016, p. 264).

The four sense elements correspond to the four types of action: (1) factual action, (2) interest-oriented action, (3) understanding-oriented action, and (4) norm-oriented action (Heinrichs 2005b, p. 29).

In view of the changes in society and in relation to spiral dynamics in connection with digitalization—and here especially with artificial intelligence—an integral frame of reference is fundamental for value-oriented corporate management.

It is important to have this holistic view not only in itself and theoretically, but to live it in a developed form (Heinrichs 2005a, pp. 107–108). This is the meaning of the mindfulness and meditative practices that also transform and support entrepreneurial actions.

The secular and real nature of the holistic reference is shown in increased intuition in the midst of everyday business as well as in a lived attitude of love toward all living things (Heinrichs 2005a, b, p. 108) (also in the sense of Hans-Peter Dürr: "Let the living become more alive") and in this respect in an understanding of economics that does not eliminate the inherent laws but forms an integral part of them.

Ivan Illich expounds upon convivialism as individual freedom, which is realized in personal interdependence and as such represents an ethical value (Illich 1973).

Convivialism thus manifests itself in an integral understanding of individualism and is a society in which individuals, groups, and communities are connected in new forms, respecting each other in their differences and cooperating for the benefit of all (Adloff and Heins 2015, p. 11).

The contrast to individualism which develops in the logic of exclusion is that this is an individualism which, in the logic of inclusion, understands the other as a condition of its own development and which does not "altruistically" include others but consciously recognizes that its own development is possible only if it does not inhibit others' development and instead supports it through positive mutualistic relationships. Development is possible only socially—with others, not against them (Meretz).

In this sense, the prisoner's dilemma paradigmatically shows the consequences of selfish, non-cooperative behavior. It leads to a lower value creation overall and in detail. Value creation should instead be achieved in an entrepreneurial manner through convivial cooperation.

With Wisdom 2.0, the contours and significance of the interrelationship of body, soul, and spirit are also becoming apparent for companies (with reference to the Wisdom 2.0 Conference 2015 with the central theme "Mindfulness and Compassion in the Digital Age"). "Mindfulness" is considered the beginning of an inner spiritual growth. It means complete attention to both the conscious and the unconscious" (Heinrichs 2018b) in the "here and now" without a dominating one-sided evaluation, i.e., without egotistically distorted desire, and enables integral and holistic thinking. More and more companies are recognizing that both the attitude of employers and employees can be changed for the better in the long term through a mindfulness approach. There is a growing awareness of the intense desire to work in companies that take people's values seriously. This makes companies more successful in attracting the best, most creative, and enthusiastic employees (Meyer-Galow 2018, p. 60).

This results in an integral business ethic based on mindfulness, which is the gateway to inner growth and entrepreneurial value creation. This stems from an integral consciousness that aims to enable value-oriented management with psychological and spiritual maturity (Meyer-Galow 2018, p. 142). "How can I live happily, and perhaps ultimately blissfully, in harmony with everything?" goes far beyond the ethical question "What should I or may I do?" and enables us to answer the latter question correctly (Heinrichs 2018a).

5.3   Intelligence: Human–Collective–Artificial Integral

5.3.1   Artificial Intelligence

A system is intelligent if it can solve problems independently and efficiently. The degree of intelligence depends on the degree of autonomy, the degree of complexity of the problem, and the degree of efficiency of the problem-solving process (Mainzer 2019, p. 3).

"Weak artificial intelligence" refers to systems that focus on the solution of concrete application problems, e.g., character or text recognition (Moeser 2018). In contrast, the goal of strong artificial intelligence is to achieve or exceed the intellectual abilities of humans. "Strong artificial intelligence" no longer acts only reactively, but also on its own initiative, intelligently and flexibly (Moeser 2018).

5.3.2   Collective and Integral Intelligence

Collective intelligence is the result of groups of individuals working together intelligently (Malone 2018, p. 20), and Malone explicitly speaks of "Supermind— The Surprising Power of People and Computers Thinking Together" (Malone 2018, p. 20).

Based on his empirical research, he identifies three factors that show a clear positive correlation to collective intelligence, i.e., the problem-solving ability of a group:

1. The average social perceptivity of the group members.
2. The degree of uniformity in the participation of the members.
3. The percentage of women in the group (correlates with average social perceptivity).

A high level of intelligence among group members therefore only has a limited influence on the problem-solving ability of a group (Malone 2018, p. 20). Rather, the ability to solve problems is crucially dependent on social intelligence. The right team composition leads to the addition of value through collective intelligence that exceeds the collective intelligence of the people involved.

According to Ashby's Law, complex and dynamic problems can only be understood and solved by a correspondingly complex and dynamic system. Consequently, the intelligence and competencies of individuals no longer suffice to develop solutions and innovations. Rather, methods are needed for the organization of supra-individual discourses. Faced with a highly networked, difficult-to-predict world with incalculable changes, recourse to explicit knowledge alone is no longer enough. Consequently, intuitive knowledge will generally gain in importance as a method of complexity reduction. Intuitive knowledge expresses the brain's ability to reduce complex relationships to the essential via unconscious pattern formation. Implicit knowledge is valuable but seldom directly accessible, i.e., intuitive

Fig. 5.3 Learning loops with human–machine interaction (own presentation based on (Malone 2018, S.234))

knowledge is implicit (Kruse et al. 2007, pp. 534–535). In this sense, analog and digital networking allow for higher complexity and are a condition of evolution, creativity, and intelligence. This applies to the networking of technical systems as well as human–machine systems.

Malone poses the central question: How can people and computers be connected in such a way that together they act more intelligently than any person, group, or computer has ever done before? and "we should move from thinking about putting humans in the loop to putting computers in the group" (Malone 2018, p. 75) (Fig. 5.3).

In this way, humans can contribute general intelligence and special abilities machines lack. Machines can provide the knowledge and special abilities humans do not have. As a result, by creating cyber-human learning loops, a group of people and computers can act more intelligently than any person, group, or computer has ever done before (Malone 2018, p. 234).

The interaction between the digital and the analog enables a real "digital transformation," which I would like to call "integral intelligence."

5.3.3 Laws of Form and Integral Intelligence

Communication between humans and machines and between machines and machines is complex. The laws of form (Spencer-Brown 1994) serve as a suitable descriptive tool and can be used to create forms of observation and depict differences as connections (Baecker 2017). It is about distinguishing and designating phenomena ("draw a distinction"), i.e., inclusion or exclusion relations (Simon 2007, pp. 52–53). It is a differential approach.

Spencer-Brown symbolizes this with a "cross." Every observation requires this "cross" to get from unmarked to marked space (Simon 2007, p. 56). This first distinction can be further developed by other inward/outward distinctions. If, for example, environments are marked, they can be reintroduced into the system as distinctions and then observed ("re-entry"). If one wants to communicate "about the outside world," one must make the outside world an element of the inside world (Simon 2007, p. 58).

The cross as a mark of distinction, and its implementation, can best be illustrated by taking an object, e.g., in this context man, framing it with the difference implicitly made long ago and asking what could have been excluded—a machine, for instance (Fig. 5.4):

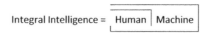

Fig. 5.4 Concept of integral intelligence (own presentation)

In place of the classical Aristotelian logic of identity, a difference-theoretical logic of identity is applied, since identity can only be had within the framework of a negation, which is to be understood as an implication. A human being is only a human being (identity) if he/she distinguishes himself/herself from the outside, which he is not (negation), but whose existence he presupposes as outside of the distinction (implication) (Baecker 2016a, p. 242).

If one looks at the difference between humans and machines, one sees that a human is alive; a machine is inanimate matter. A human being consists of organic material, a machine of plastic and metal. A human being can think and has feelings and a consciousness as well as dignity and morality, things that a machine does not have (Vowinkel 2017). If one looks at reentry, one can see that humans also have their routines or use algorithms and weightings in decision-making, which they transfer to the programming of algorithms whose application subsequently improves human decision-making. When our computers and their programs become increasingly intelligent, when they develop consciousness, then the "nontrivial machine" according to Heinz von Foerster (2003) is literally completed. Nevertheless, human intelligence as a biological system will differ from artificial intelligence in its inherent laws.

5.4   Applications

5.4.1   Neuronal Network-Based Decisions

Relationships of effects between variables in real situations are usually complex. Therefore, it is difficult to formulate well-founded hypotheses about the nature of these relationships.

With artificial neural networks ("ANN"), the user need not necessarily make an assumption about the relationship between variables. By way of ANN, the connections between variables are determined independently by a learning process and can thereby consider a multiplicity of variables (Backhaus et al. 2015, p. 296).

Artificial neural networks can use the logic of descriptive, predictive, and prescriptive business analytics methods to provide analyses, forecasts, and recommendations for action, thus enabling better decisions with advanced analytics (Fig. 5.5).

For example, bank loan granted by an artificial neural network can be decided on the basis of a dataset of creditworthy and non-creditworthy customers and their sociodemographic and economic data with an assignable classification. For such classification decisions, the possibility of so-called counterfactual explanations as explanations of decision recommendations with artificial intelligence is useful. For

Fig. 5.5 Advanced analytics
(own presentation based
Gartner's Gartner analytic
ascendancy model 2012)

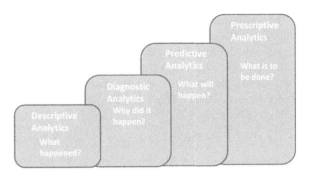

example, an applicant for a loan should know that, e.g., the loan was refused because of an income of €35,000, and with an income of €40,000 the loan would have been offered. Therefore, an explanation of the algorithm is not necessary, and an explanation is given to what was needed for the desired result (Wachter et al. 2018).

For applications in business decision situations, neural network algorithms are easily generated on a graphical user interface using the Neural Designer (What is Neural Designer?) software tool. Moreover, the Deep Learning Studio (Deep Learning Studio Desktop—DeepCognition.ai 2020) software tool shows an intuitive, simple model creation for neural networks with a drag and drop interface. In addition, neural networks can even be created with artificial intelligence, thus accelerating modeling and discovery by an effective neural network.

5.4.2 Decisions with the Analytical Network (Hierarchy) Process

Decisions at the strategic level are complex. They contain "soft" non-cardinally scaled information and ambiguity and are characterized by uncertainty. They are multi-criteria decision situations.

The analytical hierarchy process ("AHP") is suitable for solving these decision problems. This procedure was developed by Saaty (Saaty Thomas and Vargas Luis 2006) and enables decision-makers to select an alternative course of action by determining a standardized utility value.

This method's unique feature is that the correct preference judgments about the objects to be compared are not holistic but are the result of pair comparisons, enabling an intuitive evaluation. As a result, intersubjective verifiability is achieved and verifiable with a mathematically determined inconsistency measure (Ossadnik 2009, pp. 367–369).

Furthermore, scenarios with linguistic probability estimates can be created. This is particularly important if probability functions cannot be empirically determined from empirical values.

The AHP procedure can be generalized by the analytic network process and thus takes into account mutual dependencies of the criteria and so-called feedback loops based on the alternatives.

For practical applications, decision situations can be modeled and solved by utilizing software such as Expert Choice or Super-Decision. For the time being, humans model and implement the applications as well as conduct the evaluations. Consequently, these software solutions support people in decision-making, where humans still play an active and dominant role. By involving several knowledge and experience carriers, complex decisions can be made with collective knowledge and collective intuition.

5.4.3   Syntegration

Syntegration (after Stafford Beer (1994) and Fredmund Malik) is a workshop method that enables the processing of complex topics in larger groups and achieves its added value through the collective intelligence of the participants. The perspectives of up to 40 or more knowledge carriers/key persons are networked across the boundaries of the different areas so that maximum information transfer is achieved, resulting in many brains functioning as a single, highly efficient brain.

The symbol of a Syntegration is an icosahedron, where each corner represents a topic, each edge represents a participant, and the icosahedron shows the interaction of topics and participants (Fig. 5.6).

A Syntegration consists of two phases. In the first phase, a multi-stage filtering process allows participants to determine the 12 topics for subsequent discussion by a network of individual groups in the second phase. In the second phase, usually beginning the following day, these topics are dealt with in group sessions (Malik, p. 2).

According to the icosahedron, ideally, there are 30 participants, each serving as a team member in two groups, a critic in two further groups, and an observer in four additional groups (Syntegration® Effective Communication—Solidia Management Consulting 2005).

When a Syntegration ends, everyone is aware of approximately 90% of the participants' total available knowledge (Malik, p. 2) (Fig. 5.7).

Fig. 5.6 Icosahedron (own presentation based following (Malik 2013), based on (Beer 1994))

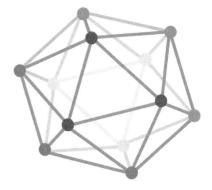

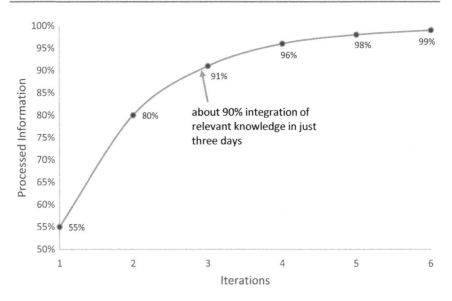

Fig. 5.7 Knowledge distribution in a group (own presentation, data base on (Malik p. 2))

The Malik consulting firm has implemented more than 600 applications of the Malik Syntegration method (including strategic issues, post-merger integration, organizational development, process optimization) (Malik SuperSyntegration (MSS)). Intelligent and highly creative solutions are created by applying the group's entire knowledge. Within 2 ½ to 3 ½ days, the innovative exploitation of the entire knowledge is achieved through the self-regulating optimization of the information flow between the participants. The entire group of participants is thus 80 times more efficient than conventional teams, while decisions are up to 100 times faster, and 70% of the measures are realized after 12 months (Malik SuperSyntegration (MSS)).

Where there is broad involvement by employees, customers, other experts as well as big data analytics, or even internationally operating companies, integral Syntegration with artificial intelligence seems to have a high potential for development.

5.4.4 Co-Creativity Through Collective Intelligence and Intuition

nextpractice, the consulting firm, focuses on "participatory development processes" and "co-creativity and collective intelligence" for innovative ideas and new forms of cooperation and leadership in companies and in society as well (nextpractice GmbH). The qualitative-quantitative analysis method nextexpertizer, the nextmoderator moderation tool, and the nextrealizer collaboration platform are of central importance (nextpractice GmbH), i.e., the interaction of software, methods, and people.

The purpose is to stimulate intelligent processes, which incorporate the explicit and implicit knowledge of organizations and markets for better orientation and the best possible solutions (next-practice GmbH). The aim therefore is to utilize not only individuals' experiential knowledge but also the distributed knowledge of collectives.

For example, the nextexpertizer tool was used to conduct 400 in-depth interviews with managers as part of the "Good Leadership" study in 2014 in an effort to draw a detailed picture of management culture in Germany. The goal was to discover which unconscious values and collective mental patterns determine the actions of managers, how the actual development of management practice is evaluated against this background, and what challenges managers expect for the future (Initiative New Quality of Work (INQA)).

The analysis procedure is primarily based on qualitative pair comparisons whose comparative elements form the search space and the associative framework of the individual surveys (Kruse 2010, p. 204). The interviews are designed to bring forth all construct dimensions that visualize the unconscious value pattern of the interviewee. Based on the large number of intuitive individual decisions and explanations and their relationships, the intuitive view of a respondent can be determined using a self-structural analysis. All respondent's individual results are subsequently combined to form a complete picture, making the common pattern of culture and value preferences visible (Initiative New Quality of Work (INQA)).

Approximately 4000–5000 terms were mathematically arranged over all test persons and in the next step consolidated into topics, resulting in six clear leadership concepts: integration in a setting characterized by solidarity, dynamic networking, iterative testing agility, cooperative team spirit, strong personality, and efficient goal achievement.

A comparison of reality with the expressed ideal of good leadership led to a paradigm shift by management, away from a purely finance-oriented value orientation and toward an integral "values" orientation of a value creation network characterized by maximum agility and willingness to learn.

5.5   Finish Line Quiz

5.01	What are key elements of integral management?	
	1	Risk taking, shareholder view, boldness
	2	Accountability, promise, and determination
	3	Integrity, reliability, trust
	4	Authority, micro- to nano-management
5.02	The theorem of surplus sense follows the evolution of mankind:	
	1	Excess of time horizon, criticism, control
	2	Excess of control, time horizon, criticism
	3	Excess of criticism, control, time horizon
	4	Excess of control, criticism, time horizon

(continued)

5.03	What is the sequence in the spiral dynamics model in interaction between individuals and the society?	
	1	Integral, followed by rational, followed by absolutistic
	2	Integral, followed by pluralistic, followed by absolutistic
	3	Rational, followed by pluralistic, followed by integral
	4	Absolutistic, followed by rational, followed by integral
5.04	What are the consequences of wisdom 2.0 for companies?	
	1	Holistic approach to include factual skills of the employees. There is an increasing importance for companies to purely focus on their staff's technical skills.
	2	Partial approach that is covered in mindfulness. There is no need for companies to care about this seriously, however.
	3	This has nothing to do with real business life.
	4	Holistic approach to include body, soul, and spirit, all embedded in mindfulness. There is an increasing importance for companies to care for their staff's values seriously.
5.05	What is collective intelligence?	
	1	Final collection of all working results from different individuals or smaller teams.
	2	Result of groups of individuals working together in an intelligent way.
	3	Nothing that can be orchestrated.
	4	All information gathered by use of ANN.
5.06	What is the importance of implicit knowledge going forward?	
	1	No change compared to the era prior to digitalization.
	2	Significant decline, because everything will become transparent and explicit.
	3	Increase, as this is the way like human brains work in order to cope with information overflow.
	4	Slight decline, as AI will cope with some of the knowledge.
5.07	What is AHP and what problems can be solved with it?	
	1	AHP is a generalization of the analytical network process. It cannot handle multiple dependencies.
	2	AHP enables decision-making on full set of "hard" information.
	3	AHP is the ambiguous hypothesis process that provides one fixed solution to decision-makers.
	4	Correct preference judgments about the objects to be compared, as the result of pair comparisons. Hence, an intersubjective verifiability is achieved.
5.08	What is the common value pattern from the "good leadership" study?	
	1	Solidary integration, dynamic networking, iterative testing agility.
	2	Cooperative team spirit, strong personality.
	3	Solidary integration, dynamic networking, iterative testing agility, cooperative team spirit, strong personality, and efficient goal achievement.
	4	Shareholder Value Management and Management by Objectives

References

Adloff, F., & Heins, V. (Eds.). (2015). *Konvivialismus. Eine Debatte. Transcript GbR*. Bielefeld: transcript (X-Texte).

Backhaus, K., Erichson, B., & Weiber, R. (2015). *Fortgeschrittene multivariate Analysemethoden.* Berlin, Heidelberg: Springer.

Baecker, D. (2016a). *Wozu Theorie? Aufsätze* (p. 2177). Berlin: Suhrkamp (suhrkamp taschenbuch wissenschaft.

Baecker, D. (2016b). *Oszillation 4.0.* Retrieved April 2, 2020, from https://www.soziopolis.de/beobachten/gesellschaft/artikel/oszillation-40/, zuletzt aktualisiert am 02.04.2020.

Baecker, D. (2017). *Produktkalkül.* Originalausgabe (Merve).

Baecker, D. (2018). *4.0 oder Die Lücke die der Rechner lässt. Originalausgabe* (p. 459). Merve Verlag (Merve): Leipzig.

Beck, D. E., & Cowan, C. (2014). *Spiral dynamics. Mastering values, leadership and change* (1st ed.). New York: Wiley-Blackwell.

Beer, S. (1994). *Beyond dispute. The invention of team syntegrity* (The managerial cybernetics of organization). Chichester: Wiley.

Deep Learning Studio Desktop - DeepCognition.ai. Deep Learning Studio Desktop. (2020). Retrieved April 02, 2020, from https://deepcognition.ai/products/desktop/

Drucker, P. F. (2002). *Managing in the next society.* Oxford: Butterworth Heinemann.

Foerster, H. (2003). *Understanding understanding. Essays on cybernetics and cognition.* New York, NY: Springer.

Goleman, D., & Griese, F. (2015). *Emotionale Intelligenz. Ungekürzte* (24th ed., p. 36020). München: Dt. Taschenbuch-Verl.

Gottfredson, L. S. (1997). Mainstream science on intelligence: An editorial with 52 signatories, history, and bibliography. *Intelligence, 24*(1), 13–23. https://doi.org/10.1016/S0160-2896(97)90011-8.

Heinrichs, J. (2003). *"Einstein der Bewusstseinsforschung"?* Retrived January 02, 2020, from https://www.johannesheinrichs.de/Philosophie-hist-allg-.43783.html

Heinrichs, J. (2005a). *Sprung aus dem Teufelskreis. Aktualisierte Neuaufl* (Vol. 1). Varna, Sofia, München, Moskau, Warschau, Chelmsford, Essex (UK), Delaware (USA): Steno (Sozialethische Wirtschaftstheorie).

Heinrichs, J. (2005b). *Demokratiemanifest für die schweigende Mehrheit: Die "Revolution der Demokratie".*

Heinrichs, J. (2016). *Integrale Philosophie.*

Heinrichs, J. (2018a). *Kritik der integralen Vernunft. Eine philosophische Psychologie.* Stuttgart: ibidem-Verlag.

Heinrichs, J. (2018b). *Landkarte des Unbewussten.* Stuttgart: ibidem-Verlag (Kritik der integralen Vernunft, eine philosophische Psychologie/Johannes Heinrichs; Das Band 2).

Illich, I. (1973). *Tools for conviviality.* London: Calder & Boyars.

Initiative Neue Qualität der Arbeit (INQA): Monitor "Führungskultur im Wandel - Kulturstudie mit 400 Tiefeninterviews". Hg. v. Initiative Neue Qualität der Arbeit

Kruse, P. (2010). nextexpertizer und nextmoderator: Mit kollektiver Intelligenz Veränderungsprozesse erfolgreich gestalten. In S. Rank (Ed.), *Change-Management in der Praxis. Beispiele, Methoden, Instrumente. Unter Mitarbeit von Beate Bidjanbeg. 2., neu bearb. und erw. Aufl* (pp. 201–218). Berlin: Erich Schmidt.

Kruse, P., Dittler, A., & Schomburg, F. (2007). nextexpertizer, nextcoach, nextmoderator: Kompetenzmessung aus der Sicht der Theorie kognitiver Selbstorganisation. In J. Erpenbeck & L. von Rosenstiel (Eds.), *Handbuch Kompetenzmessung. Erkennen, verstehen und bewerten von Kompetenzen in der betrieblichen, pädagogischen und psychologischen Praxis. 2., überarb. und erw. Aufl.* Stuttgart: Schäffer-Poeschel.

Luhmann, N. (1997). *Die Gesellschaft der Gesellschaft* (Vol. 2). Frankfurt: Suhrkamp Verlag.

mack.partners. (2020). *Spiral Dynamics Modell.* Retrieved April 02, 2020, from https://mack.partners/wissen/was-ist-integral-aqal/entwicklungsstufen-aqal

Mainzer, K. (2019). *Künstliche Intelligenz – Wann übernehmen die Maschinen?* Berlin, Heidelberg: Springer.

Malik: Malik Syntegration® Management Summary. Retrieved January 29, 2021, from https://
www.google.de/url?sa=t&rct=j&q=&esrc=s&source=web&cd=&ved=
2ahUKEwiHqsOPpcHuAhUWNuwKHf84A2AQFjAHegQIDBAC&url=http%3A%2F%
2Fwww.solarvalley.org%2Fdownloads%2Ffile%2F73%3FfileId%3D377&usg=
AOvVaw2xWetxnRGWUbO1gBxDIto0
Malik, F. (2013). *Strategie: Navigieren in der Komplexität der Neuen Welt.* Frankfurt: Campus
Verlag.
Malik SuperSyntegration (MSS). Retrieved April 02, 2020, from https://archived.malik-
management.com/de/pdf/supersyntegration/malik-super-syntegration-de.pdf and https://www.
malik-management.com/de/malik-loesungen/malik-tools-and-methods/malik-
supersyntegration-mss/
Malone, T. W. (2018). *Superminds. The surprising power of people and computers thinking
together.*
Meyer-Galow, E. (2018). *Business ethics 3.0. The new integral ethics from the perspective of a
CEO.* Berlin, Boston: De Gruyter Oldenbourg.
Meretz, S. *Commons-Diskurs: Individuum und Gesellschaft—keimform.de.* Retrieved August
07, 2019, from https://keimform.de/2016/commons-diskurs-individuum-und-gesellschaft/
Moeser, J. (2018). *Starke KI, schwache KI - Was kann künstliche Intelligenz?* Retrieved April
02, 2020, from https://jaai.de/starke-ki-schwache-ki-was-kann-kuenstliche-intelligenz-261/
nextpractice GmbH. Retrieved August 11, 2019, from https://www.nextpractice.de/
Ossadnik, W. (2009). *Controlling. 4., vollst. überarb. und erw. Aufl.* München: Oldenbourg.
Retrieved April 02, 2020, from http://sub-hh.ciando.com/book/?bok_id=22612
Saaty Thomas, L., & Vargas Luis, G. (2006). *Decision making with the analytic network process.*
New York: Springer.
Simon, F. B. (2007). *Einführung in die systemische Organisationstheorie* (1st ed.). Heidelberg:
Auer (Carl-Auer Compact).
Spencer-Brown, G. (1994). *Laws of form.* Portland, OR: Cognizer Co.
Syntegration® Wirksame Kommunikation - Solidia Mangementberatung. (2005). Retrieved
January 02, 2020, from http://www.solidia.de/die-syntegration/
Vowinkel, B. (2017). *Ist der Mensch eine Maschine?* Retrieved October 03, 2019, from https://
transhumanismus.wordpress.com/2017/06/14/ist-der-mensch-eine-maschine/
Wachter, S., Ananny, M., & Crawford, K. (2018). Counterfactual explanations without opening.
New Media & Society, 20(3), 973–989. https://doi.org/10.1177/1461444816676645.
What is Neural Designer? Retrieved August 10, 2019, from https://www.neuraldesigner.com/
learning/user-guide/what-is-neural-designer

Part II

AI and the Digital Age

Digitization: Learnings from Ancient Disruptions, AI and the Digital Trio's Functional Stage, and AI Superpowers Disrupting Us

6

Stefan H. Vieweg

6.1 Learning Objectives

1. Reflect the context of disruption—which is not a unique phenomenon—of the digital age.
2. Analyze the indicators of disruption.
3. Assess the degree of digitization.
4. Assess the challenges and chances that automation poses.
5. Explain digitization trends such as Robot Process Automation (RPA), blockchain, and quantum/supercomputing that influence artificial intelligence applications.
6. Experience the usage of AI algorithm for data analysis, its potential, and its shortcomings.
7. Differentiate the approaches between the two AI superpowers.
8. Reflect on the status of AI implementations against the background of the power struggle between social systems.
9. Critically assess the technical requirement imposed by AI in particular regarding energy.

6.2 Everything New Is Nothing New: Disruption in a Historical Context

In 2015, "disruption" was deemed to be the economic word of the year (Meck and Weiguny 2015), though if one applies a broader view, it is and has been a ubiquitous phenomenon, as humans by nature are interested to innovate. Although the

S. H. Vieweg (✉)
Institute of Compliance and Corporate Governance, RFH - University of Applied Sciences Cologne, Cologne, Germany
e-mail: dr.vieweg@vieweg-beratung.de

© The Author(s), under exclusive license to Springer Nature Switzerland AG 2021
S. H. Vieweg (ed.), *AI for the Good*, Management for Professionals,
https://doi.org/10.1007/978-3-030-66913-3_6

expression is rooted back just two decades to Clayton Christensen's "the innovator's dilemma" (Christensen 2003), the concept has been described for much longer, as the Austrian economist Joseph Schumpeter[1] named it "creative destruction." On the other side, humans have a certain inertia, stick to existing behaviors, and tend to ignore early indicators of change. As the threat initially is tiny compared to the dominant market players in terms of output and profit, these threats are identified very often in a stage where it is simply too late to restructure the business and accelerate on new business opportunities.

> *Example ice trading:* A famous case of disruption is the ice trade industry, which evolved on a global level throughout the nineteenth century when there were no refrigerators. At the eve of the twentieth century, ice trade was surging in increasing demand in particular in the US East Coast and Midwest (Cummings 1949), where it revolutionized the food industry from local production and consumption to long-distance trades and provided employment for 90,000 people in the USA alone. The abrupt end came with the new technology of refrigerators, which would not justify ice trades on a large scale. The ice trade industry collapsed after World War I into marginality (Cummings 1949). Another famous example is former film photography giant Eastman Kodak: this company dominated for decades the market, but basically failed to transition to future-proven businesses during the shift to digital photography. Although in a too simplistic approach this example is often cited to argue management's failure to see and react to the disruption, a closer look reveals that just knowing about an issue is not enough. In this specific case, management's awareness about the disruption of their industry was given (Shih 2016), though taking and timing actions accordingly basically failed. The management's task is to fully understand the implications.

The characteristics of the industries that are mostly affected by disruptions like AI and that may struggle to cope with this challenge can be generalized as follows (see Table 6.1):

Basically, what used to be a competitive advantage in a surging business environment with steady growth finds itself as a massive and destructive disadvantage at sunset. In such a situation, it is important that management not only "knows" about upcoming industry changes but "understands" what needs to be done in due time. The first-mover advantage, very well known in management concepts for market entry, needs to be reversed in regard to "first out-mover": In a sunsetting business environment, early discontinuation may provide the advantage of marginal proceeds from selling that part of the business before it is (too) late to generate an attractive price.

---

[1] 1883–1950.

Table 6.1 Disruption effects by industry characteristics (own presentation)

Industry characteristics	Growth		Decline		Disruptive threats
High entry barriers and capital lockup	+	Keeps an oligopolistic structure with few competitors and safeguards investments for incumbent players on their built-up excellence and inimitability in the specific value process chain	−	Due to specific (first mover) investments into the value process chain, reusability may hardly be possible on a competitive level due to their inflexibility	• Modularization, • commodity components, • "Softwaretization": shift from hardware to software
Large scale efficiencies	+	Extension of production unleashed productivity gains from extended run lengths	−	Inflexibility as shrinking volume production will lead to shorter run lengths, higher setup/change costs, exponential increase of cost per unit, failed fixed cost recovery	• Late customization at final assembly. • Mass customization. • Batch size one. • Self service and pull.
Finite product shelf life	O	Neutral, as products can be sold with ease	−	Variety of products shrinks, which forces small volume (but typically highly profitable) customer segments to adapt new digital substitute	• Built to order. • Iterative (agile) product development and delivery. • "To go" productions.
(Technology-driven) ecosystem	+	Unique competitive advantage provide high margins to all partners in the supply chain from suppliers, producer to retail	−	Category may vanish as retail delist products due to vanishing sales	• Onmi-channel. • Co-opetive environment.

The issue though is very often with the managers themselves: According to the proverb "Hope is the last to die," hesitation in taking brave transformation actions may deteriorate the business. Due to cognitive limitations such as the famous prospect theory of Nobel Laureate Daniel Kahneman and Adam Tversky ((1979)), people tend to gamble in the area of business decrease and losses. There is the fatal relationship between the potential scope of actions and urgency for action (see Fig. 6.1): Over time, the need to change increases, though potential actions will shrink exponentially. That means that if the need to change is perceived too late (perception threshold), the room to maneuver is too small to conduct a successful turnaround.

Fig. 6.1 Perception threshold
(own presentation)

From systemic management (Vieweg 2018), it is obvious that three core processes are ongoing in parallel in any organization:

1. The individual core process: what does a change mean to the individual person (opportunities, fears, etc.) and how does the person position herself toward the change (from driving to blocking).
2. The social core process: what does transformation do with the group of people (team to larger organizations) and their way of working together.
3. The task core process: how shall the value creation take place.

A typical antipattern is to focus on the third ("tangible," "hard facts") tasks process only, neglecting the other two which need to be addressed early on in any transformation. So, a common trap is that managers stick to "their" business and their responsibilities or try to map current responsibilities to the new business environment (due to lack of preparedness to change).

> *Example Eastman Kodak*: This is what it looked like with Eastman Kodak as well: the organizational inertia became apparent when for managers of the sunsetting high-margin specialized business the survival instinct kicked in Shih (2016). Long-serving managers have defended their "duchy" and proclaimed their participation in the new business. Apparently, as none of the last strategic moves such as merging different customer segments (due to missing volume), or following the escape pattern of seeking new growth in non-core (here: inkjet printing) businesses, were successful, the company filed for Chap. 11 under the US Bankruptcy Code bankruptcy protection in 2013

(continued)

from which only marginal parts succeeded. Another example, with some links to the above, is in the printing press manufacturer industry. Here, similar characteristics as explained in Table 6.1 can be applied (except shelf life, as this is toward consumer products, while mechanical and plant engineering is an area of business to business). High entry barriers into the complex business have created an oligopoly of few manufacturers.

In particular in Germany, three printing press manufacturers were worldwide leaders of their industry, controlling some two-thirds of the market (Schnitzler 2012)—in the pre-digitized world. These gigantic offset and web printing machines of some 30 meters (100 ft) length, often more than one hundred tons of weight, that led paper pass through at a speed of 70 km/h (44 mph), were for large-scale prints such as physical newspapers, magazines, catalogues, and telephone books. With the advent of the Internet in the early millennium years, a fatal development for their customers—the print shops—started: Print shop customers were increasingly placing their orders via "reverse auctions" (Bertram 2018), in which print shops were able to bid online for a job (typically of smaller volume) and competitors were able to further undercut the lowest price (similar to the eBay approach, but reverse). Hence, a print shop in need of a job would go to or even beyond its limit. The resulting distribution battle shifted the boundaries of different printing processes as well. The knock-on effect for the machine manufacturers followed the decrease of high-volume print runs, as physical newspaper volumes decreased: the high-volume printing processes were not competitive for short-run brochures and flyers that migrated completely to digital prints. As market for high-volume prints shrank, more and more used printing press were on the market, which prevented even further the manufacturers to sell their new ones. As the machines are built to last "forever" or at least for many years, there was no real need for print shops to buy the latest model. Figure 6.2 shows the disruptive effects of the printing press industry.

Over decades in the pre-digitized world, the printing press machine manufacturers have basically optimized their productivity by ever-increasing efficiency—leading to reduced variable unit costs at the price of high fixed costs. Ideal for a growing but fatal for a declining market (see Fig. 6.3): as long as the market size demands high output beyond the parity point, efficiency gains from ever-more integrated (automated) machines pay off with lower variable unit costs. This is bitterly reversed when the entire market shrinks, and efficiency gains are wiped away by underutilization and fixed costs that must be covered by fewer and fewer production units.

Fig. 6.2 Downwards slope in a sunsetting printing press machine industry (own presentation)

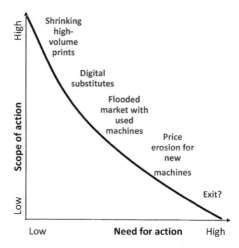

Fig. 6.3 Effects of optimizing for productivity (own presentation)

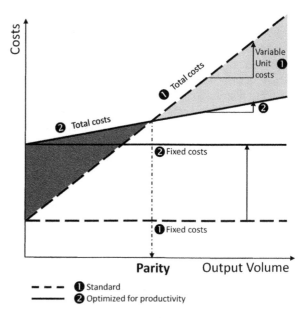

Example Heidelberger Druckmaschinen AG: In the example of Heidelberger Druckmaschinen AG, the leading manufacturer in the pre-digitized world, the effects can be seen immediately when reflecting on a few performance parameters: the share price was an all-time high of €34.338 on 20.05.2002 (4Investors 2020) and an employment high of nearly 25,000 (Heidelberger Druckmaschinen AG 2002) experienced a massive decline with insolvency

(continued)

during the financial crisis. Almost two decades later, the 170-year-old company's shares worth reached its all-time low on 18.09.2020 at € 0.50 or 1.5%(!) of that top value (Heidelberger Druckmaschinen AG 2020a). That corresponds to a decline of 21%—per year! Various restructuring programs and management shakeups and further cost cutting due to the COVID-19 pandemic crisis have led to a rearranged portfolio on digitalized business models and further optimized processes for the printing press machines and services, which are envisaged to be delivered through less than 10,000 remaining employees (Heidelberger Druckmaschinen AG 2020b).

It remains to be seen if this transformation will be successful: although the company now has an "app," sees digitization as a key element, e.g., for flexible service contracts, and even has some AI baked into their products (e.g., for technical process optimization on the machines themselves) (Heidelberger Druckmaschinen AG 2020b), the odds are on the unchanged high-volume printing market dismal outlook as such, coinciding with excessive supply on printing press machines, poor financial performance (e.g., on EUR 2.3Bn Heidelberger made a EUR six million pre-tax profit without restructuring, a third of that amount was used for a redundancy payment to an ousted board director (Heidelberger Druckmaschinen AG 2020b). . .), and missing strategy change to exploit more promising markets. The latter can be seen by Heidelberger's key printing press manufacturer competitors Koenig & Bauer Group, who focus on special (growing) printing segments such as cardboard, metal decorating, and glass direct printing (Koeing and Bauer 2019).

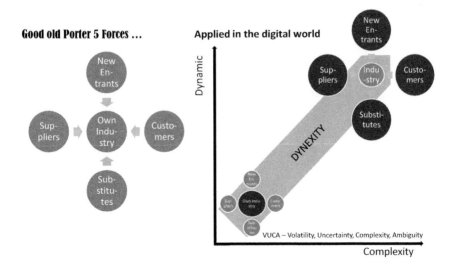

Fig. 6.4 Game-changer digitization in high dynexity context (own presentation)

In summary, the challenge of the digital area is to understand (how) to respond to new challenges. Here, the well-known Porter's five forces (Porter 2008) can be put into an adjusted context (see Fig. 6.4): while in a low dynamic and low complexity world of former times, the incumbent industry players may have dominated the competitive landscape with rare forward or backward integrations in the value chain or now entrants/substitutes, in a highly dynamic and highly complex world (so-called high dynexity), the factors outside the incumbent industry become more important and may even dominate the competition.

6.3   Digitization Potential and Expectations

"Digitization," "Internet of Things," ("IoT") or "Industry 4.0" are typical buzzwords flying around during the last decade. Almost no business of any size can escape from it, as more and more concrete applications along the value chains are digitized, even public services go digital. In many areas, this ubiquity has transformed from providing a first-mover advantage to early adopters of new technology and organizational approaches to a commodity. For example today, no retailer of size can afford to be a pure offline/onsite business. Ignoring the digitization trend leads right into the deathly downward spiral, as can be seen, e.g., in the USA with former famous Sears (that came out of a 2018 bankruptcy process at a marginal size and a high probability not to survive the COVID-19 aftermaths (Isidore 2020)). Ironically, Sears is an example of early but unsuccessful trials in e-commerce (Delventhal 2020).

The value drivers for digitization are spread across the entire value chain and for both the product development and the production/operations value delivery chains (Fig. 6.5).

According to McKinsey Global Institute (McKinsey 2016) the realized digital potential in 2016 was 18% in the USA and just 12% in Europe on average. Clearly, there is a difference between industries with information and communications technologies, finance, and knowledge-based services taking the helm (BMWI 2018). Industries such as utilities are picking up—now and with a delay of approximately one decade (!) (Bergmann et al. 2015). Although the expectations toward digitization are huge as they are in a business context, it may well be that the reality

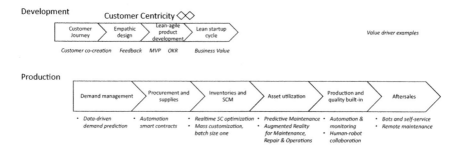

Fig. 6.5 Digitization value chains and value driver (own presentation)

will be more restricted due to the fact of missing infrastructure. For any digitalized business, data gathering, transmission, processing, and intervention is key. There is no way in providing real-time process adjustments in case of lack of communication networks to distribute such data. Ambitions on the much hoped for 5G network generation on mobile communication are exaggerated. Significant bandwidth improvement are expected everywhere, despite to fact that even in the incumbent 4G technology ("LTE") speed is suboptimal in many larger economic heavyweight countries such as Japan (#34), France (#36), the UK (#41), Germany (#44), or the USA (#62) (Opensignal 2020). The fact that the best 5G antennae will only work on a high-speed backbone network (i.e., fiber), is rarely been discussed and contributes to the rollout-issue.

6.4 Common Digitization Techniques

Digitization enables automation. Obviously, the typical benefits to expect are continuous pre-defined (higher) quality, reproducibility, higher throughput (from higher production speed and continuous uptime), and in real terms the most important factor: lower costs. Although very often, the former arguments are brought forward, at the end it is the latter, the cost argument ultimately driving the decision. This simplistic argumentation is enriched with additional arguments such as job enrichment for those remaining non-automated tasks that are taken by the remaining human workers. Although this argument can be correct too, it is not the decisive one. Otherwise, this would mean that a job would not be advertised, would be interesting for applicants, and could be filled, because the (manually human) work would not be rich enough. According to OECD's outlook on the future of work (OECD 2019), on average of all OECD countries, 14% of jobs are immediately at high risk of automation. Although this figure is smaller than in other studies, 32% of jobs could be radically transformed. This transformation does not relate to "blue-collar" workers only, but increasingly will affect those of "white-collar" knowledge workers as well, in repetitive, transactional activities.

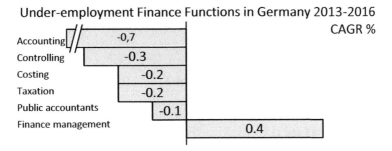

Fig. 6.6 Under-employment in finance functions in Germany 2013–2016 (own presentation based on statistics from Bundesagentur für Arbeit, aggregate from Grunwald-Delitz et al. (2018))

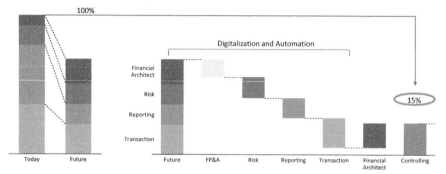

Fig. 6.7 Effect of digitization on finance tasks (own presentation based on Lahmann and Schacher (2017))

Example Controlling: This can be illustrated with the example of controlling (see Fig. 6.6): Digitization will drive automation including in finance and accounting. Transactional processes are and will be automated first (e.g., using technologies such as RPA—Robot Process Automation). Although finance roles have reached a pinnacle in 2018 (see Fig. 6.7) and under-employment in finance functions, after digitization and automation only a subset of labor resources for value added and digital orchestration will be left which may be as low as 15%!

Only intellectual very demanding, innovative activities such as financial architecture will prevail.—Financial Architecture describes the innovative creation of solution for challenges such as financing, price determination in a combined product and services offering, payment terms, and business cases for "XaaS—X as a service" businesses, in which the product is not sold to the customer, but access to the product (and additional services) is granted based on runtime service contract. In contrast, repetitive and standard rule-based activities are prone for automation and will diminish human jobs to a minimum.

6.4.1 Robot Process Automation (RPA)

One driver to that is RPA—Robot Process Automation. RPA has seen a massive boost in recent years and is growing rapidly (Gartner 2020) with realized CAGR of 65% from 2017 to 2019, and despite the economic recession in 2020 due to the COVID-19 pandemic, still a CAGR of 38% is forecast until 2021 (see Fig. 6.8), outpacing earlier projections.

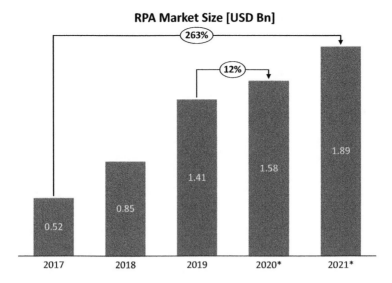

Fig. 6.8 RPA software market size worldwide (own presentation, analysis based on Gartner (2020))

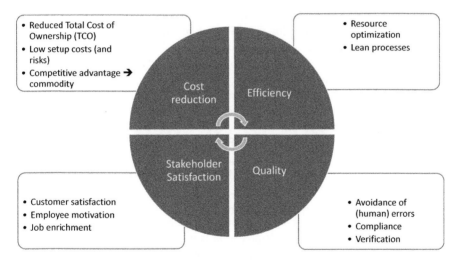

Fig. 6.9 RPA expectations (own presentation)

The reason is very simple. RPA is a transfer technology, bridging different applications without the need for heavy IT projects (that typically tend to require rare IT resources, long lead times, and large budgets). The RPA approach is to run a bot (i.e., the RPA application) on ordinary end user computers. The advantage is obviously by using the RPA that has its own user account on the company's IT systems, mirroring activities of a human worker within a predefined process using applications such as ERP systems for booking, E-mails, etc. Manual processes can

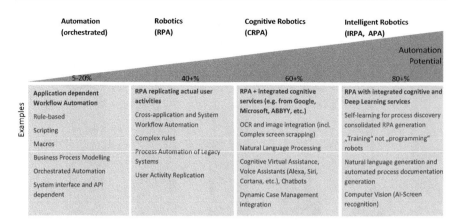

Fig. 6.10 Different characteristics of RPA (own presentation based on UIPATH (2018))

be automated within very short setup times (see Fig. 6.9). Incumbent suppliers of RPA solutions offer simple-to-use configuration tolls and/or "RPA academy" support that enables (non-IT) customers to easily set up their bot without the prerequisite of programming skills (the resource that is typically within the IT department or with the external supplier and not easily accessible). Though it is highly advisable to apply a structured approach for the RPA introduction, in an initial evaluation, potential processes that can easily be automated should be identified and validated by both the internal view of the organization and an external reflection to utilize best (implementation) practices and avoid common problems. Once the right process candidates have been identified, in the second step processes need to be captured (including data structures) and the technical feasibility be checked.

Typically, the cost for an RPA is in the order of an annual salary of one (human) resource performing the repetitive task. From thereon, the economic business case rationale with sub-annual paybacks can easily be drawn: As the RPA can run 24/7, it will give an immediate tripled capacity advantage compared to human workers. The productivity itself may add an efficiency advantage as well as error avoidance. Obviously, this expectation is only valid for such processes that have the characteristics of repetitive flow and a minimum of exception handling. Therefore, the structured approach and implementation is crucial to the RPA success. Otherwise, the implementation may entirely fail and deliver broken processes with additional (over)load for remaining staff to fix what the RPA cannot handle. In such a situation, it is not technology that failed, but the selection of adequate process parts to be automated and their implementation.

There are different stages of RPA reflecting the sophistication. More advanced technologies (IRPA, APA) use AI already (see Fig. 6.10). The higher the sophistication of the RPA (in a wider sense), the higher the potential automation can generate. The spectrum ranges from static rule-based processes within one application (e.g., spreadsheet calculation macros) onward to cross-application predefined process flows that replicate (human) user activities over to pattern recognition

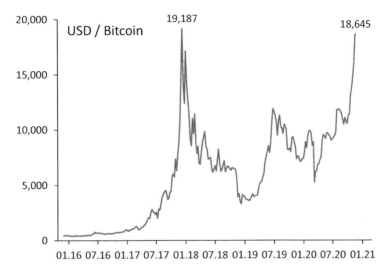

Fig. 6.11 Bitcoin price development in USD (own presentation, data based on investing.com (2020))

techniques such as optical character recognition ("OCR") or natural language processing ("NLP")[2] allowing voice recognition and voice assistant services to interact with (human) users. Chatbots are another automation application that are based on interaction between human and machines. Based on the structure that was introduced as early as 1966 (Weizenbaum 1966) and used in developments throughout, chatbots are used by businesses in a variety of interaction points with their customers. Typical examples are web chat, messenger chats, customer support, e-commerce, sales enablement, SMS (text messenger), and marketing (Chatbot 2020). The advanced process automation (APA) utilizes typical ML techniques such as supervised and unsupervised learning.

6.4.2 Blockchain

Blockchain technologies ("BCT") have attracted a lot of public attention at the end of 2017, when the crypto-"currency" Bitcoin rallied in an unparalleled surge to $20,000 (see Fig. 6.11). The year 2010 was the first-time Bitcoins could be traded. According to an anecdote (Elbers 2018), the first transaction did not really correspond to a currency, but to two standard pizzas. These were to cost 10,000 Bitcoins. One can only hope for the pizzeria that they did not sell the Bitcoins immediately:

---

[2]It is important to note that the abbreviation "NLP" is unfortunately used for two completely different subject areas. In this context, it is the AI technology of identifying and interpreting human language. It has nothing to do with the pseudo-scientific communication and psychotherapeutic approach neuro-linguistic programming (NLP).

taking into account the volatile but increasing price, e.g., in November 2020, the price for the Italian fast food, which was originally considered as the meal of the poor people, would be almost EUR 186 million.[3]

Meanwhile, there are many other crypto-currencies with different technological configurations offered, and a lively debate whether BCT-based crypto-currencies are "currencies" at all accompanied their wider spread in the market. For example, the head of the UK Financial Conduct Authority (FCA), Andrew Bailey, conveyed a serious warning with his opinion in December 2017 that "the rocketing value of bitcoin can only be temporary, and that it is stuck in a bubble. That could eventually come to an end in a spectacular burst" (Griffin 2017). Despite the critical views, crypto-currencies are a fact: as of 2020, there are multiple thousands of crypto-currencies in offer, though only three have reached a significant volume of >USD 10 Bn (coinmarketcap.com 2020).

BCT advocates refer to many other use cases rather than crypto-currencies. Examples are applications in supply chains where quality standards need to be guaranteed and tight documentation and controls need to be in place such as refrigerated transport for food and pharmaceutical products. Another example are so-called smart contracts, where (business) customer–supplier relationship management can be automated by mirroring intended transactions on a contractual basis without human interactions. A typical smart contract use case allows for automated payments as soon as negotiated conditions laid down in the contract are met like a physical good—with satnav location functionality such as GPS—being delivered to the customer site, and location update automatically logged. That log update will then trigger the payment to the supplier (Iansiti and Lakhani 2017)—a self-executing contract.

In general, for transactions between two parties that traditionally needed an intermediary, a clearing house, or trust center, BCT can provide a way without the need for such third parties. Hence, it is often called a "distributed ledger" technology ("DLT"). This would mean that banker, brokers, lawyers, and notary services are dispensable and delay-prone bureaucracy can speed up to near-real-time transactions of the Internet age. The efficiency increase comes in as lower cost and less delay; see Fig. 6.12. The key role of traditional tripartite transactions is the "party of trust" who takes the accountability that both Party A and Party B are identified and comply with their responsibilities to deliver on a contractual promise, i.e., that all information provided is correct. In case of default of one of the parties A or B, the intermediary will clear the situation by rewinding the stalled transaction. This means as well that the intermediary is in a risk position and covers said risk by asking for risk coverage premium, which adds to the overall transactional costs.

The blockchain approach uses cryptographical technology that ensures for the correctness of the information. The most important element is a hash function. Applying adequate cryptographic hash functions ("CHF"), it is possible to mark a data stream such as a text of indefinite length with a digital mark (i.e., the hash) of

---

[3]Based on data from Finanzen.net (2020).

Fig. 6.12 Principles of trusted transactions with tripartite (intermediary, above) and BCT (below) (own presentation)

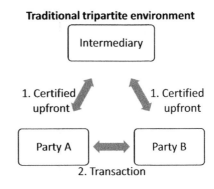

definite length. The transaction is from a current, practically irreversible perspective; Sect. 6.4.3 takes a closer look at the implications of upcoming new computer technologies such as quantum computers. There are many different algorithms around, and they cannot be explained in too much detail here. Instead, the general characteristics can be summarized as follows: It is

- Reproducible and deterministic, i.e., identical messages will generate identical hashes.
- A one-way transaction, so that with a given hash, the originating message cannot be reproduced.
- Generating different hash values for different messages; any two different messages will never share the same hash value.
- Generating basically uncorrelated new hash values, even if only minor changes in the underlying message occurred.
- Tolerant to limited computational requirements, so that generating a hash is not an issue.

As an example, the quite new SHA3–512 algorithm is taken[4] and applied on a sentence of this text, with one tiny modification—a missing dot at the end of the sentence (see Fig. 6.13).

---

[4]To test it, various tools are freely available on the Internet; for the example shown here the following service was used: https://sha256calc.com/hash/sha3-512/Applying+adequate+crypto graphic+hash+function+%28CHF%29%2C+it+is+possible+to+mark+a+data+stream+such+as+a +text+of+indefinite+length (accessed 05.10.2020).

Message	Applying adequate cryptographic hash function (CHF), it is possible to mark a data stream such as a text of indefinite length.	Applying adequate cryptographic hash function (CHF), it is possible to mark a data stream such as a text of indefinite length
		Missing dot at end of sentence
Hash (SHA3-512)	0555477f66a81f3000b737cef4 6a38c9bcd36edbef30b12b7b15 86c5ab0a9eb99c7b84a7a9748b 7bc1057009621b1c3cc8ca3819 7ade4cd7380e63f5087b5157	6e5a756f210500c8beefc9f3d2 707ac2c0899bac53218d46e6b2 601b980a3683ee8aa65bcd42a9 29f28747a6622e3ba442abcee9 fc321b5064edb621f36a0b80
		Leading to an entirely different hash value

Fig. 6.13 Hash example: Slight modification of the original message (left) leads to a significantly different hash value (own presentation)

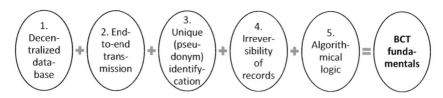

Fig. 6.14 BCT fundamentals (own presentation)

The technical approach and details of BCT cannot be explained here in too much detail, though an outline is given as key elements necessary to assess the economic and ethical implications of the technologies are as follows: BCT can be summarized with the fundamental characteristics as shown in Fig. 6.14. As by design there is no central entity that has access to the entire history of transactions, all transactions are directly stored in the blockchain and shared with all parties participating in the chain. This means that every party can verify—without request to others—the transaction history (1). Communication is directly between the parties (technically called "node") involved in a specific transaction (peer-to-peer). Information is captured at each node (2). Although blockchain is not merely an encryption method to keep information as a secret, BCT transactions and its content are visible to all members on the blockchain system. Each node is identified with a unique identification address that can be used in a decoupled mode from the real identity of that node, providing anonymity, which is based on a private (random) key and derived public addresses (3). Cornerstone is the characteristic that any eligible transaction cannot be reversed, hence providing auditing security. Once a transaction is entered into the distributed database, the underlying message or information of that transaction cannot be altered, as the credentials of the said transactional block are linked or "chained" to previous transactions (hence the name blockchain).

Modification of previous blocks will ultimately lead to an invalid status of the chain, disqualifying the modification (see Fig. 6.15). This characteristic is provided by some algorithms and computational techniques to ensure efficient handling such

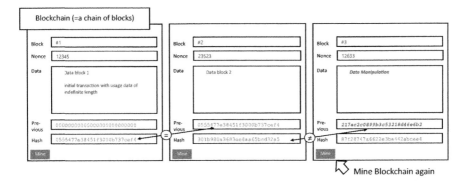

Fig. 6.15 Blockchain principle (own presentation)

as sequential ordering, network availability, as well as database stability (4). As there is clear logic, its sequences can be captured by and implemented in computer algorithms that can trigger off specific actions as previously seen in the smart contract use case (5) (Iansiti and Lakhani 2017).

Mining is one key process of BCT, in which each node in the network captures transactions between users that are verified and entered into the blockchain's distributed ledger. Therefore, miner nodes use the pool of transactions that have not yet been included in a block and start combining them into a block of multiple transactions. Each transaction from the pool is been hashed and pairwise organized and hashed again until the hash treetop is reached (also called "Merkle root" named after the cryptographic scientist Ralph Merkle (1988)). The latter is being placed together with the hash of the previous block and a random number ("nonce") in the header of the new block. Miners repeatedly hash the header by running through different nonces until a miner on the network finally creates a valid hash. In that case, the miner's node sends the underlying block to the network. All other nodes check if the hash is valid, and if so, insert the block into their copy of the blockchain and continue mining the next block.

In case of two nodes sending valid blocks into the network, miners will continue mining on their last valid block. This competitive situation between these two blocks will continue until a next block is mined on one of the competing blocks. The block is then abandoned (the "Orphan Block"), and miners of this block switch over to the successful one.

6.4.2.1 BCT Challenges

As of 2020, BCT offers both many opportunities and technical challenges. For example, the bitcoin example explained earlier has meanwhile reached a length of some 300GB of an exponential trail (see Fig. 6.16). This requires a significant computational resource.

Power consumption is a key resource, as the mining process encounters an enormous amount of computational transactions. The energy consumption for Bitcoin has reached in a base scenario 63TWh in October 2020, according to the

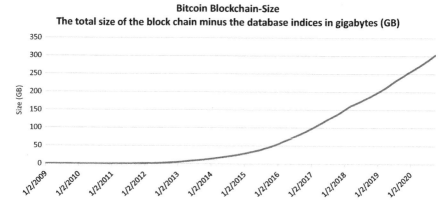

Fig. 6.16 Bitcoin blockchain size (own presentation based on cleansed data from blockchain.com (2020))

University of Cambridge's Center for Alternative Finance (CBECI 2020). This amount compares to 108% of the energy consumption of Switzerland, 12% of Germany, and 0.3% worldwide consumption (Erxleben 2019).Encountering that the Bitcoin is just one application, a multitude of computational resources and technical performance challenges (in computing capacity, network latency, and storage) need to be solved.

Another weakness is the fact that the majority of nodes in a blockchain finally define what is the ultimate "truth." So, the basic "51% rule" of nodes that defines which root is successful and which blocks are to be abandoned per se is prone to fraudulent actions in case of attractive gain from such actions. First 51% attacks were successful on blockchains such as bitcoin gold in 2018 (Dölle 2018) and Ethereum in 2019 (Jenkinson 2019). Despite the technological enhancement of prevention in that area, there remains a fundamental challenge to avoid successful fraudulent actions as they may have disastrous consequences in value and trust ruination. This can be illustrated by an example of a private real estate contract: Typically, the underlying value (of the property) is in the order of a person's largest lifetime spending. In today's standard procedures such a transaction requires specific fiduciary duty of the intermediate, the attesting notary. This highly skilled and educated lawyer—not every lawyer will be eligible to act as a notary—has responsibilities of public administration and guarantees that property transactions are correctly executed, i.e., the transfer of ownership is based on correct identification of buyer and seller, and the money due is being paid by the bona fide buyer as the proprietorship is transferred from the bona fide seller to the buyer. In case of faulty execution (e.g., proprietorship has changed without payment or vice versa), it is the notary who has to face the legal consequences; the notary can be taken to court. In case of using a blockchain technology, no such intermediary exists anymore. It is the blockchain with all transactional history that provides evidence. If this evidence is manipulated as a consequence of a fraudulent attack, there is no way to prove this fraudulent attack, nor to sue anyone, as—thanks to anonymity of the BCT—it may be extremely difficult to identify the driving forces behind that attack. Although from a current perspective, the likelihood of success of such an attack may be extremely small, but several weak points and technology enhancements indicate a real threat: as the blockchain technology requires significant computing and network resources, the risk is high for fraudulent actions. Examples include:

- Nodes are ignored/or kept from the system (i.e., cannot contribute to the majority rule).
- More "efficient" mining clouds that are more and more commonly used lead to new weaknesses of a centralized approach (i.e., the advantage of the decentralized blockchain deteriorates).
- Increasing computing performance using quantum computing will compromise existing cryptographical methods such as "brute-force attacks[5]" which are more easily being executed.

The context in which a blockchain is operated is of great importance.

Example "The DAO": The rise and fall of "the DAO" (Decentralized Autonomous Organization) in 2016 shows the implication, although the root cause of the problem was not the BCT-based currency itself (in this case Ethereum), but the smart contract built on the Ethereum blockchain (Falkon 2017): The DAO was meant to act as a venture capital fund in the Ethereum community for crypto developments. So, developers could pitch their idea to the community in order to receive funding from the DAO, which would be based on votes from community DAO token holders, who in return benefit in case of a profitable project. Two flaws in the DAO (open source) code basically led to successful fraud: the possibility of recursive calls requesting the smart contract to hand back Ether (the currency items/token in the Ethereum system) before the smart contract balance was updated, and the sequence of the smart contract sending first the Ether funds before updating the balance. Although monetary "real" damage could be avoided by some band-aid measures, it marked the end of this approach.

6.4.2.2 Blockchain and AI

AI and Blockchain can be linked to each other and complement each other: Basically, blockchain technologies provide trust on data and transaction that applicants can rely on their correctness and immutability. The (resource) price for that proposition is very high, as can be seen by blockchain lengths or energy consumption. Here, AI provides the complementary characteristics that can—correct implementation

---

[5]Brute-force attacks basically consist of a systematic alteration of input parameter such as password combinations until the correct combination is found.

Table 6.2 Complementary characteristics of blockchain and AI (own presentation, based on Corea (2017))

Blockchain to support AI with TRUST	AI to support Blockchain with EFFICIENCY
Providing trust from an immutable audit trail	Energy consumption for the resource-intensive mining process by AI-based optimizing techniques
Better data quality (trusted data) improves AI effectiveness	Scalability based on AI "federated" learning on new data sharing approaches keeping blockchain length at check, rather than keeping non-value legacy blocks
Ease of AI acceptance in providing (personal) data	Security to avoid fraudulent attacks on the application layer on top of the blockchain
Provide bots artificial trust in machine-to-machine interactions	Minimizing mining (and cost) efforts by predicting likely successful nodes
Limit AI action space by applying smart contracts to specific actions	Data exchange controls (data gates) for blockchain protected personal data sharing

assumed—lead to higher efficiency and a stronger overall proposition (see Table 6.2, left side). Hence, a certain convergence of both drivers of the digitization can be expected (Corea 2017).

6.4.3 Quantum Computer, Supercomputer, and the Implication of Computing Performance

Digital technologies such as AI and blockchain require a high amount of computing power, as well as complex models in scientific (e.g., astrophysics, quantum mechanics, and meteorology) or industrial applications (geological exploration, aircraft development, and weapon systems). The exponential development in that field over decades has reached a level that is headed by the Japanese RIKEN Fugaku Supercomputer (Morgan 2020) since June 2020: scratching at the exaflops definition[6] and a cost of close to USD 2 BN, up to 80 MW of electrical power consumption is leading an accelerated race for computational dominance (see Fig. 6.17), so that in consequence, the leading position is shorter (<1 year) than in former years. In public, this is a tripartite race between Japan, the USA, and China. Power consumption is a key issue: the fastest computer (by FLOPS—floating point operations per second) in 2020 (Fuguka, JP, 415 PFLOPS) is 762 times more energy hungry than the most efficient supercomputer (MN-3, JP 1.6PFLOPS).[7] Compared to the human brain—which is an often-used analogy, though with many flaws which to discuss are beyond the topic here—it would still show up to 4.700 higher efficiency.[8]

---

[6]"exa" (10E18) is a thousand "peta" (10E15), which is a thousand "tera"(10E12), which is a thousand "giga" floating point operations per second (FLOPS).

[7]Own calculation based on https://www.top500.org/lists/green500/2020/06/ (accessed 06.10.2020).

[8]Own calculation assuming 1.500 PFLOPS at 15 W, a typical setting found across the literature.

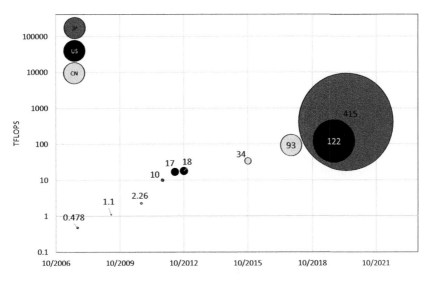

Fig. 6.17 Supercomputer Top#1 Rankings. Bubble size reflecting efficiency (in MFLOPS/W: the larger the bubble, the higher the efficiency) (own presentation, data based on Top 500 (2020))

Computing performance is key for big data analysis, highly complex tasks, deterministic (as shown in the blockchain mining example) and cryptographical applications.

Quantum computing is an emerging dimension that strives for supremacy over classical computer architecture. The hope is that specific computational tasks can be executed exponentially faster than using classical computers—even supercomputers. Classical computing is based on the basic elements of a bit which holds a single binary value such as "0" or "1," whereas quantum computers take the theory of quantum mechanics that uses basic elements called quantum bits—or qubits—that can hold both values at the same time. In a coherent setting of multiple qubits, multiple options can be processed simultaneously. This can be explained by assuming that qubits are measurement particles within a given system with a certain state. The base state before measurement cannot be precisely defined; they can only be described with probabilities. Multiple qubits can be entangled with each other, i.e., they influence each other and are not independent. As a consequence, there are simultaneous correlations, which is in harsh contrast to our day-to-day experience of "larger" particles: e.g., an object has a (mechanical) impulse and, with its velocity and mass, has an impact on a second object when it hits the latter—its deformation will be the consequence thereafter. In quantum mechanics, the simultaneous interaction of quantums—although in physical distance to each other—is hard to understand, at least Albert Einstein is cited to speak about "spooky remote effects" (Wobst 2020). A quantum computer assumes all possible states in parallel, e.g., if 53 qubits are entangled and influence from outside, there are $2^{53} \approx 10^{16}$ different states possible, all of which are considered in parallel. The challenge is to influence the states in various stages such that the desired combination (called "interference") is identified. That parallel information processing will exponentially reduce the time it would take even for the fastest classical computing systems to solve a computational problem.

Example Google AI Quantum and Sycamore: The first narrow setting of such supremacy of quantum computing was demonstrated in 2019 by a US-centric international team around the Google AI Quantum and nine US and three German scientific institutions (Arute et al. 2019). Based on a narrow computational task (that is specifically hard for classical computers, and advantageous for quantum computing), the "Sycamore" quantum processor—an array of up to 53 qubits—took about 200 seconds for the task that the then faster state-of-the-art classical supercomputer (Summit, USA, which is number 2 in Fig. 6.17, which is "just" 2.7 times slower than the ruling #1 Fugaku) would take approximately 10,000 years (#1 Fugaku would require still some 3,700 years, accordingly). This dramatic increase in speed—although applicable only for a dedicated experimental setting—is first public evidence of the widely perceived computing paradigm of quantum computing supremacy. Critics from competitors such as IBM claimed that this experiment could have been solved within 2.5 days (Savage 2020). While there is an intense race for ever-increasing computing performance, there are assessments of 10–15 years (from 2020) still to go when quantum computing will be available on a broadened basis. Though, a variety of initiatives and networks are preparing for it already now (Solomon 2020) and paving the way of using this emerging technology: as quantum computers have an entirely different architecture, and going along with that an entirely different way of utilizing the full performance spectrum, development environments need to be set up and readily in place once the technology will be available on a large(r) scale.

An often-cited problem that might occur once quantum computing is the new state of technology is hacking existing cryptographical applications that are basically used everywhere today for hashing, digital signatures, and encryption. The different cryptographical approaches are very often based on an asymmetric public key cryptography ("PKC") that allows us easily to share information in an authentical and secure environment . . . . until said approach can be compromised (easily).

Public key infrastructure ("PKI") is based on a set of a private key and a public key. As the name indicates, private keys are kept as a secret by the user and is not shared with the outside world, whereas the public key can be shared with others easily. The beauty of the approach is that it does not require a symmetric exchange of keys (e.g., only one key used for encryption and decryption) that leads to massive logistical and procedural issues to ensure that only the correct identity has used the cryptographical key for the intended purpose. PKC is an irreversible approach, i.e., a cryptographical transaction such as encryption of a message of creation of a digital signature cannot be reversed with the key used; it needs the counterpart key.

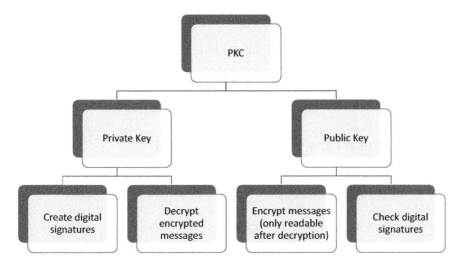

Fig. 6.18 Principle of a public key cryptography (own presentation)

Figure 6.18 illustrated the two different principal functions of using cryptographical keys—encryption of messages (to keep the content as a secret) and creation of a digital signature (providing authentication, which is providing the evidence that the party claiming a certain identity indeed is the identity claimed to be). The basis for asymmetric cryptographical procedures is that the so-called one-way function provides one simple and efficient way to calculate (i.e., multiplication of prime numbers), but the reverse is extremely hard (i.e., factorization of a large number). The longer the key, the harder the factorization effort. Hence, there is an ongoing need to extend key lengths, as computational performance is increasing.

With current computational performance, cyber-attacks typically do not pay off as the burden is simply too high; it would take much too long to hack a cryptographic secret. In an environment where exponentially more computational performance is prevailing, brute-force attacks are likely to pay off and may compromise existing data security infrastructures fundamentally. Invented in the late 1970s by the three MIT mathematicians Rivest, Sharmir, and Adleman, the famous RSA approach ("RSA"), which is a deterministic approach based on a set of mathematical functions, is used today in various applications from e-mail, electronic banking, and electronic passports to Internet transmission protocols. The RSA algorithm has been frequently cracked on various increasing key lengths: Competitive challenges (against a prize setting in the beginning) have shown factorization for keys up to a length of 768 bit (EMC 2020). Hence, there is an ongoing need to extend key lengths, as computational performance is increasing. As of 2020, in Germany the recommendation is to use key lengths of 2048 bits (BNA 2014).

With the emergence of quantum computing, the logic of longer keys will not be feasible anymore, as there is a massive impediment to the PKC performance as such. Already today, typically RSA is not used to encrypt messages as such, but for performance reasons just to encrypt a symmetric key (i.e., both sides use the same key).

Though, it needs to be reflected that with increasing sophistication of attacking existing cryptographical approaches, there is as well the innovation of those approaches that provide new—more secure—opportunities.

6.5   Technical and Economic Trends in AI

AI is a highly dynamic area of technology. Although the idea of AI roots back into the 1940s, it is just in recent years with the emergence of the Internet services, so-called social media, and the commercialization of customer data that AI has become a mainstream technology. Spoiled by specific flagship applications such as autonomous driving, AI is an integral part of the complex solution. Meanwhile, there are so many AI deployments in various areas of the daily lives that it seem to be fair to call it a ubiquitous technology: examples are individualized content (commercials) offered on websites; navigation systems with speech recognition; speech assistant services such as "Alexa," Google Home," or "Siri"; optical character recognition when transferring a PDF (bitmap) into something machine-readable, facial detection for authentication checks, or body scan (Presize.ai 2020) to allow optimal apparel sizing in online shopping . . . The list is endless and very often the consumer even does not know that AI is included in the service offering provided.

During the last few years, there is a publicly visible race between two nations and societal systems for the supremacy of AI: the USA and China. Other countries started to catch up, in particular Russia. Europe is still defining their way forward (EU 2020), whereas low-cost Eastern Europe EU countries emerged to the workshop for many international groups on programming—including AI applications. Russia's AI spend in 2017 on domestic investments was just USD 12 m, still encountering the projected private sector spend increase to $500 m; this is a fraction of the billions spent in the USA and China (Bendett 2018). Though, the ambition was set by the Russian President in 2017 in an online session "Russia Focused on the Future" to more than one million participants when Putin said "Artificial intelligence is the future not only of Russia but of all of mankind, [. . .]. Whoever becomes the leader in this sphere will become the ruler of the world" (Gigova 2017). Russia has an AI strategy plan and policies released in 2019 (OECD.AI 2020). Due to the fact that Russia repeatedly misused data from end user for state-directed observations, the trust in Russian software diminished heavily. Russia was blamed for fraudulent interventions in the US election 2016 (Ross et al. 2016).

Not to forget in this race the UK: It should be realized that cybernetics started off there in the late 1940s with the scientist W. Grey Walter (1910–1977) in what became later the Bristol Robotics Laboratory: his simplified first "tortoise" robots had a minimum of self-determination and "learning" on identifying just with two sensors and three motors its way to the light, even if there are obstacles in its way (Holland 2003). Since then, the UK is at the forefront of robotics development.

Despite this, the following section's focus will be on the competition between the USA and China, as they are primarily driving AI on a worldwide basis. Though, it is strongly recommended not to forget that there are more than just two superpowers in that race.

The key competition between the USA and China basically kicked off with an experiment in 2016 with Alpha GO (the Google AI). Go is a highly complex board game, originated in China and with an extremely long history. Unlike other board games such as Chess, Go is extremely difficult to transform into an automated machine, as there are "endless" combinations possible and the rules are very complex. That is having a computer outpacing the (human) grand master (at that point in time it was the South Korean Lee Sedol, a 9 out of 9 dan professional player and one of the best players overall) is a provocation to one of the Chinese heritages. Apparently, the Chinese government has changed its approach toward AI when the Google AI team managed to score victory over one of the world's best human GO players. Although Alpha GO is just a game, its success is a turning point as AI became ready for the market—as Chinese government recognized that AI is serious. From there on, the Chinese dictator and government have put AI as a cornerstone of the "New Silk Route", China's political program to gain supremacy over the West in general, and the USA in particular.

6.5.1 China and the "Market Leninism"

The progress in China is unparalleled. This can be easily illustrated with the ranking of top-valued companies that are not yet on the stock market—the famous unicorn[9] list: not only that increasingly Chinese companies are on the top 10 list, the largest pre-IPO valuation ever with some USD 140 BN, Bytedance, is a Chinese company (Bocksch 2020).

As of 2020, China has surpassed the USA in particular areas of AI, such as facial detection solutions. For example one leading company, Megvii (Megvii 2020), was founded in 2011 by three students. Its core competency is in deep learning. Leveraging its proprietary AI productivity platform Brain++, Megvii focuses on three key verticals: personal IoT, city IoT, and supply chain IoT. Their solution is able to identify persons within 100 msec, even on a mobile device and better than a human could do. Megvii partners with Storefriendly to deploy AI-powered unmanned warehouse storage solution in Singapore (Wallstreet online 2020).

China has some advantages on AI development, compared to the USA:

1. As AI success is heavily dependent on data, China's population with three to four times more users than the USA is an immediate advantage.
2. In their emergence as economic power, China has skipped some developments such as credit card payments (that are very famous in the USA) and went straight

---

[9]A company with a valuation above USD 1 Bn is deemed to be a unicorn.

to mobile payments, leaving China with some 50 times more mobile payment transactions than in the USA.

Overall, the population and market size provide some tenfold volume of data, compared to the USA. As a common proverb indicates: "Data is the new oil" (and China is the new Saudi-Arabia) (Lee 2018), China is in the pool position to develop and advance AI systems, as these systems can learn better (from more data) than any other region. This rapid uptake of new technology leads to better performance. For example, in facial detection solutions such as Megvii, the impressive performance is possible in detection of Chinese people in particular. Other ethnical settings lead to different performance (see Sect. 8.5).

By 2020, China has already surpassed the USA in facial detection systems (Mozur 2019). Other applications such as credit checks on the mobile have transformed a typical long-lasting process into a real-time rating and decision process. Credit check can be provided within less than 10 sec on 5000 parameters using AI, compared to the traditional 10-parameter risk assessment checks from banks). In particular, the mobile as such provides already rating information from battery charging level (low level is seen more critical than fully loaded ones) or operating system version (as this indicates if the potential lender can afford the credit, i.e., the newer the better) directly to the usage pattern (i.e., how confident or resistant a user is inputting data).

The usage of these advances needs to be reflected in a societal context. In China, which is a non-democratic political system, and a typical collectivist society (according to Hofstede), the group prevails over individuals by far. In such a context, state-based supervision is not necessarily negatively perceived, though it encompasses a massive risk of scrutiny on the individuals. China has established public naming of individuals' wrongdoing by electronic screens at crossroads: individuals passing on a red traffic light will be publicly named on such screens—based on facial detection systems. Although in 2020 no direct punishment on such wrongdoing has been introduced (yet?), it is a tiny step and a great danger that the political loyalty will benefit and opposite opinions will be punished—with high social credit points, discounts in public transport, with low social points probably travel ban. Hence, AI emerges into an Orwell-type mighty instrument (Qiang 2019).

China shows a paradoxical situation: economic success in a communistic system is what Orville Shell, the US author, activist, and academic,[10] calls "market Leninism" (Schell and Delury 2014): Apparently it is possible to establish in a one-party system a sector of innovation and technology. It was always thought to be impossible, but apparently it is feasible. China has a clear target to reach AI supremacy by 2030. AI helps China to establish a ubiquitous surveillance of their citizens, in order to establish social stability and to suppress criticism on the political system. China has meanwhile (2020) installed more than 415 million CCTV cameras in the public,

---

[10]Former Dean of the University of California Berkeley Graduate School of Journalism, and Arthur Ross Director of the Center on US–China Relations at the Asia Society in New York.

and 18 out of the 20 most surveilled cities worldwide are Chinese (Bischoff 2020). According to the human activist and University of California, Berkeley, researcher Xiao Quiang, China's ruling dictatorship has set up the project "Sharp Eyes" with cameras everywhere, so that with the help of AI facial recognition in real time, a total surveillance is possible (surveillance state). The test laboratory is in the province of Xingjiang in the Northwest of China, where some 25 million people live, half of them being a specific group of Muslims. In 2009, a turmoil in the provincial capital Urumqi kicked off a long time of suppression. AI systems are used to surveil and predict citizens' tendency to what Chinese government calls terrorism. Based on the findings of the AI systems, detected people are pulled into so-called re-educational camps, without any legal basis, e.g., for wrongdoing. Even outside of the camps the citizens are affected by highest levels of surveillance and basically risk collective penalties.

6.5.2   USA and the "Surveillance Capitalism"

The history of AI and robotics originates from great minds such as scientists like Norbert Wiener to visionary science fiction authors like Isaac Asimov (Seiler and Jenkins 2014). They have paved the way throughout decades, as have lessons learnt at Cold War times and the race to the moon in the 1960s. The entrepreneurial spirit of the "American Dream," excellent education at top-ranked universities, and funding through military budget led to an innovative environment that formed Silicon Valley and that has created the world's largest and most successful IT businesses[11]—for now—and many startups driving innovation.

AI technological approaches on the one hand try to mirror human cognitive behavior in terms of learning strategies. On the other hand, the intent is to exceed human cognitive performance in specific tasks.

Some learning strategies apply similar approaches like most children do by trial and error in a joyful interaction with their surroundings. AI learns on its own (unsupervised learning) from data, which is commonly known as deep learning approach.

Example Atari Breakout: As an example, in 2013 scientists applied AI on the formerly famous Atari-video computer game "Breakout" with one target: to win. The task is to hit a ball with a racket and smash it against a multilayer wall of bricks that is to be destroyed. The ball would bounce back so that the player needs to defend effectively in not losing a ball. For a human player, it is really hard to gain excellence and almost impossible to win. The AI took 100 games to learn how to hit the ball with the racket and not to lose the ball. After

(continued)

---

[11]Very often seen as "GAFAM" (Google, Apple, Facebook, Amazon, and Microsoft).

300 games, the computer surpasses human performance, and after 500 games, AI has found a creative way to victory: a tunnel through the different layers of bricks is drilled and many bricks are destroyed with just one hit of the ball (Mnih et al. 2015).[12] While one decade ago, hardly anyone would have thought that AI could work, today it is used in almost every part of the society.According to the Future Today Institute, the great promise of AI is that computers are able to see problems in an entirely different perspective than humans do. Probably it will be possible to find another and initially seemingly impossible solution for big tasks such as climate change or a radically different approach in the treatment of incurable cancers. In purely practical terms, AI promises to enable humans to come up with more creative solutions, which in turn leads us to ingenious solutions (Webb 2019).

Some of those practical applications on more creative solutions are in healthcare cancer treatment (Dobbins Lehman 2020): In order to predict the development of cancer over time and with that prevent unnecessary surgery, at MIT and the Massachusetts General Hospital, Boston, a deep learning algorithm analyzed all medical records with hundreds of thousands of images of patients who had been operated because of a highly dangerous focus on breast cancer in a certain time. It was found that 90% did not need to be operated; only 10% had cancer.

Another example is autonomous driving: here, the challenge for AI is to understand the surroundings. While in other parts of the world such as China and Europe, this application is maximum in prototype stage, in the USA first commercial offers on self-driving freight dispatch such as Embark Trucks (Ohnsman 2019) exist already. Although the US traffic and road situation cannot be compared with other parts of the world, hence solutions working in the USA on hundreds of miles straight highways may not work in Germany's narrow and curvy villages, the pace on execution shows clear first-mover mentality.

In the USA, a surveillance movement started during the last decade. Although the motivation is entirely different from the one in China (to keep society at check and avoid any opposition to the ruling party).

The largest US Internet companies like GAFAM—Google, Apple, Facebook, Amazon, and Microsoft—hold massive data about their users; with each and every even tiny interaction, the company can increasingly better see who their users are and what they do (Domingo 2015). So, the users' behavior is being recorded, what they enter in the application's interface (even if they discard entries before sending), which content they look at, and various environmental parameters such as smartphone and operating system version (Chen 2020), etc. Using AI, various data are being customized and individualized for the user. On the one hand, that is a convenience and better experience for the user, as the user does not have to perform

---

[12]A video and original source code can be found here: https://www.youtube.com/watch?v=V1eYniJ0Rnk (accessed 08.10.2020).

such filtering and research by herself. On the other side, there is a tremendous risk that the real companies' intent—which is typically the maximization of profit and hence cash—conflicts with the users' intent. Instead of society using so-called social media, it is exactly the other way round: social media (and the companies behind them) is exploiting society; hence the term "surveillance capitalism," which was created by the former Harvard professor Shoshana Zuboff, reflects this situation (Zuboff 2019). Table 6.3 gives an overview of so-called social media offerings and the companies behind them. As the surveillance capitalism is based on data, the larger the data access, the better. That ultimately leads to a monopolization of the market: larger companies such as GAFAM with their ubiquitous reach into the users' life are best positioned to succeed in a market, either by surpassing smaller competitors or by large-scale takeovers of innovative, smaller companies.

A massive ethical problem emerges here, as it is not only the surveillance and offering customized content to users, it is basically the influence such filtering of data has on the users' behavior as such. That is the so-called social media have transformed from an individualized content provision to manipulate user behavior and decision-making. Although that was initially merely intended to maximize the (GAFAM) company's profit through advertisements, meanwhile there is a political dimension to it, since political parties use such services for the purpose of citizen manipulation. At least since the aftermath of the 2016 US presidential election scandal around Facebook and Cambridge Analytica, the problem emerges, and critical minds raise the discomfort of the subversive way GAFAM influence on politics and the deterioration of the democracy.

Google has set up an AI environment that allows us to identify as much as possible about the user. Google wants to track as much as possible about their users, even non-facts such as wishes, thoughts, and dreams (Fung 2019). Hence, the company tracks data relating to every aspect of their users' entire life. Google were initially against advertising, as it would destroy the decency of the Internet and thus their search engine—hence the original claim "Don't be evil."[13] But when the dotcom bubble burst in early 2000, Google—already the world's most popular search engine at the time—also came under pressure from investors who wanted to see more profit. So, they thought about the side effects of digital tracking, which is a technical basic fact. From these traces, the activities of the users can be predetermined. This was developed secretly; the drastically increasing profit was only announced in 2004 (1510% increase since 2001[14]) with the IPO. Google's business model is also used by others, e.g., Facebook: These companies then bought data from other high data volume businesses, e.g., from credit card issuers. Behavioral prediction applications can help reduce uncertainty. In advertising and

---

[13]Google was founded in 1998 by the students Larry Page and Sergei Brin, initially without a clear business model. The founders' guiding mantra at that time was "Don't be evil." See Vise (2005).

[14]February 16, 2016. Google's net income from 2001 to 2015 (in million US dollars) [Graph]. In Statista.   from   https://www.statista.com/statistics/266472/googles-net-income/   (accessed 19.10.2020).

Table 6.3 So-called social media offerings and the companies behind (own presentation, data sources based on We Are Social, & Hootsuite, & DataReportal (31. Januar, 2020). Ranking der größten Social Networks und Messenger nach der Anzahl der Nutzer im Januar 2020 (in Millionen) [Graph]. In Statista. https://de.statista.com/statistik/daten/studie/181086/umfrage/die-weltweit-groessten-social-networks-nach-anzahl-der-user/, (access 19.10.2020); LinkedIn. (26. August, 2020). Anzahl der registrierten Nutzer von LinkedIn nach Weltregionen Jahr 2020 (in Millionen) [Graph]. In Statista. https://de.statista.com/statistik/daten/studie/192879/umfrage/vergleich-der-besucherzahlen-von-linkendin-nachweltregionen/, (access 19.10.2020))

So-called Social Networks with the Most Users Worldwide 2020
Ranking of the largest social networks and messengers by number of users in January 2020 (in millions)

So-called social network	Company behind	Country	Number of users in Jan 2020 (in millions)	Market share (%)	Thereof Facebook	Thereof Tecent
Facebook	Facebook Inc.	USA	2449	17%	✓	
YouTube	Google LLC	USA	2000	14%		
WhatsApp	Facebook Inc.	USA	1600	11%	✓	
Facebook Messenger	Facebook Inc.	USA	1300	9%	✓	
Weixin/ WeChat	Tencent	China	1151	8%		✓
Instagram	Facebook Inc.	USA	1000	7%	✓	
Douyin/ TikTok	ByteDance	China	800	6%		
QQ	Tencent	China	731	5%		✓
LinkedIn	Microsoft Corporation	USA	704	5%		
QZone	Tencent	China	517	4%		✓
Sina Weibo	Sina Corporation	China	497	3%		
Reddit	Advance Publications	USA	430	3%		
Snapchat	Snap Inc.	USA	382	3%		
Twitter	Twitter Inc.	USA	340	2%		
Pinterest	Pinterest Inc.	USA	322	2%		
Kuaishou	Beijing Kuaishou Technology Co., Ltd	China	316	2%		
					44%	17%
	Total	USA	10,527	72%		
		China	4012	28%		

marketing, for example, people did not know how the products were actually used. They rigorously exploit society's experienced trust in technology that has made the user world safer, more efficient, and more comfortable over the last few decades—in other words, has constantly improved it.

Though, there is a turning point when the fine border line between information for users for their own independent decision-making and manipulation is crossed.

In 2010, Facebook launched a "social influence and political mobilization" study (Bond et al. 2012) to investigate whether it can influence user behavior by providing dedicated messages to them. Randomly chosen 61 million Facebook users saw a button "I voted," some with faces of their Facebook friends that have voted; others saw the button without the friends' faces. Finally, Facebook proclaimed having mobilized 340,000 to vote. Although these numbers were impressive, linked to the overall sample population it represents "just" 0.6%. Nevertheless, it clearly marks evidence of the potential to manipulate. This can be seen e.g. from various studies that too much consumption of social media radicalizes and makes people unhappy and more aggressive (and strengthens belief in abstruse conspiracy theories).[15]

GAFAM have built up a surveillance system that becomes even more powerful through speech assistance systems such as Alexa (Amazon), Siri (Apple), or Google Home (Google). They penetrate very deeply into the personal lives of their users, not only in a snapshot, but in particular by detecting changes over time. The systems learn from slight changes in e.g. the voice and can use this information to analyze the user's condition such as sniffles or shaky voice as an indicator of a cold or other mental disposition. At the end, this is the identical micro-behavioral targeting, based on a detailed understanding of the personality of the user (Zuboff 2019). This targeting is what Cambridge Analytica has done in its massive scandal in 2018, although with a political rather than a marketing objective.[16] As Cambridge Analytica was mainly financed by a conservative billionaire (Robert Mercer (Confessore and Gelles (2018)), it is obvious that anyone with enough money can acquire AI and scientists to manipulate the public and to undermine democracy. Instead of having learnt from the scandal, the control of information dissemination for manipulation is continuing at a high pace, including discriminating systems and wrong decision-making based on algorithmic decision systems ("ADS") (Crawford et al. 2018), e.g., that are used in litigation, and flawed predictions that ultimately eliminate human rights, purely based on data and algorithms that may be inappropriate to a given situation.

Although there is a significant risk of misuse of AI (and hence, ethical approaches are required, which will be discussed in later chapters), the potential is enormous as well. As Kai-Fu Lee puts it: "Never has the potential for the rise and failure of mankind been greater" (Lee 2018).

Meanwhile, we are in a fourth wave of AI implementation (see Fig. 6.19) that allows broader implementations. Some of the examples have been shown in the

---

[15]As an example, see Kaczinski et al. (2019).

[16]In that scandal, data from 87 million Facebook users were misrouted to the Cambridge Analytica, which used these data in 2016 to manipulate the US elections and the Brexit referendum in the UK. it led to a $ 5 BN penalty for Facebook having not protected their users' data sufficiently enough.

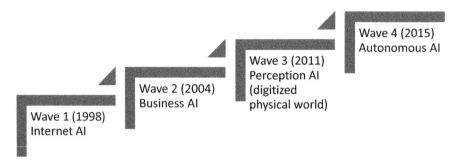

Fig. 6.19 Stages of AI (own focused diagram, stages according to Lee (2018))

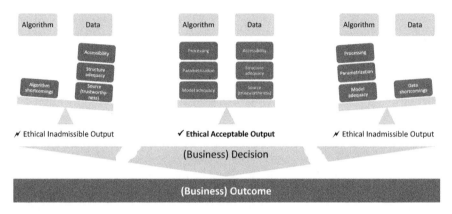

Fig. 6.20 The art and science of AI (own presentation)

previous sections. Not to forget, that it is still all "weak AI" and not a "strong AI," mankind-like AI—for now.

6.6 Example of AI Application: The Effect of Algorithm and Dataset

In this section, dependencies of algorithms and data settings will be explained using a concrete example. There are additional resources available to experience the impact directly. Specific coding skills are not a prerequisite, though it is unavoidable to get a little more down to the execution level.

Any computational approach is based on two key ingredients: data and algorithms (Fig. 6.20).

It needs to have both components in balance and appropriate. None of the components can fully compensate the weakness of the other side. For sure, there are technical means of handling incomplete or compromised datasets; though if the entire dataset is pruned to a certain direction (leading to discrimination of certain groups), even the smartest algorithms would not be able to compensate without "clean" data.

In order to demonstrate the effect, the AI development environment Kaggle (belonging to Google) is used and a test setting applied to different parameterized algorithms as well as different data sections. The demonstration can be redone and modified by using the provided notebook, accordingly.

6.6.1 AI Development Platform

At the latest with the emergence of the Internet, IT development followed not only a proprietary track but open development communities have created an infrastructure that is widely used (see as well Sect. 9.4). One example is Linux that is not only the dominant operating system for servers (and supercomputers), but its kernel is used in the Android (Google-owned) mobile operating system that was initiated in 2007 in the sunsetting of Nokia's dominancy on the mobile phone market (with their proprietary operating system Symbian) and the rising Apple iPhone (with the proprietary operating system iOS) smartphone era. So as well in AI, there are a variety of open-source-hosting platforms that enable teams to develop software in a highly efficient way. Those platforms are meanwhile in ownership of large Internet companies such as

- Github[17]: 2.9 million users, owner: Microsoft,
- Kaggle[18]: one million users, owner: Google and
- Bitbucket[19] one million teams/ten million users, owner: Atlassian.

This environment enables fast learning and adjustments. For example, Kaggle frequently initiates competitive challenges in which many teams across the world participate in.

6.6.2 Demonstration Using an AI Notebook and Specific Dataset

In this demonstration, an AI notebook on Kaggle has been used, based on the most popular programming language Python. The original notebook that is used to compare the prediction accuracy of an AI solution is based on different algorithms on a students' dataset (Cortez and Silva 2008). The aim is to predict the students' achievements in secondary education, based on real-world data such as student grades, demographic, social, and school-related features. Models used include

---

[17]https://github.com/ (accessed 19.10.2020).

[18]https://www.kaggle.com/ (access 19.10.2020).

[19]https://bitbucket.org/ (access 19.10.2020).

- Binary (pass/fail),
  five-level classification (very good, good, satisfactory, sufficient, fail) and regression analysis.
- Four data mining models:
  Decision trees
  Random forest
  Neural networks
  Support vector machines

On purpose, the different ML models are not explained in detail here. It is referred to the Python standard library `scikit-learn`,[20] an open source platform, where different machine learning algorithms and predictive data analysis tools are provided (see Table 6.4).

There are many more ML models and DL platforms available such as the Tensorflow,[21] keras,[22] or pytorch.[23] Models out of these DL libraries can be integrated into the demonstration notebook as required.

To illustrate the performance of different algorithms, two measures of accuracy are used: the model mean absolute error (MAE) and the root mean square error (RMSE).

In the notebook,[24] the different steps of importing relevant modules and the dataset are provided. An initial analysis of the 395 records-long dataset regarding demographic distribution does not reveal obvious relationship between one (independent) factor and the dependent final grade "G3"—except the correlation with previous grades. The latter are less of interest, as it would rather provide insights into why students fail. Hence, the other, weaker.

Figure 6.21 shows some of these graphical analyses as well as the correlation table.

As ML models typically cannot deal with categorical or ordinary variables, the data are transferred using one hot encoding to derive binary values.

Analyzing the most important correlation (see table) of the (one hot encoded) variables with G3 shows in the original dataset that students with less previous failures score higher, educated families result in higher grades, students who wish to go for higher studies score higher, students who go out a lot score less, and students without romantic relationship score higher (see Fig. 6.22).

To assess the accuracy of the different models, the median prediction has been taken as the naïve baseline, which results in (due to the normalization from one hot encoding, results are directly in %):

---

[20] https://scikit-learn.org/stable/ (accessed 19.10.2020).

[21] www.tensorflow.org (accessed 19.10.2020), a Google initiative.

[22] Keras.io (accessed 19.10.2020), platform-independent MIT-initiative, meanwhile integrated API into Tensorflow.

[23] pytorch.org (accessed 19.10.2020), a Facebook initiative.

[24] https://www.kaggle.com/svtest/eda-and-ml-sv-v1/edit?rvi=1 (accessed 19.10.2020).

Table 6.4 ML algorithms in the Python-based SCIKIT-LEARN library

SKI-Learn Library: ML Models	
1. **Supervised Learning**	2. Unsupervised learning
1.1. Linear models	**2.1.** **Gaussian mixture models**
1.2. Linear and quadratic discriminant analysis	2.2. Manifold learning
1.3. Kernel ridge regression	2.3. Clustering
1.4. Support vector machines	2.4. Biclustering
1.5. Stochastic gradient descent	2.5. Decomposing signals in components (matrix factorization problems)
1.6. Nearest neighbors	2.6. Covariance estimation
1.7. Gaussian processes	2.7. Novelty and outlier detection
1.8. Cross decomposition	2.8. Density estimation
1.9. Naive Bayes	2.9. Neural network models (unsupervised)
1.10. Decision trees	
1.11. Ensemble methods	
1.12. Multiclass and multilabel algorithms	
1.13. Feature selection	
1.14. Semi-supervised	
1.15. Isotonic regression	
1.16. Probability calibration	
1.17. Neural network models (supervised)	

Source: https://scikit-learn.org/stable/user_guide.html (access 19.10.2020)

```
Median Baseline Mean Absolute Error
     MAE = 3.7879%
Median Baseline Root Mean Square Error
     RMSE = 4.8252%
```

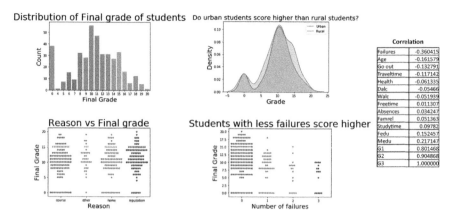

Fig. 6.21 Initial analysis of test dataset (own presentation, data source: https://www.kaggle.com/svtest/eda-and-ml-sv-v1/edit?rvi=1, access 19.10.2020)

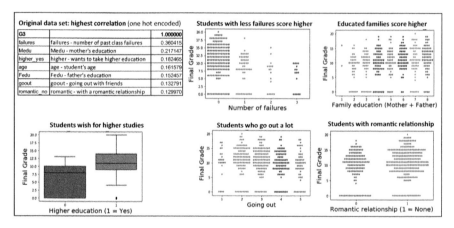

Fig. 6.22 Most important correlation in the original dataset (own presentation, source: https://www.kaggle.com/svtest/eda-and-ml-sv-v1, access 19.10.2020)

The model initiation is configured as follows:

```
model1 = LinearRegression() # no parametrization
model2 = ElasticNet(alpha=1.0, l1_ratio=0.5)
model3 = RandomForestRegressor(n_estimators=100)
model4 = ExtraTreesRegressor(n_estimators=100)
model5 = SVR(kernel='rbf', degree=3, C=1.0, gamma='auto')
model6 = GradientBoostingRegressor(n_estimators=50)
```

As can be seen in Fig. 6.23, linear regression model would outpace all other tested algorithms, as it results in the smallest mean absolute error, as well as in the smallest root mean squared error.

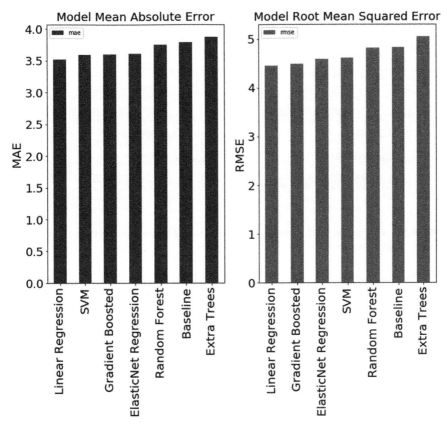

Fig. 6.23 Accuracy (%) from the original parameterization and dataset (own presentation, source: https://www.kaggle.com/svtest/eda-and-ml-sv-v1/edit?rvi=1, access 19.10.2020)

Considering mass data application in an operational setting and requirement of resource efficiency (time and computational resources required), it would be likely that the chosen model in that case would be a regression analysis.

Though, if the algorithms' parameters are slightly modified as follows[25]:

```
model2 = ElasticNet(alpha=0.4, l1_ratio=0.4)
model3 = RandomForestRegressor(n_estimators=110)
model4 = ExtraTreesRegressor(n_estimators=200)
model5 = SVR(kernel='rbf', degree=10, C=5.2, gamma='auto')
model6 = GradientBoostingRegressor(n_estimators=20),
```

entirely different results will show up; see Fig. 6.24.

---

[25]This can be seen in the notebook at line 702.

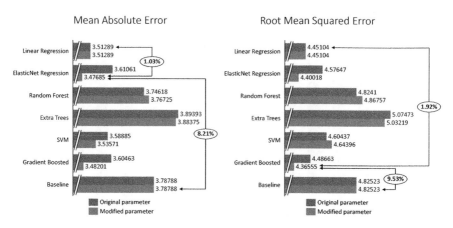

Fig. 6.24 Accuracy (in %, MAE and RMSE) of original and modified parameter set on the original data set (own presentation)

This would mean that instead of recommending the usage of the linear regression, ElasticNet of Gradient Boosted ML models are better suited to solve the problem of accurate predictions, as linear regression is just third rank in MAE.

The result is as well dependent on the training strategy; hence, it is dependent on the real data that is used to train the model(s) and the data used for prediction. For demonstrational purposes, from the dataset with 395 records, only records from entry 100 onward are taken, i.e., 296 records in total are used.[26] This selection leads to an entirely different set of key correlation factors (see Table 6.5). While the expected high correlation of performance from previous failures still is prevalent or relevant such as higher ambitions, it can be seen that new characteristics such as fathers being teachers or extra payment for courses are more important than age or behavioral aspects such a going out with friends or having a romantic relationship. That is if from the original prediction (based on the best setting of model parameter) the conclusion would be to urge students on their behavior, another section of the data would suggest that other factors such as extra payment for courses would probably drive motivation and the final grade.

Applying the modified dataset leads to a new naïve baseline[27]:

```
Median Baseline Mean Absolute Error
    MAE = 3.3514%
Median Baseline Root Mean Square Error
    RMSE = 4.6789%
```

---

[26]See notebook at line 705.

[27]See notebook line 712.

Table 6.5 Data-dependent different key correlation factors (own presentation)

G3		1.000000

Original data set

Failures	Failures—number of past class failures	0.360415
Medu	Medu—mother's education	0.217147
higher_yes	Higher—wants to take higher education	0.182465
Age	Age—student's age	0.161579
Fedu	Fedu—father's education	0.152457
Goout	Goout—going out with friends	0.132791
romantic_no	Romantic—with a romantic relationship	0.129970

Extracted data set (starting at record #100)

Failures	Failures—number of past class failures	0.361262
higher_yes	Higher—wants to take higher education	0.184882
Medu	Medu—mother's education	0.169926
Fedu	Fedu—father's education	0.157593
Fjob_teacher	Fjob—father's job	0.138645
paid_yes	Paid—extra paid classes within the course subject	0.122317

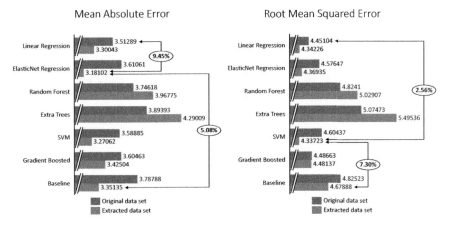

Fig. 6.25 Accuracy (in %, MAE and RMSE) of original and modified dataset on the original data parameter set (own presentation)

The different models' (in their original configuration as stated above) performance, based on the different datasets, can be seen in Fig. 6.25:

The results show that again linear regression would not be the best choice; in the extracted dataset the Elastic Net (again) would provide best accuracy that is 9.5% better than the original linear regression.

6.6.3   Takeaways from the Demonstration

As was demonstrated with the AI notebook applying different algorithms on datasets, the results in terms of accuracy vary, depending on the specific configuration. Hence, neither algorithm nor data can be taken as "neutral" or "clean." It needs to be ensured that both the model and its parameterization as well as the data fit for a meaningful and rationale prediction. In other words, AI per se is neither good nor bad; the context the technology is applied in is paramount to set the ethical implications of that technology usage.

Even if in the demonstration the absolute error seems to be small around 3.5%, it may have massive implications on people if, e.g., such an AI prediction is used for decisions affecting a larger population as in the COVID-19 pandemic crisis, where a false detection of a ten million population could mean that hundred thousands of (erroneously as infected detected) citizens suffer from restrictions.

6.7   Technical Constraints of AI Exploitation

The computational restrictions are not only on the algorithm and data side; they are prevalent on the hardware side as well. Going along, the ecological implications are massive.

Since the approaches in particular for deep learning ("DL") are extremely resource intensive, the demand is increasingly surpassing the available supply or resources, as found out by the MIT's Initiative on the digital economy research (Thompson et al. 2020) (see Fig. 6.26). Taking 1995 as baseline of 100% for hardware and software requirements, obviously this has increased until 2017 by a factor of 1000 for hardware (which is impressive by itself as it corresponds to an

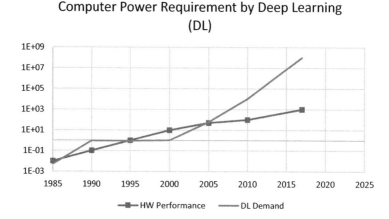

Fig. 6.26 Discrepancy between hardware performance and demand by DL (own simplified presentation based on data in Thompson et al. (2020))

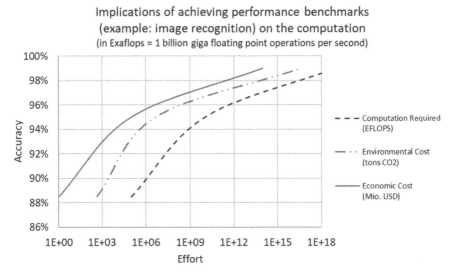

Fig. 6.27 Implications of achieving performance benchmarks (conservative polynomial, not exponential projection) (own, simplified presentation based on data in Thompson et al. (2020))

increase of 37% p.a.[28]!), but for DL-related software this is 100 million times (or 131% p.a.)! This may limit the extension of performance targets in terms of accuracy, as computational resource requirements increase with the accuracy demand.

Applying a projection of required resources in terms of computational performance, the implicated ecological cost and the economic impact are tremendous: even in a slightly conservative assumption of a polynomial (instead of an exponential) resource requirement, Fig. 6.27 unveils a massive increase in resource requirements, if accuracy of the AI application is to be improved from moderated levels as of today. The consequence of this when driving for better accuracy is to focus on better training and search strategies (i.e., improving the algorithms) for the DL applications. Otherwise, it simply does not pay off to do so.

From an ethical perspective, apparently there is the intrinsic risk of going with solution that is "just good enough" and not to strive for the best accuracy, as such a solution is simply not affordable. The collateral consequences in terms of discrimination, irrational sanctions, or other harm to people due to an AI application that has just a moderate accuracy are real. Hence, it needs to take concrete preventive measures, some of which will be discussed in Chap. 11.

---

[28]CAGR: compound annual growth rate.

6.8 Finish Line Quiz

6.01	\multicolumn{2}{l}{What are disruptive threats to industries with heavy upfront capital lockup?}
	1	"Plain vanilla" hardware that can be configured through software.
	2	Late customization at final assembly.
	3	Omnichannel.
	4	Built to order.
6.02	\multicolumn{2}{l}{Where to find the perception threshold?}
	1	Between normative and liquidity crisis.
	2	Between liquidity crisis and bankruptcy.
	3	Between normative and strategic crisis.
	4	Between liquidity crisis and insolvency.
6.03	\multicolumn{2}{l}{According to a study from McKinsey, the digitalization degree …}
	1	… in US/Europe in 2016 was c. 90%/90%, respectively.
	2	… in US/Europe in 2016 was c. 90%/25%, respectively.
	3	… in US/Europe in 2016 was c. 48%/15%, respectively.
	4	… in US/Europe in 2016 was c. 18%/12%, respectively.
6.04	\multicolumn{2}{l}{According to the OECD (2019), the % share of immediate job risk due to automation and the % share of radically transformed jobs are:}
	1	0%/12%
	2	4%/22%
	3	14%/32%
	4	24%/42%
6.05	\multicolumn{2}{l}{According to the anecdote, what would be the valuation of the first Bitcoin transaction (2 pizzas @ 10,000 Bitcoins) in current terms?}
	1	EUR 9.10
	2	EUR 9100
	3	EUR 9100,000
	4	EUR 91,000,000
6.06	\multicolumn{2}{l}{What is the current (October 2020) length of the Bitcoin blockchain and how much energy is required?}
	1	3 GB/1% of Switzerland's electrical energy consumption
	2	30 GB/10% of Switzerland's electrical energy consumption
	3	300 GB/100% of Switzerland's electrical energy consumption
	4	3000 GB/10x of Switzerland's electrical energy consumption
6.07	\multicolumn{2}{l}{What is hashing?}
	1	Slight modification of the original message leads to a significantly different hash value.
	2	Slight modification of the original message leads to a slight different hash value.
	3	Significant modification of the original message leads to a slight different hash value.
	4	Modification of the original message will not alter the hash value.
6.08	\multicolumn{2}{l}{How does BCT and AI interact with each other?}
	1	Both terms are synonyms and actually the same.
	2	BCT supports AI with trust, AI supports BCT with efficiency.
	3	BCT supports AI with efficiency, AI supports BCT with trust.

(continued)

	4	Both terms have no complementary characteristics and hence there is no use in combining them.
6.09		What is the basic function of a PKC system?
	1	Private key to create a digital signature/public key to encrypt message.
	2	Public key to create a digital signature/private key to encrypt message.
	3	Public key to check a digital signature/private key to encrypt message.
	4	Private key to check a digital signature/public key to decrypt message.
6.10		Who is the dominant player in supercomputing over the last few decades?
	1	USA
	2	China
	3	Japan
	4	All the above.
6.11		As of 2020, what is Russia's AI position on the global market?
	1	An AI strategy to catch up with the USA and China exists.
	2	Russia is world leader in AI.
	3	Russia is not interested in AI at all.
	4	Russia and the USA are head to head on AI.
6.12		What is a key AI application in which China is leading?
	1	Natural language processing (NLP)
	2	Optical character recognition (OCR)
	3	Facial detection
	4	China has not yet reached primacy in any AI application.
6.14		What does the term "surveillance capitalism" indicate?
	1	So-called social media are exploiting consumers—the consumer is de facto the product.
	2	So-called social media is the product which just supports consumers to pursue their interests.
	3	In the USA, a state-regulated surveillance approach executed by private firms.
	4	The term does not refer to AI discussions.
6.15		The worldwide social media market share (2020) of Facebook and Tencent is about. . .
	1	15%/15%
	2	25%/15%
	3	45%/15%
	4	55%/25%
6.16		What is the critical point with ADS (algorithmic decision systems)?
	1	They can be used for litigation.
	2	Flawed predictions.
	3	Ultimately elimination of human rights.
	4	All the above.
6.17		Which combination of data and algorithm is required for ethical acceptable output from AI systems?
	1	Data: Model adequacy, parameterization, algorithm: Trustworthy source, accessibility
	2	Data: Structure adequacy, parameterization, algorithm: Trustworthy source, accessibility

(continued)

	3	Algorithm: Model adequacy, parameterization, data: Trustworthy source, accessibility
	4	Algorithm: Structure adequacy, parameterization, data: Trustworthy source, accessibility
6.18		Who are the companies behind popular platforms to develop and share experiences on AI (algorithm and data)?
	1	Kaggle—Google, Github—Atlassian, Bitbucket—Microsoft
	2	Kaggle—Google, Github—Microsoft, Bitbucket—Atlassian
	3	Kaggle—Atlassian, Github—Microsoft, Bitbucket—Google
	4	Kaggle—Atlassian, Github—Goggle, Bitbucket—Microsoft
6.19		What is a typical finding regarding AI algorithm and dataset?
	1	AI solutions are agnostic to datasets and algorithm parameterization.
	2	Only algorithm parameterization is crucial for the AI output.
	3	Only dataset selection is crucial for the AI output.
	4	Different datasets and algorithm parameterization lead to different results. Hence, a robust configuration needs to be found and trained in order to allow for non-discriminating output.
6.20		What are key technology constraints and/or implications with AI?
	1	Hardware demand increased by 37% p.a., DL by 131% p.a., which is sustainable as it has been over the last 25 years.
	2	With increasing accuracy demand, the computational operations (measured in Exaflops) massively increase, hence the environmental costs (tons CO_2) as well as the economical costs.
	3	Hardware demand increased by 37% p.a., DL by 131% p.a., in particular, the DL algorithms and search strategies need to be enhanced.
	4	Answers 2 and 3 are correct.

Correct answers can be found in www.vieweg-beratung.de/downloads

References

4Investors. Retrieved September 29, 2020, from https://www.4investors.de/aktien/heidelbergerdruck.php

Arute, F., Arya, K., Babbush, R. et al. (2019). Quantum supremacy using a programmable superconducting processor. *Nature 574*, 505–510. https://doi.org/10.1038/s41586-019-1666-5. Retrieved October 06, 2020.

Blockchain.com. (2020). Retrieved October 06, 2020, from https://www.blockchain.com/charts/blocks-size

BMWI (ed.) (2018). *Monitoring-Report Wirtschaft DIGITAL 2018*. Retrieved September 29, 2020, from https://www.bmwi.de/Redaktion/DE/Publikationen/Digitale-Welt/monitoring-report-wirtschaft-digital-2018-langfassung.pdf?__blob=publicationFile&v=4

Bendett, S. (2018). *In AI, Russia is hustling to catch up*. Retrieved October 8, 2020, from https://www.defenseone.com/ideas/2018/04/russia-races-forward-ai-development/147178/

Bergmann, M., Kiel, E., & Vieweg, S. (2015). Wege zur erfolgreichen Transformation im Messwesen der Energiewirtschaft. In Köhler-Schute, C. (Ed.), *Smart metering*.

Bertram, F. (2018). *Druckmaschinenhersteller Zurück im Geschäft. Focus Money 15/2018*. Retrieved September 29, 2020, from https://www.focus.de/finanzen/boerse/druckmaschinenhersteller-zurueck-im-geschaeft_id_8703594.html

BNA. (2014). *Bundesnetzagentur für Elektrizität, Gas, Telekommunikation, Post und Eisenbahnen: Bekanntmachung zur elektronischen Signatur nach dem Signaturgesetz und der Signaturverordnung (Übersicht über geeignete Algorithmen)* vom 21. Januar 2014. Retrieved October 08, 2020, from BAnz AT 20.02.2014 B4). https://www.bundesanzeiger.de/pub/publication/YJvG4TRGdmanKwPYS7t;wwwsid=2582896526AA003291C606E54EA27FBE.web07-pub?0

Bond, R., Fariss, C., Jones, J. et al. (2012): A 61-million-person experiment in social influence and political mobilization. *Nature, 489,* 295–298. https://doi.org/10.1038/nature11421. Retrieved October 08, 2020.

Bischoff, P. (2020). *Surveillance camera statistics: which cities have the most CCTV cameras?* Retrieved October 21, 2020, from https://www.comparitech.com/vpn-privacy/the-worlds-most-surveilled-cities/

Bocksch, R. (2020). *Die Top 10 der Einhörner.* Retrieved September 04, 2020, from https://de.statista.com/infografik/7475/die-10-am-hoechsten-bewerteten-einhoerner/

CBECI. (2020). Retrieved October 06, 2020 https://www.cbeci.org/

Chatbot. (2020). Retrieved October 05, 2020, from https://www.chatbots.org/

Chen, C. (2020). *TikTok seems to be copying and pasting your clipboard with every keystroke.* Retrieved October 08, 2020, from https://www.privateinternetaccess.com/blog/tiktok-seems-to-be-copying-and-pasting-your-clipboard-with-every-keystroke/

Christensen, C. M. (2003). *The innovator's dilemma: The revolutionary book that will change the way you do business.* New York: Collins Business Essentials.

coinmarketcap.com. (2020). Retrieved October 05, 2020, from https://coinmarketcap.com/

Confessore, N., & Gelles, D. (2018). *Facebook fallout deals blow to Mercers' political Clout.* Retrieved October 19, 2020, from https://www.nytimes.com/2018/04/10/us/politics/mercer-family-cambridge-analytica.html

Corea, F. (2017). *The convergence of AI and blockchain: What's the deal?* Retrieved October 06, 2020, from https://medium.com/@Francesco_AI/the-convergence-of-ai-and-blockchain-whats-the-deal-60c618e3accc

Cortez, P., & Silva, A. (2008). Using data mining to predict secondary school student performance. In A. Brito, & J. Teixeira (Eds.), *Proceedings of 5th FUture BUsiness TEChnology Conference (FUBUTEC 2008),* pp. 5–12, Porto, Portugal, EUROSIS, ISBN 978-9077381-39-7. Retrieved October 19, 2020, from http://www3.dsi.uminho.pt/pcortez/student.pdf

Crawford, K., et al. (2018). *AI now report.* Retrieved October 15, 2020, from https://ainowinstitute.org/AI_Now_2018_Report.pdf

Cummings, R. O. (1949). *The American Ice Harvests: A historical study in technology, 1800–1918.* Berkeley and Los Angeles: California University Press.

Delventhal, S. (2020). *The story shows many aspects of failure.* Retrieved September 29, 2020, from https://www.investopedia.com/news/downfall-of-sears/

Dobbins Lehman, C. (2020). Artificial intelligence to support independent assessment of screening mammograms—The time has come. *JAMA Oncology, 6*(10), 1588–1589. https://doi.org/10.1001/jamaoncol.2020.3186. Retrieved October 08, 2020.

Dölle, M. (2018). *Kettenreaktion - Wie 51-Prozent-Angriffe Bitcoin & Co. Bedrohen.* Retrieved October 06, 2020, from https://www.heise.de/select/ct/2018/14/1530921921642329

Domingo, P. (2015). *The Master Algorithm - How the quest for the ultimate learning machine will remake our world.* New York: Basic Books.

Elbers, M. (2018). *Bitcoin Kurs von 2009 bis 2018.* Retrieved October 05, 2020, from https://www.kryptopedia.org/bitcoin-kurs-2009-bis-2018/

EMC. (2020). *RSA.* Retrieved October 08, 2020, from http://www.emc.com/emc-plus/rsa-labs/historical/rsa-768-factored.htm

Erxleben, C. (2019). *Bitcoin-Stromverbrauch: Die Kryptowährung benötigt mehr Energie als die Schweiz.* Retrieved October 06, 2020, from https://www.basicthinking.de/blog/2019/07/16/bitcoin-stromverbrauch-vergleich/

EU. (2020). *Shaping Europe's digital future.* Retrieved April 01, 2020, from https://ec.europa.eu/info/strategy/priorities-2019-2024/europe-fit-digital-age/shaping-europe-digital-future_en

Falkon, S. (2017). *The story of the DAO—Its history and consequences.* Retrieved October 06, 2020, from https://medium.com/swlh/the-story-of-the-dao-its-history-and-consequences-71e6a8a551ee

Finanzen.Net. (2020). *Bitcoin 20.11.2020.* Retrieved November 20, 2020, from https://www.finanzen.net/devisen/bitcoin-euro/chart

Fung, B. (2019). *CNN Business: Unhackable – The unlikely activist behind the nation's toughest pricacy law isn't done yet.* MacTaggert, Alastair in. Retrieved October 15, 2020, from https://edition.cnn.com/2019/10/10/tech/alastair-mactaggart/index.html

Gartner. (2020). *Spending on robotic process automation (RPA) software worldwide from 2017 to 2021.* Gartner September 2020 in Statista IS 942569. Retrieved October 05, 2020.

Gigova, R. (2017). *Who Vladimir Putin thinks will rule the world. 02.09.2017.* Retrieved October 08, 2020, from https://edition.cnn.com/2017/09/01/world/putin-artificial-intelligence-will-rule-world/index.html

Griffin, A. (2017). *Bitcoin buyers should prepare to lose all their money, Independent* 15.12.2017. Retrieved October 05, 2020, from https://www.independent.co.uk/life-style/gadgets-and-tech/news/bitcoin-buyer-investment-risks-lose-money-value-drop-bubble-crytocurrency-a8112396.html. (access 05.10.2020).

Grunwald-Delitz, S., Schäffer, U., & Weber, J. (2018). *Wir nähern uns dem Gipfel – Eine Bestandsaufnahme der Controllerzahl in Deutschland, CM 1/2018.*

Heidelberger Druckmaschinen AG. (2002). *Heidelberger Druckmaschinen AG - Geschäftsbericht 2001/2002.*

Heidelberger Druckmaschinen AG. (2020a). *Heidelberger Druckmaschinen AG – Company Profile.* Retrieved September 29, 2020, from https://www.heidelberg.com/global/en/about_heidelberg/company/company_profile/history/chronology.jsp

Heidelberger Druckmaschinen AG. (2020b). *Heidelberger Druckmaschinen AG Annual Report 2019/20.* Retrieved September 29, 2020, from https://www.heidelberg.com/global/media/en/global_media/investor_relations/ir_reports_and_presentations/2019_42/200609_cfs_1920_report.pdf

Holland, O. (2003). Exploration and high adventure: The legacy of Grey Walter. The Royal Society. https://doi.org/10.1098/rsta.2003.1260. Retrieved October 08, 2020.

Iansiti, M., & Lakhani, K.R. (2017). *The truth about blockchain.* HRB Jan-Feb 2017. Retrieved October 05, 2020, from https://hbr.org/2017/01/the-truth-about-blockchain

Investing.com. (2020). *BTC/USD – Bitcoin US Dollar.* Retrieved November 20, 2020, from https://www.investing.com/crypto/bitcoin/btc-usd-historical-data

Isidore, C. (2020). *Sears' survival is in doubt.* CNN Business May 20. Retrieved September 29, 2020, from https://edition.cnn.com/2020/05/20/business/sears-bankruptcy/index.html

Jenkinson, G. (2019). *Ethereum classic 51% attack—The reality of proof-of-work.* Retrieved October 06, 2020, from https://cointelegraph.com/news/ethereum-classic-51-attack-the-reality-of-proof-of-work

Kaczinski, A., Henning-Thurau, T., & Sattler, H. (2019). *Social media & society report.* Retrieved October 19, 2020, from https://www.marketingcenter.de/sites/mcm/files/downloads/research/lmm/literature/kaczinski_hennig-thurau_sattler_social_media_and_society_report_2019.pdf

Kahneman, D., & Tversky, A. (1979). Prospect theory: An analysis of decision under risk. *Econometrica, 47*(2), 263–291. https://doi.org/10.2307/1914185. Retrieved September 02, 2020.

Koeing & Bauer. (2019). *Koenig & Bauer AG.* Retrieved from https://www.koenig-bauer.com/fileadmin/user_upload/04_Unternehmen/Investor_Relations/Berichte/Berichte_2019/Koenig-Bauer-GB2019_en.pdf. Annual Report 2019.

Lahmann, S., & Schacher, P. (2017). *Digitaler Wandel im Controlling.* Controlling Konferenz 2017. Retrieved February 20, 2020, from https://www.icv-controlling.com/fileadmin/

Veranstaltungen/VA_Dateien/Controller_Tagung_CH/Vortr%C3%A4ge_2017/Pr%C3%A4sentation_EY.PDF

Lee, K. F. (2018). *AI superpowers: China, Silicon Valley, and the New World Order.* Boston, MA: Houghton Mifflin Harcourt.

McKinsey. (2016). *Digital Europe: Pushing the frontier, capturing the benefits.* New York: McKinsey Global Institute.

Meck, G., & Weiguny, B. (2015). *Disruption, baby, disruption!* Retrieved September 22, 2020, from https://www.faz.net/aktuell/wirtschaft/wirtschaftswissen/das-wirtschaftswort-des-jahres-disruption-baby-disruption-13985491-p2.html

Megvii. (2020). Retrieved October 08, 2020, from Megvii.ai

Merkle, R. C. (1988). A digital signature based on a conventional encryption function. Advances in cryptology—CRYPTO '87. *Lecture Notes in Computer Science, 293,* 369–378. https://doi.org/10.1007/3-540-48184-2_32. Retrieved October 06, 2020.

Mnih, V., Kavukcuoglu, K., Silver, D. et al. Human-level control through deep reinforcement learning. *Nature, 518,* 529–533 (2015). https://doi.org/10.1038/nature14236. Retrieved October 08, 2020.

Morgan, T. P. (2020). *With Fugaku supercomputer installed, RIKEN takes on coronavirus.* Retrieved October 06, 2020, from https://www.nextplatform.com/2020/05/18/with-fugaku-supercomputer-installed-riken-takes-on-coronavirus/

Mozur, P. (2019, April 14). *One month, 500,000 face scans: How China is using A.I. to profile a minority.* Retrieved October 08, 2020, from https://www.nytimes.com/2019/04/14/technology/china-surveillance-artificial-intelligence-racial-profiling.html

Opensignal. (2020). *Opensignal 2020.* Retrieved February 20, 2020, from https://www.opensignal.com/reports/2018/02/state-of-lte

OECD.AI. (2020). *Powered by EC/OECD (2020), STIP Compass database.* Retrieved February 21, 2020.

OECD. (2019). *OECD Employment Outlook 2019: The future of work.* Retrieved October 01, 2020, from https://www.oecd-ilibrary.org/employment/oecd-employment-outlook-2019_9ee00155-en

Ohnsman, A. (2019). *Self-driving startup Embark Raises $70 Million, Opens Freight transfer hubs for Robot Big Rigs.* Retrieved October 08, 2020, from https://www.forbes.com/sites/alanohnsman/2019/09/25/self-driving-startup-embark-raises-70-million-opens-freight-hubs-for-robot-big-rigs/

Porter, M. E. (2008). The five competitive forces that shape strategy. *Harvard Business Review.*

Presize.ai. (2020). Retrieved October 08, 2020, from Presize.ai

Qiang, X. (2019): The road to digital unfreedom: President Xi's surveillance state. Retrieved October 08, 2020, from https://www.journalofdemocracy.org/articles/the-road-to-digital-unfreedom-president-xis-surveillance-state/

Ross, B., Schwartz, R., & Meek, J. (2016). Officials: Master Spy Vladimir Putin now directly linked to US hacking. *ABC News.* Retrieved October 08, 2020, from https://abcnews.go.com/International/officials-master-spy-vladimir-putin-now-directly-linked/story?id=44210901

Savage, N. (2020). Google's quantum computer achieves chemistry milestone. Retrieved October 06, 2020, from https://www.scientificamerican.com/article/googles-quantum-computer-achieves-chemistry-milestone/

Schell, O., & Delury, J. (2014). *Wealth and power - China's long march to the twenty-first century.*

Schnitzler, L. (2012). *Druckmaschinen - Die Deutschen verpassen den Anschluss.* Wirtschaftswoche 03.05.2012. Retrieved September 29, 2020, from https://www.wiwo.de/unternehmen/it/druckmaschinen-die-deutschen-verpassen-den-anschluss/6564098.html

Seiler, E., & Jenkins, J. H. (2014). *Frequently asked questions about Isaac Asimov.* Retrieved October 18, 2019, from http://www.asimovonline.com/asimov_FAQ.html#starters2

Shih, W. (2016). The real lessons from Kodak's decline. *MIT Sloan Management Review, 57*(4), 11.

Solomon, H. (2020). *Canadian quantum computing firms partner to spread the technology.* Retrieved October 08, 2020, from https://www.itworldcanada.com/article/canadian-quantum-computing-firms-partner-to-spread-the-technology/436742

Thompson, N.C., Greenewald, K., Lee, K., & Manso, G. F. (2020). *The computational limits of deep learning.* Retrieved October 19, 2020, from https://arxiv.org/pdf/2007.05558.pdf

Top500.org. Retrieved October 06, 2020, from https://www.top500.org/lists/green500/2020/06/

UIPATH. (2018). *Robot process automation.* Retrieved February 20, 2018, from https://www.uipath.com/automate/robotic-process-automation

Vieweg, S. (2018). Streamlining von Support-Funktionen vor dem Hintergrund der Digitalisierung - Aufbau von Shared Service Centern und Business Process Outsourcing. In M. Pfannstiel & P. Steinhoff (Eds.), *Der Enterprise Transformation Cycle.* New York: Springer.

Vise, D. A. (2005). The Google Story: Inside the Hottest Business. *Media, and Technology Success of Our Time.*

Wallstreet Online. (2020, August 25). *Megvii partners with storefriendly to deploy AI-powered unmanned warehouse storage solution in Singapore.* Retrieved October 08, 2020, from https://www.wallstreet-online.de/nachricht/12863963-megvii-partners-with-storefriendly-to-deploy-ai-powered-unmanned-warehouse-storage-solution-singapore

Webb, A. (2019). *The big nine. How the tech titans and their thinking machines could warp humanity.* New York: Public Affairs/Hachette.

Weizenbaum, J. (1966). ELIZA—A computer program for the study of natural language communication between man and machine. *Communications of the ACM, 9*(1), 36–45. https://doi.org/10.1145/365153.365168.

Wobst, R. (2020). *Hohe Wellen. Sind heutige Verschlüsselungsverfahren akut bedroht.* Heise online. Retrieved October 08, 2020, from https://www.heise.de/select/ix/2020/8/2007211154790390069

Zuboff, S. (2019). *The age of surveillance capitalism: The fight for a human future at the new frontier of power.* New York: Public Affair.

AI and the Ethical Challenge

Stefan H. Vieweg

7

7.1 Learning Objective

1. Illustrate the dimensions of AI disruption on societies, in particular on the importance of human work in a historical context.
2. Discuss the ethical implications of such disruption.
3. Taking the two AI superpowers—the USA and China—illustrate the different ethical challenges derived from the level of pervasiveness of AI technologies that influences lives of individuals and societies.
4. Reflect the historical circumstances that have contributed to China's situation regarding corruption and lack of trust within the society.
5. Critically reflect the effects of the "Sharp Eye" project and the implementation of a total surveillance using AI technologies.
6. Elaborate on the (US) business model of "Big Tech" companies using AI technologies to exploit their consumers.
7. Identify the cornerstones of data privacy approaches such as the CCPA.
8. Identify the ethical key challenges.

7.2 Introduction

In Sect. 6.5, an overview was given on the technological edge of AI development. It was pointed out that not all technically possible applications may have a positive effect on the environment and society. As was discussed in Sect. 1.5.3, the consequences must be reflected likewise. Ultimately, the problem is to identify— as a society

S. H. Vieweg (✉)
Institute of Compliance and Corporate Governance, RFH - University of Applied Sciences Cologne, Cologne, Germany
e-mail: dr.vieweg@vieweg-beratung.de

© The Author(s), under exclusive license to Springer Nature Switzerland AG 2021
S. H. Vieweg (ed.), *AI for the Good*, Management for Professionals,
https://doi.org/10.1007/978-3-030-66913-3_7

1. Which beliefs and ethical norms shall be applied in order to maximize the desired ethical dimension like deontological or utilitarian ethics (which was shown in Sect. 1.4).
2. Where to limit technology in order to prevent or minimize the unwanted effects.

This self-discipline in algorithm design, data gathering, and processing and utilization of the AI technology will be a key challenge for economies and societies. It would be naïve to assume for a "one-fits-all" approach. Acceptability can only be achieved in a societal context and will vary across the globe. From that point of view, in the following section a fundamental challenge regarding human work will be addressed in general, and specific ethical challenges in the dominating superpowers China and the USA will be discussed.

7.3   Automation (and AI) Effects on Human Work and Jobs

In Chap. 6, it was laid down that disruption is not a new phenomenon, but clearly, the ongoing digitization "revolution" has a massive disruptive power. One key aspect that affects societies is the implication on (human) work, job security, and with that the possibility for people to make up their living. For the last few (probably hundred) years, humans live in an unparalleled increase of prosperity, despite the many wars and destruction (Morris 2010). In a historical context, over centuries, world powers come and go (Kennedy 1987). With digitization, a new age is arising as human thinking is extended with AI, so that entirely new and more effective approaches to solve problems are possible.

Some famous current quotes compare AI as new electricity: "Just as electricity transformed almost everything 100 years ago, [...] AI will transform in the next several years." (Ng 2017) or—according to Microsoft's CEO Brad Smith, as new combustion engine (Jones 2019). Whatever metaphor is used, the impact will be pervasive to people's lives.

A key aspect is the consequence to human jobs. Relevant studies show a range between 15% [OECD (Nedelkoska and Quintini 2018)] to 47% [Programme on Future of Work (Frey and Osborne 2013)] of job losses. Though scientists cannot predict when, where, and how many jobs are lost. Some projections are more concrete in showing that 50% are lost within the next 15 years (Lee 2018). The situation is similar to the situation during the Industrial Revolution of the nineteenth century, when e.g. in the UK wages stagnated over decades, prosperity was on a downward slope, whereas technologies emerged.

In concrete terms today, AI has started to and will continue to replace office jobs that are based on quantitative, analytical processes, in particular of transactional and recurring nature that can be automated: e.g., administrative reporting, foreign exchange, analysts, or customer service (see Sect. 6.4.1 as well). For some manual jobs requiring a high level of hand–eye coordination, robots are not yet that good. AI surpasses human capabilities in analytical areas and will be a tool for highly

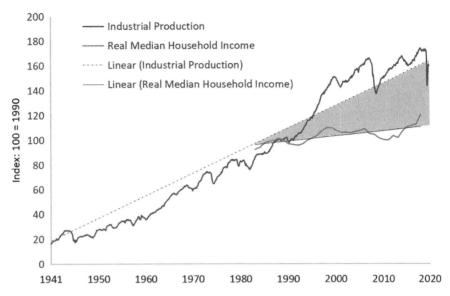

Fig. 7.1 Productivity and household income in the USA (own presentation based on data from U.S. Census bureau, retrieved https://fred.stlouisfed.org. (access 21.10.2020))

sophisticated jobs such as lawyers, doctors, scientists, and journalists; hence, the (human) support functions for those occupations will vanish.

This has a massive impact on society as such (reference is made to the Tragedy of the Commons; see Sect. 4.5). As an example, the situation in the USA is illustrated by comparison of the distinctive productivity increase and the restrained household income development (see Fig. 7.1). The gap between the benefits of productivity increase, which represents 1.5% p.a. (CAGR), is not reflected in the household income that increases only by less than half of that: 0.65% p.a. (CAGR). The spread between the two means that fewer and fewer parts of that society participate from the advances of technology achievements. Sooner or later, there will no longer be a wealthy middle class that earns its living with routine work (McAfee 2019). The reason for this productivity increase is twofold: first from automation and second from offshoring jobs to lower pay level countries. In a US study using Frey and Osborne's automation assessment model and Blinder's model of offshorability, the risk of job losses on US county level is in the range of 36–67% for automation and 11–22% range for offshorability, respectively (Devaraj et al. 2017). These findings are in harsh contrast to public opinion and politicians' argumentation that led to a trade war between the USA and China since 2017. At least in some industries, the standard of living has already diminished over time.

Example US Truckers

As a consequence of deregulation of work, increased automation, and diminished unionization, they earn only some 40% (price-adjusted) of what the proceeds were some 40 years ago (Viscelli 2016). Given the fact that many workers in the USA live from paycheck to paycheck with a "free cash flow" of just very few hundreds of dollars per month, this indicates financial instability that even adds vulnerability in disruptive times and job insecurities.

The disparity between the upper 10% (typically defined with annual income of min. USD250,000) or upper 1% (>USD one million) and the middle class constitutes a massive risk for societal problems.

1. Although the past has shown a sound increase in prosperity, as the spread between the very few very rich on the one side and the numerous societal backbones of a stable middle class widens.
2. The latter destabilizes and suffers in not being able to cope with living standards.
3. The generations' dream of being able to achieve a better living standard than the parents will diminish.

From that perspective, the theory of value-adding economies, which was developed by Karl Marx (Kurz 2013) some 150 years ago, seems to reflect the potential disruptive power of the concentration of capital and resources versus human work. Spoiled by competition and a Darwin-like selection brutality, companies are forced to introduce new production processes and new products in order to reduce costs as only the fittest will survive. Markets (i.e., the match of demand and supply) coordinate companies' output (products and services). "Because of the anarchic nature of the system, crises occur periodically; development is cyclical" (Kurz 2013). The value added in the form of profit is disproportionately allocated merely in capital growth (of very few) and expanding even higher production means for even more productivity through automation. This has a countereffect: the mass of workers—and with them their purchasing power—diminishes in consequence of replacement of human work by machines. But it is the consumption that is the ultimate source of profit, and that has gradually dried up. Hence, shrinking consumption means shrinking profit rate and in the long run it even conjures up the end of capitalism.

From this perspective, while AI is not the only source of this disruption in the labor market, it accelerates the transformation massively. This will tear society apart. The rich will become richer, and the poor will not be able to free themselves from misery (Lee 2018).

7.4   China and the Total Surveillance State

To reflect China's trajectory of developing and utilizing AI technologies, it is important to have the historical and societal context in mind: Since the setup of the "People's Republic of China" in 1949 and Mao's Cultural Revolution thereafter, surveillance, persecution, denunciation, and suppression of dissidents emerged in China in order to safeguard the political system based on one party—the Chinese Communist Party. Since, a system of observation and control was instilled throughout the society, so that inappropriate behaviors were detected and sanctioned quickly. Initially, this mass surveillance system was established on a word-of-mouth basis (Chang 2016) and continues as local party officials implement the social credit system (that was announced for 2020) by weekly on-site inspections of every household. The political argumentation for such a massive surveillance and the introduction of the social credit system is to make citizens obedient, role-model people, and at the same time fight crime and corruption (Lippold 2019).

Reflecting the Chinese society is in a Hofstede-sense (Hofstede et al. 2010), China's culture—in contrast to many Western countries—can be described as

- Collectivistic culture that put the group's interest in front of the interest of their individuals.
- With significant power distance, where many individuals accept the concentration of power with a very few.
- A long-term orientation (or Confucian dynamics) that emphasizes persistence, status, respect for tradition, protection of face, and reciprocation of gifts and favors.

As the aftermath of the Culture Revolution and the pervasive question of whom to trust eroded the public morality (Wang 2019). Combined with the fast transformation from an agricultural society, which was based on trusted personal networks ("guanxi"), to an industrial superpower with anonymous urbanization, trust and morality faded while uncertainty increased massively. Prominent cases of fraud and corruption in the mining, food, and drug industries with fake substandard products sparked consumer anger and deteriorated China's reputation. The dimension of the problem—both in materiality and in duration—is illustrated with two examples:

> **Example milk Scandal 2008**
> In 2008—shortly after the Summer Olympic in Beijing—the baby milk (infant formula) scandal became public: milk powder was purposely tainted with the cheap chemical melamine to fake protein level. This led to 294,000 affected babies, 54,000 of which were hospitalized and at least 6 died from kidney stones (The Guardian 2008). The scandal comprised basically the key

(continued)

producers and extended to other food products such as eggs as well. In consequence, trust in food safety deteriorated within China as well as international trade, as it caused an import ban from various countries worldwide and effected product recalls from international brands such as Unilever (Sinn 2008) or Heinz (AFP 2008) and finally a general alert from the US FDA (Food and Drug Administration) against food products from China, as "the problem of melamine contamination is not limited to infant formula products" and "the problem of melamine contamination in Chinese food products is a recurring one" (FDA 2009). In addition, people's faith in the political leaders deteriorates (Elegant 2008).

Example Vaccine Scandal 2018
In 2018—a decade later-, the Changseng Biotechnology vaccine scandal, in which more than 200,000 Chinese children were administered with rabies vaccines from production runs that were not effectively quality controlled (The Lancet 2018). The mistrust in the Chinese system continues.

What can be seen from these examples is that corruption is a pervasive problem in China that roots from:

1. The one-party political system that prohibits opposition and hence has no effective corrective measures (e.g., that are provided by separation of powers, judicial independence, free elections, and free journalism). Although in such a centralized directorship, decisions can be forced and pushed through much quicker than in a multi-party political system, there is no incentive for the ruling party to improve structures in the best interest of the public. The incentive is purely in manifestation of the ruling party's own privileges. A common assumption within China and abroad that with economic liberalization a politic mind shift and reforms toward respect of human rights will eventually occur was falsified since the aggressive program shift put forward as of 2013 by China's new autocratic leader (see Sect. 6.5.1).
2. The aftermath of the Culture Revolutions' system of mistrust, observation, and control that incentivized denunciation and forced cooperation with political officials to avoid sanctions—the basis for corruption.
3. The rapid (forced see #1 above) industrialization that did not allow for the development of adequate social and economic standards and efficient structures such as independent controls. This spoiled the misconduct, as infringements kept often without punishment (Wang 2019).
4. The countrywide migration streams to urban mega-cities with up to 27 million population (Shanghai, #3 on worldwide basis, 33 cities above three million) (Comparitech 2020) that has distorted the rural family bonding: e.g., caretaking

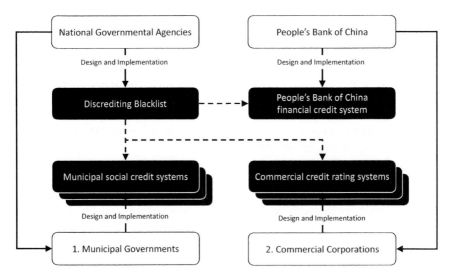

Fig. 7.2 Social credit systems for natural persons in China [own simplified presentation based on (Chuncheng 2019)]

children in multi-generations households is impossible, as the younger migrate to urban areas leaving their original families behind. So, strangers as nannies would look after children purely for their own economic benefit without social links to the children's parents.

The fast-pace digitization has created even more online-fraud attacks without effective penalization, with particularly elderly people targeted as victims.

Reference is commonly made to the Western countries' credit systems that allows access to capital resource through high credit scores of creditworthiness, and which is seen as a role model for China to cope with fraud and corruption (Wang 2019).

From that perspective, high expectations and acceptance rate from the Chinese public for the social credit system can be better understood; some studies score public acceptance as high as 80% (Kostka 2018).

Chinas' social credit system that is being rolled out benefits expected and sanctions unwanted behavior.

There are different types of social credit system (Chuncheng 2019) (see Fig. 7.2):

1. The judicial system, led by the Supreme People's Court that designed and implemented the discrediting blacklist (and a red list for high scores) that publicly lists individuals and corporations and that leads to massive restriction and repressions in wrongdoers (e.g., no access to credits, air and high-speed trains, private schools and universities, etc.) and businesses (in a self-regulated manner as the publicly provided display shall motivate businesses to score high for competitive reasons). By March 2019, 13 million publicly blacklisted people are penalized by denial of access to loans, attractive jobs, or transport services

(20 million air tickets denied, in addition high-speed train tickets) (Matsakis 2019).

2. Municipal local systems that aim for reinforcement of social governance with potential effects on credit scores. Everyone is tracked, and some local systems are designed so that for each individual up to the age of 80 years (Lippold 2019) specific "voluntary" work and specific behavior is required in order not to lose scores. As local officials are likewise affected with the scoring systems, they are incentivized to put pressure on the local community members. Hence, a system of fear is established (Lippold 2019).

3. People's Bank of China financial credit system in particular to foster the market infrastructure by credit reports (individual and businesses) as well as scores for individuals (Chuncheng 2019).

4. Commercial corporations' credit rating system, which initially started on a voluntary basis (mobile users could opt out), offering in particular privileges to high scorers such as waiver of deposits on rents. For example as of October 2019, Alipay had 520 million customer records on their "Sesame" credit system (Lippold 2019).

To implement the social credit system, AI extends the depths of tracking individual's behavior based on geotagging, facial recognition, and payments (see above). Beyond the question of appropriateness there are cases reported where the database is incorrect (either not updated and people are kept on the blacklist even when the originating issue was resolved, or—as the case may be—driven by other motives): e.g., the case of the Chinese lawyer Li Xiaolin, who was rejected to purchase a flight ticket in 2016, as his name continued to be listed on the blacklist for failure of having carried out a court order in 2015, although he has resolved it already (Wang 2017).

On the public side, with the program "Sharp Eyes" a large-scape surveillance program is being rolled out in major Chinese cities (see Sect. 6.5.1).

Example CCTV Surveillance and Crime Rate in China
The line of argument that more surveillance means more security cannot be derived from the data (see Fig. 7.3). Obviously, there is no direct correlation between CCTV per capita and crime index. The correlation is $r = 0.1$; regression analysis with a slight positive slope (0.06) shows an adjusted R^2 of -1.6%, so there is no significant evidence in regard to "the more CCTVs the smaller the crime rate."

Another example of AI-based surveillance activities in China is linked to the police-led mass DNA collection campaign across mainland China, where DNA samples of male citizens are basically forcedly collected outside a forensic investigation. Via the police's database, these samples can be linked to multigenerational

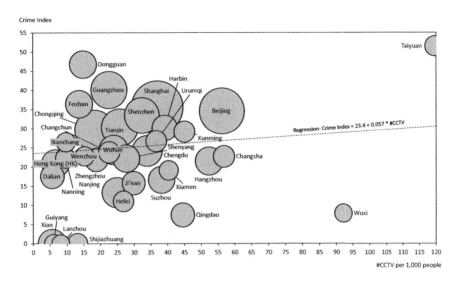

Fig. 7.3 Crime rate and CCTV surveillance in China's major cities, bubble size relative to population (Beijing: 20.4 million) [own presentation, data based on (Comparitch 2020)]

family trees so that any DNA sample from an unknown male can be linked back to a specific family and even to an individual man (Rudolph 2020). This program seems to be part of an even larger biometric profiling of innocent citizens that includes retinal scans, fingerprints, and vocal recordings. This police-run genomic surveillance violates Chinese domestic law and the multitude of UN Declarations and international human rights norms, as inclusion of innocent civilians in forensic databases presents a gross violation of privacy (Leibold and Dirks 2020).

Critically to reflect is the tendency that through the Chinese expansion program—the "New Silk Route," which started in 2013—many developing countries are following (or are forced to follow) the Chinese interpretation of usage of AI: by 2020, 58 countries such as Pakistan, Venezuela, and many African states in which China has provided cheap credits for local infrastructure programs. With the funds, China offers surveillance technology as well to help the ruling (very often not democratic) leaders to keep citizens at check.

These developments show significant ethical challenges, which directly link back to the fundamentals of business ethics (see Chap. 3 as well):

- Is it justified to do business with the Chinese agencies that support mass surveillance, which violates existing laws and ultimately enables discrimination, suppression clan custody, and excessive preventive justice measure before a criminal offense occurred?

  US companies like biotech giant Thermo Fisher Scientific (Leibold and Dirks 2020) did in case of DNA mass surveillance, and Apple CEO Tim Cook is looking forward to a "common future in cyberspace with China" (Wang 2017).

- Is it in the supplying business ethical obligation to limit the support for specific use and to abandon delivery in case of customer's misuse? How would a coordination look like that is acceptable in a competitive environment?
- How can a responsible support for an emerging nation look like to avoid misuse of technology in the long run?

7.5   USA and the "Surveillance Capitalism"

With the advent of AI technology capturing basically all details of consumers' lives, ethical concerns emerge as to how far a pervasive influence manipulates individuals and with that the societies in general.

In particular, elections are the most endangered, as could be seen in the presidential elections in 2016. Both candidates were very close in votes—variance less than 100,000—in just three states, i.e., the final decision depended only on these very few votes in these states. Applying dedicated manipulation of the voters like mobilizing to vote or to keep them away from the election, the final results can easily be biased. Despite AI-based manipulation, there have been (and continues to be) other means of said manipulation as well like putting hurdles in place for voters by simply restricting polling places makes it difficult for voters to cast their vote if they have to travel long distances and to wait in long queues, or—as the intent was from the ruling 2020 administration—to reduce postal services despite the rush to postal voting in times of COVID-19.

AI-based manipulation is very effective, since the large-scale Internet giants, GAFAM in particular, have access to most sensitive information about their consumers (hence the voters) such as their activities, preferences, attitudes, behaviors, beliefs, interests, and even the wishes and fears. From AI-based data analysis the companies can identify how religious a particular consumer is, how deep and to whom the consumer has connections with, and who is a homophobic, racist, or a conspiracy theories follower. Given the fact that Internet giants control the communication channels in the so-called social media as well, the de facto power to manipulate is with them.

Initiatives such as the data protection initiative from the US actionist Alistair Mactaggert and his multi-million dollar legislative initiative—the California Consumer Privacy Act ("CCPA")[1]—to curb the Internet giants was successful in 2018. "The CCPA gives California consumers the right to learn what information a business has collected about them, to delete their personal information, to stop businesses from selling their personal information or use it for cross-context behavioral advertising, and to hold businesses accountable if they do not take reasonable steps to safeguard their personal information" (Mactaggert 2019). This success came as a surprise to many Internet companies and was opposed from, e.g., from

---

[1]This approach corresponds to the earlier introduced European General Data Protection Regulation (GDPR).

Facebook, Google, and AT&T, as it attacks the foundation of their current business models, and attempts were made to weaken the law. The initiative continues for a Version 2 of the CCPA with even stronger consumer rights related to their personal and sensitive data including

- Knowing who has access to those data.
- Non-discrimination possibilities to correct, delete, and take it with them to other businesses.
- Business responsibilities to disclose any politically motivated use of that data.
- Ensure data security.
- Businesses to only collect specific data (Mactaggert 2019).

Some companies like Microsoft have positioned themselves as giving moderate consent in order to regain consumer trust and to provide (new) services for business clients (Microsoft 2020).

AI is an ubiquitous fact in business today and does not relay to tracking of online activities of consumers. Although very often consumers would not know it or are not really aware of the implications. Examples (originating in the USA, but not limited to its use there) are recruiting automation, in which interviewees are analyzed regarding their facial expression, gestures and body language, sentiment and tone, keywords, etc. The interview processes may be scaled (one interviewer to many interviewees in one online session with automated analysis of interviewees' reactions) or may be fully automated right away using bots. Various US-based suppliers like Gecko.AI, HireVue or Mya have AI-based RPA solutions for video-based/recorded interviewing and assessments that are used by international business customers such as Adecco, Dow Jones, L'Oreal, KraftHeinz, Sodexo, Unilever, and Vodafone[2]. The economics are promising as there is 90% of decrease in time to hire.

Although candidates may be informed about the fact that AI-based technology is used and it is voluntary, de facto there is no real choice in a situation where applicants would want to opt out when they are seeking a job.

As with China, the developments in the USA show significant ethical challenges, which directly link back to the fundamentals of business ethics (see Chap. 3 as well). Major ethical challenges can be summarized as follows:

- How to ensure that AI-based machines are means for the people and not the other way around?
- How can a deterioration of societies by a few "Big Tech" companies be avoided, and the free political and societal environment be supported?
- How can the autonomy of individuals be strengthened in free access to unbiased and "disfaked" information in an environment of manipulation through AI-based services?

---

[2]See websites of mentioned suppliers: www.gecko.ai; www.mya.com; www.hirevue.com

- How can transparency on usage of sensitive data about the personality of individuals be ensured effectively so that non-discriminating and fair decisions in full conformance with basic (human) rights can be taken?
- How can the effective accountability from those who use sensitive personal data be incentivized and enforced?

7.6 Finish Line Quiz

7.01	How does the household income increase resonate with the productivity increase via automation (based on US statistics).	
	1	Household income raise matches productivity increase.
	2	Household income raise doubles productivity increase.
	3	Household income raise is less than half of productivity increase.
	4	There was no productivity increase.
7.02	What is the projected range of job losses due to AI-based automation?	
	1	5–15%
	2	10–30%
	3	10–40%
	4	15–50%
7.03	What is the logic of the long-term deterioration of current market systems?	
	1	Due to de facto forced introduction of newest productivity measures (such as AI), job losses will reduce consumption and hence the ultimate source of corporate profit.
	2	Due to voluntary introduction of AI, jobs will be enriched, will stimulate consumption, and ultimately increase corporate profit.
	3	AI does not have any direct effect on the job market.
	4	Due to de facto forced introduction of AI, jobs will be enriched, will stimulate consumption, and ultimately increase corporate profit.
7.04	What is an underlying situation in China that should be reflected in an analysis of the reasons for China to establish a surveillance state?	
	1	Erosion of trust within the society after the culture revolution.
	2	Erosion of formerly trusted personal networks (guanxi) within the fast transformation from an agricultural society.
	3	Fraud within an anonymous urbanization.
	4	All the above.
7.05	How many root causes for corruption in China were discussed?	
	1	1
	2	2
	3	3
	4	4
7.06	What is the correlation between the number of CCTV surveillance cameras in China and the crime rate?	
	1	The more CCTV cameras installed, the less the crime rate.
	2	Indifferent to slightly positive correlation, i.e., more CCTV does not lead to less crime.
	3	High positive correlation: The more CCTV, the higher the crime rate.

(continued)

	4	No correlation at all.
7.07		What are fundamental ethical questions in an international context?
	1	Is it justified to do business with, e.g., the Chinese agencies that support mass surveillance?
	2	How can misuse of technology be prevented in the long run?
	3	How can the delivery in case of customer's misuse be abandoned?
	4	All the above.
7.08		What type of information about consumers is tracked by AI?
	1	Only activities and clearly articulated interests (e.g., search entries).
	2	Activities, preferences, attitudes, behaviors, beliefs, interests, and even the wishes and fears.
	3	Activities, preferences, and interests.
	4	Activities, preferences, behaviors.
7.09		What in substance is covered by the CCPA?
	1	Data access: Knowing who has access to / right to correct them. Discrimination-free possibilities to correct / delete / take it with them to other businesses.
	2	Political motivation: Business responsibilities to disclose any politically motivated use of that data.
	3	Specific use only: Only collect specific data.
	4	All the above.
7.10		Give examples of already available AI usage in the HR process!
	1	Video bots for recruiting.
	2	Scaled video (one to many) sessions with automated analysis.
	3	Chatbot for employee self-service.
	4	All the above.

Correct answers can be found in www.vieweg-beratung.de/downloads

References

AFP. (2008). *Heinz stops buying Chinese milk products.* Retrieved October 21, 2020, from https://web.archive.org/web/20081003125923/ http://afp.google.com/article/ALeqM5jKovOtOFykh1iHvH3ZZcFIiknRsQ.

Chang, J. (2016). *Wild swans: Three daughters of China.*

Chuncheng, L. (2019). Multiple social credit systems in China. *Economic Sociology: The European Electronic Newsletter, 21*(1): 22–32. Available at SSRN, Retrieved October 21, 2020, from https://ssrn.com/abstract=3423057 or https://doi.org/10.2139/ssrn.3423057.

Comparitch. (2020). Retrieved October 21, 2020, from https://www.comparitech.com/vpn-privacy/the-worlds-most-surveilled-cities/#Methodology.

Devaraj, S., Hicks, M. E., Worell, E. J., Faulk, D. (2017). *How vulnerable are American communities to automation, trade, & urbanization?* Retrieved October 21, 2020, from https://projects.cberdata.org/reports/Vulnerability-20170719.pdf.

Elegant, S. (2008). *China's poisoned-milk scandal: Is sorry enough? Time.* Retrieved October 21, 2020, from https://web.archive.org/web/20090104090026/http://www.time.com/time/world/article/0%2C8599%2C1843536%2C00.html.

FDA. (2009). Import Alert #99–30, "Detection without physical examination of all milk products, milk derived ingredients and finished food products containing milk from China due to the presence of melamine and/or melamine analogs". Retrieved October 21, 2020, from http://webarchive.loc.gov/all/20090501094113/https://www.fda.gov/ora/fiars/ora_import_ia9930.html.

Frey, C. B., & Osborne, M. A. (2013). *The future of employment: How susceptible are jobs to computerization.* Retrieved October 19, 2020, from https://www.oxfordmartin.ox.ac.uk/downloads/academic/The_Future_of_Employment.pdf.

Hofstede, G., Hofstede, J.G., & Minkov, M. (2010). *Cultures and organizations: Software of the mind.* Revised and expanded 3rd Edition, New York: McGraw-Hill.

Jones, L. (2019). *Microsoft's brad smith says AI will be as transformative as the internal combustion engine.* Retrieved October 19, 2020, from https://winbuzzer.com/2019/11/06/microsofts-brad-smith-says-ai-will-be-as-transformative-as-the-internal-combustion-engine-xcxwbn/.

Kennedy, P. (1987). *The rise and Fall of great powers.* New York: Random House.

Kostka, G. (2018). *China's social credit systems and public opinion: Explaining high levels of approval.* Available at SSRN, Retrieved October 21, 2020, from https://ssrn.com/abstract=3215138 or https://doi.org/10.2139/ssrn.3215138.

Kurz, H. D. (2013). *Die Entzauberung des Kapitalismus.* Retrieved October 21, 2020, from https://www.faz.net/aktuell/wirtschaft/wirtschaftswissen/die-weltverbesserer/karl-marx-die-entzauberung-des-kapitalismus-12668047.html?printPagedArticle=true#void.

Lee, K. F. (2018). *AI superpowers: China, silicon valley, and the new world order.* Boston: Houghton Mifflin Harcourt.

Leibold, J., & Dirks, E. (2020). *Genomic surveillance: Inside China's DNA dragnet.* Retrieved October 21, 2020, from https://www.aspistrategist.org.au/genomic-surveillance-inside-chinas-dna-dragnet/.

Lippold, M. (2019). *Wie China seine Bürger überwachen will.* Retrieved October 21, 2020, from https://www.n-tv.de/politik/Wie-China-seine-Buerger-ueberwachen-will-article21359017.html.

Mactaggert, A. (2019). *The California privacy rights and enforcement act of 2020.* Retrieved October 21, 2020, from https://oag.ca.gov/system/files/initiatives/pdfs/19-0019%20%28Consumer%20Privacy%20-%20Version%202%29.pdf.

Matsakis, L. (2019). *How the west got China's social credit system wrong. Wired.* Retrieved October 21, 2020, from https://www.wired.com/story/china-social-credit-score-system/.

McAfee, A. (2019). *More for less.* New York: Scribner.

Microsoft. (2020). *CCPA offering.* Retrieved October 26, 2020, from https://docs.microsoft.com/en-us/microsoft-365/compliance/offering-ccpa?view=o365-worldwide.

Morris, I. (2010). *Why the west rules – For now.* Picador.

Nedelkoska, L., & Quintini, G. (2018). Automation, skills use and training. *OECD Social, Employment and Migration Working Papers,* No. 202, OECD Publishing, Paris, Retrieved October 19, 2020, from https://doi.org/10.1787/2e2f4eea-en.

Ng, A. (2017). Retrieved October 19, 2020, from https://www.gsb.stanford.edu/insights/andrew-ng-why-ai-new-electricity.

Rudolph, J. (2020). *ASPI: Inside China's nationwide DNA collection program.* Retrieved October 21, 2020, from https://chinadigitaltimes.net/2020/06/aspi-inside-chinas-nationwide-dna-collection-program/.

Sinn, D. (2008). *Lipton milk tea powder recalled in Asia.* CBS News. Retrieved October 21, 2020, from https://www.cbsnews.com/news/lipton-milk-tea-powder-recalled-in-asia/.

The Guardian. (2008). *Chinese figures show fivefold rise in babies sick from contaminated milk.* Retrieved October 21, 2020, from https://www.theguardian.com/world/2008/dec/02/china.

The Lancet. (2018). Vaccine scandal and confidence crisis in China. *The Lancet, 392*(10145):360. Retrieved October 21, 2020, from https://doi.org/10.1016/S0140-6736(18)31695-7.

Viscelli, S. (2016). *The big rig: Trucking and the decline of the American Dream.*

Wang, M. (2017). *China's chilling 'social credit' blacklist.* Retrieved October 21, 2020, from https://www.hrw.org/news/2017/12/12/chinas-chilling-social-credit-blacklist.

Wang, X. Y. (2019). *China's social credit system: The Chinese citizens' perspective.* Retrieved October 21, 2020, from https://blogs.ucl.ac.uk/assa/2019/12/09/chinas-social-credit-system-the-chinese-citizens-perspective/.

Part III

Practical Examples

AI in the Financial Industries: Between Apathy and Hysteria

8

Susan Spinner

8.1 Learning Objectives

1. Reflect the paradigm shift posed by the fundamental topics of climate change and artificial intelligence and the consequences for business decisions.
2. Review the extreme positions of apathy and hysteria as a non-option.
3. Aggregate the opportunities of a digital transformation and new requirements on changing roles, skills, and cultural awareness.
4. Reflect implications of biases in data and AI algorithms, which can lead to massive (even if unintended) discrimination, therewith posing a significant risk in businesses and beyond.
5. Identify some de-biasing approaches such as XAI—Explain AI.
6. Elaborate on core human virtues and explain why courage may be most important.

8.2 The Paradigm Shift

Not long ago this title "Between Apathy and Hysteria" would have seemed very dramatic, but recently many practitioners and academics alike, who have touchpoints to new technology, may identify with those extremes.

This has happened because many people sense a shift, a very significant paradigm shift in daily reality. The world order that many of us viewed as a constant just a few years ago has not only been put into question, but in many instances has already been altered.

S. Spinner (✉)
CEO and Managing Director CFA Society Germany, Frankfurt am Main, Germany
e-mail: info@cfa-germany.de

© The Author(s), under exclusive license to Springer Nature Switzerland AG 2021
S. H. Vieweg (ed.), *AI for the Good*, Management for Professionals,
https://doi.org/10.1007/978-3-030-66913-3_8

And parallel to this alteration of world order, are two meta-driving forces of change which are creating upheaval in all parts of our lives: climate change and artificial intelligence.

8.3   Climate Change and Artificial Intelligence: Reasons for Hysteria?

Two existential questions can be observed:

1. How can humans continue to thrive in a sustainable way on this planet, in a way that also preserves the health of the planet?
2. How can we safeguard and cherish our humanity in an ever-more digitally driven world?

Since both forces could, at least in theory, wipe out humanity entirely, it is not surprising that there may be feelings of hysteria.

This can be witnessed in the panicked discourse surrounding climate change, and while this drama is perhaps even necessary to affect positive change more quickly, cooler heads must prevail (no pun intended).

There is a second mega-trend confronting individuals, businesses, and societies likewise: artificial intelligence and the ethical implications that are involved in its application, here through a finance lens.

While during 2019, movements such as "Fridays for Future" put the spotlight on the ecological risk factor (that affects the financial industries as well as everyone else), attention during 2020 was clearly lured away by the COVID-19 pandemic, which added social risks to our worries. But the problem is not gone. Not at all. "The Pandemic Is a Dress Rehearsal. The world is entering a transformative era. Prepare for more chaos and instability" (Mead 2020). And just as with the comparatively "small" problem of the COVID-19 situation, there are no functioning means to manage such a situation confidently, on a global scale. So, what about global warming: if the global community fails to deliver on the Paris 2015 intent to limit global warming below 2 °C, (financial) risks will turn into reality and key (financial) assets will literally be diluted (e.g., see the dramatic simulations from MIT Sloan Management School and the Climate Change Initiative[1]). Although the problem is a truly global one, thus far local advantage-thinking and action has been more prevalent.

As with the potential disaster of global warming, the potential widespread dangers of artificial intelligence are not always visible, nor are the potentially negative effects easily forecasted or quantified.

---

[1]The climate interactive world simulations, e.g., demonstrate the effects in the City of London where the House of Parliament and Westminster Abbey would be flooded in a 4 °C warming scenario. See https://climatechangeinitiative.org/. (access 02.09.2020).

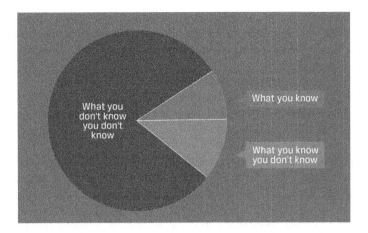

Fig. 8.1 VUCA- Volatility, uncertainty, complexity, and ambiguity, Source: CFA Society Germany

In fact, the large asymmetry of information between those digitally in the know and those not, and the speed at which advances in artificial intelligence are taking place, means that most individuals cannot keep pace with the technology and tend to tune out completely and get on with their otherwise busy lives (see Fig. 8.1).

This is the VUCA[2] (Bostrom 2003) world, where what you know you know is declining and what you know you do not know seems to be growing, yet it is likely still shrinking due to the unknown unknowns, which could well be growing exponentially, but how can we know? Just thinking about this is truly mentally fatiguing. . .

8.4   Apathy, the Other Extreme

Here is an AI scary story that some may be familiar with. A robot has been programmed to make paper clips in a factory. He is very good at it and makes them far more quickly and accurately than a human could. But unfortunately, no one thought about a program to turn off the robot, *and his directive to make paper clips has no limit.* So the robot begins to make paper clips beyond the factory, after he has turned the factory itself into a large paper clip. In fact, he starts to make ever larger paper clips, until the earth itself is one immense paper clip and the robot is eyeing neighboring planets as his next conquest (Bostrom (2003).

This fits with the quote from Eliezer Yudkowsky "the Artificial Intelligence does not hate you, nor does it love you, but you are made out of atoms that it can use for something else."

---

[2]"VUCA" – Volatility, uncertainty, complexity, ambiguity.

This is pure science fiction and also ignores Asimov's famous "Three Laws of Robotics," but combined with quotes like Elon Musk's, that "AI poses the greatest threat to humanity", it is not surprising that one might feel panic, or simply not want to think about it at all.

Yet neither of these extremes is conducive to productive solutions.

How instead can we get to what can be called the *sweet spot between hysteria and apathy*, a place where transparency thrives and a framework of trust in systems is still possible? A place where human intelligence *guides* artificial intelligence and not the other way around—a question that, for example, CFA Institute is actively looking at, by updating the required skills and tools for investment professionals.

With this in mind, it is helpful to first broadly discuss what is currently happening in artificial intelligence within the context of finance and what implications that may have.

Many financial AI applications thus far are related to fraud detection, credit scoring, and robo-advising and have been more focused on retail rather than institutional applications. But this is changing rapidly as banks and investment firms seek to deploy the technology across research, sales, trading, and compliance (Greenwich Associates 2020).

In 2018, CFA Institute conducted a global survey of investment professionals, which showed that 73% of the respondents stated that their firm was looking to apply technology to client engagement or to use machine learning in portfolio construction. A more recent study from early 2019 showed financial industry leaders identifying the growth in AI and machine learning as the greatest source of disruption for investment professionals in the next 5–10 years.

This development has the potential to bring significant advances and improvements to the world of finance. Routine tasks that can be automated will free up humans to work on more complex and hopefully rewarding tasks.

So, what is not to like? The pace, for a start. It is apparent that AI is evolving much faster than our legal frameworks, regulatory oversight, and popular understanding of these technologies can.

This is true in finance too. Many financial firms have legacy technology which is difficult to align with new methods and their progress has been primarily reactive. And unlike 20 years ago, when the best and brightest headed to finance because it was so lucrative, many financial firms currently struggle to attract the IT talent needed to realize the full power of AI and big data in their business models. In fact, those working at the top technology companies globally, like Google and Microsoft, continue to enjoy a real advantage, as those employees specialized in AI at these companies have access to knowledge and skills not yet taught even in the top universities around the world (CFA 2019) (CFA Institute AI Pioneers in Investment Management). And most of these elite employees are not looking to move into finance. Moreover, Google and Microsoft have managed to lure in developers' skills on a worldwide basis by acquiring the open software development platforms for data scientists (see Sect. 6.6.1: Kaggle, started in 2010, with more than a million users worldwide, was acquired by Google's parent company Alphabet Inc.

in 2017; Github, started in 2008, with its c. 40 million user base, was acquired by Microsoft in 2018).

This means that finance firms continue to play catch-up. One hope which seems to be persuasive is that finance latecomers will benefit from the trial and error of the early tech entrants and be able to leapfrog forward with a new successful technology. But this requires large and sustainable budgets and also talent to stay in the game, something that will eventually weed out many firms. It is forecast that only about 15 asset management firms will ultimately remain globally. This sobering statistic is balanced by an encouraging broad demand for asset management currently, with significant increases in assets over the last few years[3].

An ongoing strategy for FinTech platforms is *component replacement*, aimed at introducing functionality that is cheaper, faster, or safer, relative to legacy platform components. Blockchain-based/distributed ledger technology systems could significantly reduce the need for specialized custodial institutions since, in principle, market participants would be able to exchange and record transactions securely in the cloud (see Sect. 6.4.2 as well). Blockchain is currently too slow and expensive to replace existing practices on a large scale. In the future however, blockchain could serve as the core technology for platforms that require verification and trust. *Trust is the air that capital markets need to breathe*, so this technology could prove to be a game-changer.

That is, unless quantum computing lives up to its claims, that has it potentially hacking the blockchain within 5 years. But that is a subject for another story [see details on e.g. 51% attack in Sect. 6.4.2 and (Cambridge Quantum Computing 2020)].

In the current regulatory landscape, platform completion and component replacement in FinTech seem likely to occur mostly through platform partnerships. Not long ago so-called robo-advisors were touted as a major threat to established investment firms. Instead, they have proven to be more complementary, rather than disruptive, with large firms simply buying up the most promising FinTech startups and adding the new technology to their own services.

Finally—and perhaps most significantly—even though they are not natural participants today, once market participants begin to trust the data handling and AI capabilities of the large Internet platforms, they could become core components of FinTech platforms for the same reasons they are trusted in the social, retail, and device domains. Why would financial players choose to build Google's or Amazon's artificial intelligence and machine learning capabilities from scratch, especially when they struggle to match the talent already.

But this has not stopped banks from thinking about or starting to use artificial intelligence technology throughout their organizations: in lending, in detecting

---

[3]On a global level a year-on-year increase of 15% in 2019 according to BCG 2020 Global Asset Management—Protect, Adapt, and Innovate. https://image-src.bcg.com/Images/BCG-Global-Asset-Management-2020-May-2020-r_tcm9-247209.pdf, (access 02.09.2020), though with clear requirements of innovation and customer-centric practices required.

fraud, in operations, in human resources, account opening, payments, and else-where—anywhere where automated tasks are conducted (see Sect. 6.5.1).

This digital transition provides a significant opportunity for investment professionals to position themselves optimally in this new environment, where investment roles, technology roles, and innovation roles will be dominant.

According to the recently released CFA Institute study " Investment Professional of the Future" (CFA 2019), the combination of human intelligence, or H-I, and artificial intelligence, A-I, will add more value than either component alone because it ideally leverages the benefits of both. Ethical orientation, transparency, communication, empathy, tacit knowledge, and trust interaction are the key human elements that technology cannot (yet) reproduce.

Teams will be more important than star individual portfolio managers and diversity in teams will be sought to achieve the best results. Professionals will have to understand how technology is being used in his or her company and then be able to translate this into customized information and results for clients. According to Investment Professional of the Future, such T-shaped skills, combining both broad and specific knowledge, are the most coveted. At the same time, leadership skills are more desired than ever and the workplace itself is expected to grow in importance and have a far higher influence on the employee experience as in the past.

This provides an exceptional opportunity to create company cultures that are positive and dynamic, with a clear human-centric impact, especially after the COVID-19 pandemic lockdown.

This is the future that probably all of us aspire to, but first we need to take a look at where we are now, which is not as clear-cut.

8.5   Current State in the (Traditional) Financial Industries

While many finance firms may not be as advanced as their high-tech counterparts, there is still a pointed need to create a greater transparency in finance with respect to AI.

> "Fact: We have already turned our world over to machine learning and algorithms. The question now is, how to better understand and manage what we have done?" *(Chudakov 2012) (see Sect. 1.5.3 on the Collingridge problem as well)*

Between the simple fixed algorithms and true AI *"lies an opaque place that we've already entered with little thought or debate, much less agreement as to aims, ethics, safety, best practice. If the algorithms around us are not yet intelligent, meaning able to recognize "that calculation or action doesn't look right: I'll try it again", they are starting to learn from their environments. And once an algorithm is learning, no longer is there a chance to know exactly what its rules and parameters are, nor can anyone be certain of how it will interact with other algorithms, the physical world, or us.*" (Smith 2018).

For example, according to the science historian George Dyson, some high frequency trading, or HFT firms have been allowing their algorithms to learn "just letting the black box try different things, with small amounts of money, and if it works, reinforce those rules. We know that's been done. Then you actually have rules where *nobody* knows what the rules are: the algorithms create their own rules— you let them evolve the same way nature evolves organisms." (Dyson 2019).

In his 2011 novel *The Fear Index*, Robert Harris (Harris 2011) imagines the emergence of the singularity or human-level machine intelligence—from exactly this type of random organic digital evolution.

While this type of mass machine procreation is still largely fictional and more of a future concern, the widespread problems of big data are already evident now.

A series of data slip-ups have been mostly visible from large tech corporations, who have been intent for years on claiming their digital turf, by amassing huge amounts of proprietary data.

What is becoming very apparent is that if machines are provided biased or flawed data, they are going to produce biased or flawed results.

In one example, three different AI systems by IBM, Microsoft, and Megvii have been found to correctly identify a person's gender from a photo at a rate of 99%— which sounds impressive, but only if that person is a white male (Cossins 2018). In other cases, e.g., for women of color, the accuracy of facial recognition drops significantly.

In fact, there have been a series of such embarrassing episodes. It seems hard to believe that sophisticated programmers could allow this to happen routinely, until one considers the source; literally—that 95% of algorithms are programmed by men[4], many of whom are weird (WEIRD: *W*hite, *E*ducated, *I*ndustrialized, *R*ich, *D*emocratic).

Furthermore, there is a significant bias on developers' age toward below the age of 45 where almost 91% are covered (see Footnote 62).

Should it be at all surprising, with these kinds of statistics, that there are so many issues with bias? Even if it is highly likely unconscious?

The concerns that there are not enough female and minority voices influencing machine learning seem to be understandable.

As one algorithmic program reviewed more than 100,000 labeled images from around the Internet, its biased association became *stronger* than that shown by the dataset — *amplifying rather than simply replicating bias.*

As Sara Wachter-Boettcher, the author of *Technically Wrong*, asks: "Does it matter that the things that are profoundly changing and shaping our society are being

---

[4]According to the 2020 Developers Survey, nearly 92% are men (42 k responses), 71% are white or European descent (38 k responses), second largest group South Asian with 10%. See https://insights.stackoverflow.com/survey/2020#developer-profile-gender-professional-developers2. (access 02.09.2020).

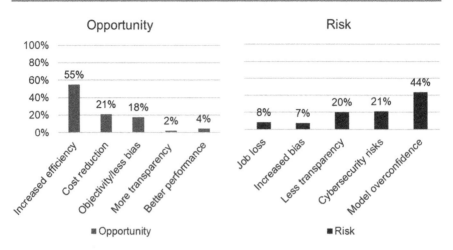

Fig. 8.2 AI opportunities and risks of AI implementation in investments (own presentation from CFA Society Germany poll 2019)

created by a small sliver of people with a small sliver of experiences?" (Wachter-Boettcher 2018).

Yet it is often not recognized as an issue because we tend to see machines as being objective.

This supposed objectivity is called "math-washing," and has become prevalent, because a program is widely considered to be a more neutral decision-maker than a human. As a professor at MIT said (Byrnes 2016): we have a tendency to idolize programs like Facebook as being entirely objective because they have mathematics at their core.

In fact, we know this is not true. In fact, it could be even "more dangerous" because it is hard to know why a machine has made a decision, and because it can get more and more biased over time. Yet the perceived risk of bias has remained low, as one can see from the following survey.

CFA Society Germany members were recently polled on the following question:

"In your view, what is the greatest opportunity and the greatest risk of AI implementation in investment?" Fig. 8.2 shows the results.

8.6   Approaches toward a Sustainable AI Framework

To confront this, we need robust standard AI frameworks that underscore the importance of ethical behavior and our shared human values.

Such a framework should explain first and foremost the human involvement, including the goal and/or purpose of the algorithm.

What is the definition of success? Key in this discussion is to establish a sense of *transparent human accountability*, so that responsible individuals can be clearly identified in cases of both success and failure.

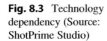

Fig. 8.3 Technology dependency (Source: ShotPrime Studio)

Then have a look at the data; as we know "data is the new oil" and without relevant data that is of high quality, meaning that it is representative, accurate, unbiased, and timely, even the best intentioned algorithm can go wrong.

In addition, some vendors are using data that was bought from someone else, who bought it from someone else. They cannot trace the data. That brings a new ethical issue that will need to be addressed.

And to put this challenge in perspective, according to IBM, over 90% of all data in existence has been collected in the past 2 years (Beatty 2016).

And even if a high level of data quality and integrity is attained, that data will still be a reflection of the past or of the status quo and cannot necessarily be extrapolated into the future.

Then the model itself must be understood; what are the assumptions being used in the model and why? What is the margin of error and how are errors corrected?

Finally, governance structures must be created within companies to assure not only that all the above is considered, but that it is appropriately applied, documented, and consistent with the strategies, goals, and culture of the firm.

These findings must then be communicated routinely to the developers of the AI so that appropriate alterations can be made.

And while individuals must be held clearly accountable within firms, firms themselves must be held clearly accountable to the public (Diakopoulos 2016; Guszcza et al. 2018) (Fig. 8.3).

This requires intelligent regulation; we need auditing processes that work like a TÜV[5] for algorithms. There are already some private companies doing this algorithmic auditing, but these methods must be more standardized in the future, to improve comparability.

---

[5]TÜV – Technischer Überwachungs-Verein, a German provider of testing, inspections, and certification services, being worldwide second by revenue [all TÜV-branches Nord, Rheinland, Süd in 2017, according to (TIC Council 2018, TÜV 2017)]. The reputation of a TÜV certificate has been very high for decades, despite the disastrous bursting of the Vale in Brazil in early 2019, shortly after TÜV Süd issued a certificate for that dam (see Chap. 1).

The EU will likely remain the standard bearer for data protection and recently has also created broad ethical guidelines, with seven key requirements for AI. GDPR is currently the world data protection standard. Google itself has said that it is no coincidence that its global Data Safety Engineering Center is located in Munich, as "Europe is the global leader in data security and Germany is Europe's leader" (Google 2019).

In the USA, the research group DARPA at the Department of Defense is working on the ambitious project XAI for "EXPLAINABLE AI," with the results intended to be relevant not just for defense but other areas including finance too (Fig. 8.4).

Being able to understand and interpret the outcome of AI models is essential to their future use: if people cannot trust the outputs of these models, the models will be rejected. Transparency and explainability are two key ways to build this trust. Explainability is also key for legal compliance—as in finance, where lenders are often required to tell applicants why they are being refused for a loan—and is crucial to debug AI systems.

Accenture Labs are working on designing explanation subsystems that help interpret the outputs of already created "black box" models that are not transparent by design, such as neural networks (McGrath et al. 2018).

This approach is known as counterfactual explanations (Wachter et al. 2017), which provide the minimal changes required on the input data in order to obtain a different result. For example, a counterfactual explanation for a rejected loan application would tell the user what changes they would have to make to the "inputs" of the application, like their income, assets, and so on, in order to have the application approved (see Sect. 6.6 as well on the concrete dataset example).

This all seems very reasonable and even promising, but many companies using AI techniques are not currently operating in this way. In fact, there has been something of a Wild West atmosphere in the AI space; just as the term "manifest destiny" defined the right of settlers in the Wild West of the USA to claim lands and move indigenous peoples, so are many of the current entities in the AI space behaving like they have the right to explore, use data, and innovate at any cost.

It is clear that there are ethical considerations to AI, and we are needing to adapt our current application of business ethics to AI.

Getting Back to Classical Ethics

As broadly known, the three common schools of ethical thought are virtue ethics, consequentialist or consequence-based ethics, and deontological or duty-based ethics (see Sect. 1.4 for details).

While the attention to *duty or consequences is fundamentally a focus on compliance*, virtue ethics looks at whether an action is consistent with being a virtuous person; it is looking at the character of the individual.

Clearly, in companies, the emphasis *on compliance* has been most profound and the concept of *virtue ethics* as having a role in business has been historically ignored. Only in recent years, since the great financial crisis, have companies broadly accepted how much culture matters and how much that is reflected in the characters of its employees. Not just the process and the result count, but also the individuals in

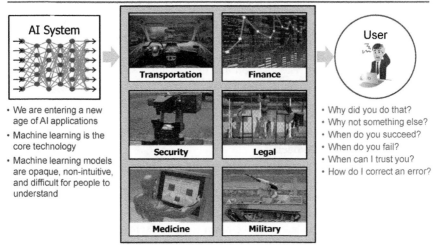

- We are entering a new age of AI applications
- Machine learning is the core technology
- Machine learning models are opaque, non-intuitive, and difficult for people to understand

User

- Why did you do that?
- Why not something else?
- When do you succeed?
- When do you fail?
- When can I trust you?
- How do I correct an error?

- The current generation of AI systems offer tremendous benefits, but their effectiveness will be limited by the machine's inability to explain its decisions and actions to users.
- Explainable AI will be essential if users are to understand, appropriately trust, and effectively manage this incoming generation of artificially intelligent partners.

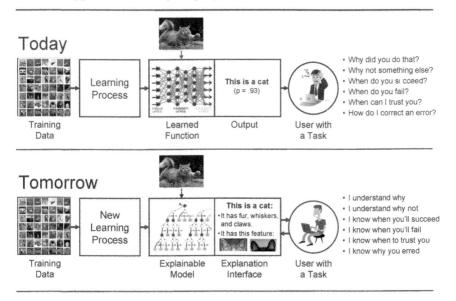

Fig. 8.4 XAI—Explainable AI. [Source: (DARPA 2019)]

teams and especially the management should reflect ethical values. In the firm of the future, this positive culture is forecasted as a key element of success.

Classically, Aristotle most famously said "We are what we repeatedly do"; he believed that virtuous behavior can be developed through repeated ethical actions and a virtuous character leads to ethical actions.

I have been teaching an "Ethics for Finance" class at the Goethe Business School for several years and lecture on how modern portfolio theory could in many ways be called legacy portfolio theory, as many of its premises have been shown to be outdated; we know that rationality and the rational "homo oeconomicus" are no longer looking so smart. The unemotional utilitarianism self-interest which formed the backbone of business school educations for decades became something of a self-fulfilling prophesy, as generations of companies supported the idea of business being *amoral*, not immoral. Amoral meaning that there is no moral premise whatsoever. This sort of thinking allowed for the Wall Street film character Gordon Gekko to actually serve as a role model.

But people are not rational, as Daniel Kahneman (Kahneman and Tversky 1979) made famous, and business is not void of morality.

Yet humans have been fascinated with objective rationality for centuries and the aspiration to achieve it has inspired many great thinkers. With the advent of digital technology and machine learning, we seem to have exchanged our worship of the rational analog homo oeconomicus for the worship of the supposedly neutral and rational digital AI. But AI programs are made by humans and data is input by humans. Most AI can only detect patterns, based on these human factors. At least thus far.

8.7 Required Change of Mindset

So, a change of mindset is needed and, with this, an end to math washing.

We need to keep ourselves informed and hold humans accountable for the AI that is being produced and we must be able to solve *the problem of many hands*, meaning that responsibility for an error must be able to be traced through multiple parties.

More fundamentally, we need to more generously appreciate the essential role of human beings and *human intelligence* in our civilization.

We need to look again to our *core human virtues*, the four classic cardinal virtues being: temperance, prudence, courage, and justice.

Coming back to the *sweet spot* between apathy and hysteria; in order to move solidly into this better space, we need however one human virtue most: courage (Fig. 8.5).

"Courage is the most important of all the virtues because without courage, you can't practice any other virtue consistently." (Maya Angelou).

Everybody caring about the future needs the courage to contribute and thrive in this new world, and it has never been more important to value and cherish our collective human intelligence.

The machines are not going to take over unless we let them.

We may need to establish the collective courage to mandate that just because we *can* do something, it does not mean we *should*.

Fig. 8.5 Courage is most important of all the virtues (Source: Shutterstock/Mikael Damkier)

8.8   Finish Line Quiz

8.01	What is the argument to assume a paradigm shift through AI?	
	1	There are new opportunities coming up with AI technologies.
	2	There is no paradigm shift at all.
	3	AI and climate change are the two topics that alter the world order.
	4	Climate change leads to a paradigm shift, not AI.
8.02	What are typical escape patterns in a paradigm shift?	
	1	Ethical viable decisions based on rational analysis of risks and opportunities.
	2	Frequent alteration of decisions based on initial rational analysis of risks and opportunities.
	3	Hysteria—ignoring the problem as such, or apathy—emotionally charged overreaction.
	4	Apathy—ignoring the problem as such, or hysteria—emotionally charged overreaction.
8.03	What are typical financial AI applications that were initially introduced?	
	1	Customer service chatbots, portfolio construction, scoring, and rating.
	2	Fraud detection, credit scoring, robo-advising.
	3	Customer service chatbots, credit scoring, robo-advising.
	4	Fraud detection, portfolio construction, robo-advising.
8.04	What is the projection of how many asset management firms will survive on a global basis?	
	1	15,000

(continued)

	2	1500
	3	150
	4	15
8.05	\multicolumn{2}{l}{What is the recommended skillset in the AI era from an investment management perspective?}
	1	No specific skillset is required.
	2	I-shape skills
	3	T-shape skills
	4	Star individual portfolio managers are more important than ever.
8.06	\multicolumn{2}{l}{What is the focus of virtue ethics?}
	1	The character of an individual.
	2	Compliance.
	3	Whether an action is consistent with being a virtuous person.
	4	Answer 1 and 3.
8.07	\multicolumn{2}{l}{What is behind the "problem of many hands" in an AI era?}
	1	Responsibility for an error must be able to be traced through multiple parties.
	2	It is solved, as AI will get the "many hands" out of its way.
	3	AI need to coordinate the "many hands" of different interests.
	4	A final party need to take final responsibility.
8.08	\multicolumn{2}{l}{Which human virtue is required most?}
	1	Temperance.
	2	Prudence.
	3	Courage.
	4	Justice.

Correct answers can be found in www.vieweg-beratung.de/downloads

References

Beatty, M. (2016). *IBM cloud object storage.* Retrieved September 2, 2020, from https://www.slideshare.net/MichaelBeatty/ibm-cloud-storage-cleversafe.

Bostrom, N. (2003). *Ethical issues in advanced artificial intelligence.* Retrieved September 2, 2020, from https://www.researchgate.net/publication/229001428_Ethical_Issues_in_Advanced_Artificial_Intelligence.

Byrnes, N. (2016). *Artificial Intolerance – Artificial intelligence is being integrated into our lives, but there's a lot we don't understand about how these systems work. How do we feel about that?*

CFA. (2019). *AI pioneers in investment management.* Retrieved September 2, 2020, from https://www.cfainstitute.org/-/media/documents/survey/AI-Pioneers-in-Investment-Management.ashx.

Chudakov, B. (2012). *The tool that tells the story: New narratives and metalives in the age of connected devices.*

Cossins, D. (2018). Discriminating algorithms: 5 times AI showed prejudice. *Artificial intelligence is supposed to make life easier for us all – but it is also prone to amplify sexist and racist biases from the real world.* NewScientist. Retrieved September 2, 2020, from https://www.newscientist.com/article/2166207-discriminating-algorithms-5-times-ai-showed-prejudice/#.

CQC. (2020). *Cambridge quantum computing.* Retrieved September 2, 2020, from https://cambridgequantum.com.

DARPA. (2019). *XAI*. Retrieved September 2, 2020, from https://www.darpa.mil/program/ explainable-artificial-intelligence.

Diakopoulos, N. (2016, February). Accountability in algorithmic decision making. *Communications of the ACM, 59*(2): 56–62, https://doi.org/10.1145/2844110. Retrieved September 2, 2020, from https://cacm.acm.org/magazines/2016/2/197421-accountability-in-algorithmic-decision-making/fulltext.

Dyson, G. (2019). The third law. In J. Brockman (Ed.), *Possible minds: Twenty-five ways of looking at AI*. New York: Penguin Press.

Google. (2019). *Verstehen. Entwickeln. Fähigkeiten vermitteln. Partnerschaften eingehen.* Retrieved September 2, 2020, from https://safety.google/engineering-center/.

Greenwich Associates. (2020). *Artificial intelligence will soon disrupt institutional Finance.* Retrieved September 2, 2020, from https://www.greenwich.com/press-release/artificial-intelli gence-will-soon-disrupt-institutional-finance.

Guszcza, J., Rahwan, I., Bible, W., Cebrian, M., Katyal, V. (2018). *Why we need to audit algorithms.* Retrieved September 2, 2020, from https://hbr.org/2018/11/why-we-need-to-audit-algorithms.

Harris, R. (2011). *The fear index*. London: Hutchinson.

Kahneman, D., Tversky, A. (1979): Prospect theory: An analysis of decision under risk. Econometrica, 47(2), 263. Retrieved September 2, 2020, from https://doi.org/10.2307/1914185.

McGrath, R., Costabello, L., Chan, L.V., Sweeney, P., Kamiab, F., Shen, Z., Lecue, F. (2018). Interpretable credit application predictions with counterfactual explanations. *arXiv*:1811.05245. Retrieved September 2, 2020.

Mead, W. R. (2020). The pandemic is a dress rehearsal. The world is entering a transformative era. Prepare for more chaos and instability. *WSJ* August 3, 2020. Retrieved September 2, 2020, from https://www.wsj.com/articles/the-pandemic-is-a-dress-rehearsal-11596495140.

Smith, A. (2018). *Franken-algorithms: The deadly consequences of unpredictable code.*

Stackoverflow: 2020 Developers Survey. Retrieved September 2, 2020., from https://insights. stackoverflow.com/survey/2020#developer-profile-gender-professional-developers2.

TIC Council. (2018). *Factsheet TIC Council The new voice of the testing, inspection and certification (TIC) industry.* Retrieved October 25, 2020, from http://www.ifiafederation.org/content/ wp-content/uploads/Factsheet__TIC_Council.pdf

TÜV (2017). *TIC council fact sheet.* Retrieved September 2, 2020, from http://www.ifia-federation. org/content/wp-content/uploads/Factsheet__TIC_Council.pdf.

Wachter, S., Mittelstadt, B., & Russell, C. (2017). Counterfactual Explanations without Opening the Black Box: Automated Decisions and the GDPR. *Harvard Journal of Law & Technology, 2018*:arXiv:1711.00399. Retrieved September 2, 2020.

Wachter-Boettcher, S. (2018). *Technically wrong: Sexist apps, biased algorithms, and other threats of toxic tech.* New York: W.W. Norton & Company.

Ethical Best Practice Applying AI in a Socially Sensible Manner

9

Stefan H. Vieweg

9.1 Learning Objective

1. Reflect the required broad understanding (not only knowledge) of key scientific disciplines to assess the potential and risks of technology such as AI.
2. Understand the ethical dimension of a technology decision.
3. Identify new options in decision-making as business leader.
4. Apply an inductive logic—what can be derived for a socially acceptable AI application?
5. Assess different setups of AI innovation in a global setup.
6. Propagate ethical sound solution in applying AI technologies that respects non-technical limitations.

9.2 Introduction and Motivation

In the following chapter, an actual real-life case of implementing AI in a socially sensible manner will be presented and some important inductive implications will be drawn. In the example there are two protagonists:

The first one, *Florian Schild*, is an entrepreneur who is founder of the startup *boot.AI* that offers AI-based knowledge sharing, analysis, and implementation services.
The second protagonist is the seasoned CEO of one of *boot.AI*'s clients. He runs a larger production company.

S. H. Vieweg (✉)
Institute of Compliance and Corporate Governance, RFH - University of Applied Sciences Cologne, Cologne, Germany
e-mail: dr.vieweg@vieweg-beratung.de

Having studied mathematical engineering at the Universität der Bundeswehr Munich, the entrepreneur's motivation is to combine different sciences, particularly electrical engineering, mathematics, computer science, physics, and aerospace engineering. Why is this of interest? In general terms, thorough foundation disciplines such as mathematics do not fit to the applicational view of engineers or physics. A mathematician reviewing a physicist's formula would probably heavily complain as the expressions and conditions are not mathematically exact. The mathematician would focus on correct expressions, conditions, and settings. In contrast to that, engineers would rather take an output-oriented stance, use all data that they can get hold on, and apply a recipe-type pragmatism of utilizing mathematical procedures (probably not fully knowing about why they can or cannot use them). The task for a mathematical engineer is to combine these antagonists. Increasingly, this is a similar task that can be observed in various companies. Typical for-profit organizations have very much a functional setup ("silos" such as marketing, sales, operations, and finance), which means that a (local) optimum is likely to be achieved within one function, though it does not necessarily lead to the best solution for the company as a whole (Tsvasman and Schild (2019)). Example: if the purchasing department squeezes the suppliers by forcing lower prices, that may show a great success (i.e., less cost) … for the managers in the purchasing department (and their bonuses). Though, it may lead to unidentified quality problems that will backfire, e.g., in the production or after sales. Hence, the local (here: purchasing) optimum is not necessarily the sweet spot for the entire organization. The real situation, though, is often similar to the example above: a cross-functional understanding of what the other part is driving does not exist. Countermeasures are coming more and more in play such as orchestrating cross-functional agile teams in an appropriate scaling agile environment (which will not be discussed here further) and/or technology such as AI. AI technology can only be successful, if in an organizational setup three key factors fit: (1) algorithms, (2) data, and (3) processes. AI drives an end-to-end view of value creation throughout the organization. As an example, again our producing company: If the core (physical) production process is accompanied by an AI-based information flow including predictive or prescriptive analytics, this will inevitably mean that to ensure an efficient end-to-end value flow, predictions about future (customer) demand (based on insights from marketing), the raw materials ordering process (in the purchasing department) all along the production line, and supply chain right to the delivery of finished products at the customers side are required. In other words, this is a cross-functional solution (and global optimum—to take the mathematician's view).

9.3   Ethical Opportunities of AI: A Real-Life Story from an SME Production Company

As mentioned before, this real-life story is about a *boot.AI* client, the CEO of a biochemical production company.

Example of a Mid-Sized Biochemical Production Company
The company has some 14,000 employees (out of which 140 work in the headquarters in a small city in a rural area in Bavaria, Germany) worldwide with eight production sites in Germany and selling in 100 countries. The CEO is 59 years old and supervises the ordinary course of business. He inherited the business from his father and runs this family-controlled company in second generation. After World War II this company developed really well and evolved as a hidden champion. So basically, the company is his life. Every now and then, the CEO read about AI in the news and media, though he never anticipated that this has anything to do with his company. The company is running, so why bothering about AI?

On Christmas Eve, his daughter, who works at Microsoft, talks about the impressive progress in AI in her area and she asked her father if AI would not be something to look at for his firm as well. The CEO, an "old school" manager with gravitas and wearing a tie even on weekends at the dinner table, clearly denies. He plans to hand over the business to his nephew soon, so it will be him to look after these things. Therefore, the daughter approached her cousin and asked him to have a look into the AI potential for her father's firm. As a consequence, her cousin invited various IT consulting companies (all of which are in top league rankings). Those consultants—all in smart business suits but without emotions toward the company—came in with a focused approach to trim the company for efficiency. So, they checked where to retrieve data. In other words, their approach was *data-driven AI*.

In this specific case, there was an essential problem with the data-driven AI approach: *NO DATA!*

The consultants have not found anything that they could have worked with. In an isolated view—according to the motto "much helps much"—this would suggest AI can only contribute an added value if a lot of data is accessible. In contrast to that, this would lead to a discrimination to those circumstances where data are rare. The good news is that there are well-functioning alternatives to the data-driven approach.

Example US Moon Mission For example, recalling the US moon missions in the late 1960s: they succeeded by putting "intelligence" in another area, the process design (and trajectory of the vehicle) and (mathematically very beautiful) algorithms that could cope with slim processing capabilities in the Apollo Guidance Computer and the Lunar Module Guidance Computer, respectively (Will 2018), which were used in the space vehicles with much less than any of today's smart phones and a minimal dataset.

So, the alternative to a pure data-driven approach is the *process-driven* view. This enables beneficiaries as well in a slim data setting (in contrast to a big data approach with some brute force digging algorithms trying to detect common pattern).

To follow up with the company example from above, in order to be able to generate data, sensors are required to detect relevant items and transfer this detection into measurements that are captured with data. So, the biochemical company requires a supply chain with sensor-equipped machines and infrastructure to generate relevant data along the value chain. Generated data will be used in algorithms, which at the end is defined sequence of data manipulation based on mathematical models. Even if one famous technique—neural networks—is used, that does not ex ante define the interaction and manipulation points as such, but which provides a defined framing (such as the number of layers of the neural network). Based on the algorithm's output, the supply chain can be automated such as based on predicted consumption of certain raw materials (based on specific environmental conditions such as temperature, air pressure, humidity, and actual machine conditions indicators such as filling levels of tanks and speeds), an automated ordering process with the supplier could be triggered.

Within the example company, the CEO has rejected this type of automation, as he does not like that. His nephew approached the startup boot.AI via some contacts.

Approaching the company site can be illustrated as such: the company is located in a rural area in the backyards of Bavaria. The company has telecommunication networks based on DSL technologies; the CEO still uses only ISDN. Reflecting briefly on the topic of digitization, this company is in a typical setting that can be found at least in Germany in many areas: wired (copper-cable based) infrastructure is rarely available or not capable of handling massive data volumes as expected in full-blown IoT implementations. So, 5G, the new mobile telecommunication standards, is very promising with high data transfer rates[1] allowing real-time applications such as autonomous driving. From this point of view, it is very interesting, but as higher frequencies and smaller cells are used with 5G, this requires a proper backbone infrastructure—based on fiber[2], which is not available either in those rural areas (and may not for a very long time going forward)! So, all in all, there is an infrastructure problem!

Passing nice green meadows and approaching this small city, the large company building where 140 employees work comes in sight. The CEO opens the door and guides us to his office—nicely furnished with posh but oldish, green leather upholstered armchairs of dark brown wood. The CEO opens

(continued)

---

[1] Although reality may vary: compared to UMTS (3G) with some 42 Mbit/sec, 4G (LTE) with max. 500 Mbit/sec and 5G with up to 20 Gbit/sec (though, current implementation may be more around 1-2Gbit/sec), see https://www.5g-anbieter.info/speed/wie-schnell-ist-5g.html. (access 04.09.2020).

[2] https://blog.qsc.de/2019/05/ohne-glasfaser-infrastruktur-kein-5g-mobilfunk/. (access 04.09.2020).

straight away that he has not asked for that meeting; it was initiated on his nephew's request. Although this situation is probably suboptimal for a young startup, the question was posed to the CEO where he sees problems and areas to improve. He denied and claimed not having any problems. Such behavior triggered an alarm immediately: If a manager claims not having any issues, then that person may have one indeed. He disclosed—not without pride—some KPIs of his firm. As it happened to be, boot. AI had insights into another biochemical group that has digitized their supply chain from customer ordering process straight to the delivery of finished products at the customer site. That company can predict the most adequate raw materials supplier and track individual delivery units.

Reflecting these two realities shows that it requires more than technology to implement AI solutions: empathy! It starts off with talking to the affected and involved people and to understand their objectives (based on their values), their individual ways to achieve those, and their particular needs along. It is to show possible approaches from other (best) practices. This approach also opens new business opportunities as in that particular case, an IT (consultancy) giant who provides IT technology services to SMEs as well abstained for offering in that particular case, as the case was "too small" for them...

So, as boot.AI asked if at all some data are available throughout the supply chain, it turned out that on a very small level, though, there was an IT administrator, a server, and one machine with three sensors measuring filling levels, an odometer measuring velocity, and a temperature sensor.

Although this is not very comprehensive and conclusive, boot.AI offered to build within a few hours a very simple model using those sensor data in order to demonstrate what would be possible utilizing that in-process information for optimizing the flow toward the quality goals of the company. (Quality does not start at the end of a finished product! Well implemented, it is an intrinsic capability of an organization providing as much transparency as possible to spot problems early on and fixing them before an odd product reaches the finishing line.) In this particular case, it turned out that the raw material components had different temperatures when entering specific sections of the production process. Their temperature has an influence on the process quality downstream as they have temperature-dependent consistency (viscosities). So, within a few hours the possibilities of advancing the production quality just by measuring early on were demonstrated. The CEO was immediately impressed, and he asked what could be done if he would have more sensors, as he has heard that more modern machines have various sensors and provide such information. So far, he had a market overview on

(continued)

production machines from an efficiency (physical throughout) point of view, but did not encounter the added value on the information. He is used to take economic investment decisions like investing some €400,000 into a new machine as the better physical throughput will save him operational costs in a very short time; the business case pays off.

From the demonstration and analysis, it turned out that just 16 sensors would be required to establish the information flow to ensure timely interventions in the process. That would mean that the process would be highly automated, and the quality of the end product can be calculated.

The CEO's reaction was outraged, as this would be impossible. Why? "At this company site, 140 employees are employed, 40 of whom are dedicated solely to checking, testing the quality of the product at the end of the machine. Now you come along and say that if I have the 16 sensors, then I might not need these people anymore. That can't be true," he said.

The CEO and the entrepreneur then decided that proof for this thesis should be provided in a laboratory test setting. In other words, a small machine that, so to speak, reproduces the large machine was to be used to prove that the quality of the products produced could be predicted almost exactly. For half a year, this machine was actually loaded with different products and in the end an algorithm was developed which allowed to add arbitrary raw materials to the production process and to predict 99.9% of the product characteristics.

And that was a complete mind shift for the CEO: he said that 50% of all products produced in the first batch are defective. The company spends a lot of resources—time and money—on engineering to make sure the product is good again. If this were to be eliminated, the current activities could be monitored with only 2 remaining employees instead of 40.

The CEO immediately became aware of the scale and the economies of scale: 100 sites, 40 employees per site, reduced to 2 remaining employees each, represent an enormous potential. And the loss of 38 employees would be applicable just in one department of the entire company.

Here, it is important to note that there is not necessarily an automatism of decision-making: instead of just looking on the economic dimension of an opportunity (here cost cutting by laying off employees), there is the social dimension of sustainability as well that needs to be encountered in decision-making.

In the setting of this example: the company is the largest employer in that rural town, absorbing some 50% of totally available workforce. Laying off people on a large scale could mean that the entire site may go down the drain.

So, the CEO claimed that this new knowledge is a "weapon." He spotted two things immediately:

(continued)

The new approach can be scaled immediately: if he uses the sensor-equipped machines and feeds the algorithm, he would be able to roll this resource optimization across the entire group worldwide.

Currently, he has an advantage compared to his peer competitors, which he can utilize wisely. Given that the company is in a world-leading market position without immediate cost pressure, there are more options to utilize this advantage.

And that was when the CEO loosened the tie a little bit: He sat and swayed a little bit back and forth in his chair and he got a little grumpy when he said "but that also means that I can fire 38 people. Yeah, but what could I do, I could educate." But when asked whether he wants to turn trained biologists and chemists into computer scientists, he said that this was unlikely.

What else could they do? A list of approaches was compiled. The CEO saw one possibility in making concrete contributions to some of the 17 Sustainable Development Goals ["SDG" (UN 2020)] of the United Nations. Among them are the fight against poverty and hunger, gender equality, health promotion, education, responsible consumption, and production... Two of these goals were selected to work on these issues with the competitive advantage that the company currently has as a world leader. The CEO wants to use this advantage to build a new concept now with sustainability: In the meantime, his machines are at a standstill 1 day a week. The employees in the quality laboratory now only work 4 days a week (except for those who operate the machines) on the same salary—very courageous. He knows that he has no financial disadvantage; it just works more efficiently. And he is thinking about how this new mindset can also be transferred to society.

9.4   Consequences and Looking Forward

In general, society has to deal with the fact that work will be eliminated in the future through further automation, of which AI is a part. This is a very uncomfortable truth that many people do not want to hear. But if we look into the past, we will very quickly come across similar developments. So of course, the industrial revolutions (Perez 2002) are often cited in this context. What does it really mean, specifically for the human work. To illustrate the impact of technology, the changes in agriculture over the last 100 years shall be taken as an example (see Fig. 9.1): Apparently, many individual manual activities in arable farming, which was conducted in the early twentieth century, i.e., just 100 years ago by people and/or horses, have been entirely replaced by a continuous stream of increasing powerful machines such as 5%

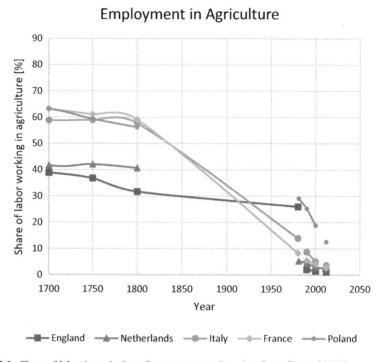

Fig. 9.1 Share of labor in agriculture [own representation, data from (Roser 2013)]

p.a. increase in tractor performance,[3] or combine harvesters to fully automatic harvesting robots for the tomato or asparagus harvest[4]. Also, in cattle breeding, automated feeding systems and milking machines up to fully automated milking systems are standard in the dairy industry of Western industrialized countries; milking of individual cows by hand is no longer economically relevant there. Accordingly, considerably less manpower is required per output unit.

Following the diesel scandal in 2015 and the significant increase in global warming and climate issue awareness, in some countries such as Norway electric mobility is already taking shape and is a de facto increasing reality. In 2019, 42% of all newly registered cars were e-cars, compared to 5.5% in 2013 (Krempl 2020). In 2019, the EU has at least prominently proclaimed the "Green Deal" (EU 2019). This challenge is facing changes that will in turn cost many jobs in traditional sectors such as the automotive industry.

---

[3] As an example: John Deer Model B from 1942 provided 20 hp. (kW), whereas Model 9620RX as of 2020 has 620 hp. (456 kW) which is factor 31 in 78 years or a CAGR of 5%. Source: https://www.oldtimerplus.de/inserate/traktoren/john_deere/99751, https://www.deere.de/de/traktoren/gro%C3%9Ftraktoren/serie-9r/9620rx/. (access 11.09.2020).

[4] https://www.hepcomotion.com/de/fallstudien/ernteroboter-koennte-gruenen-spargel-guenstiger-machen/. (access 09.09.2020).

Fig. 9.2 Human capabilities and automation (own presentation)

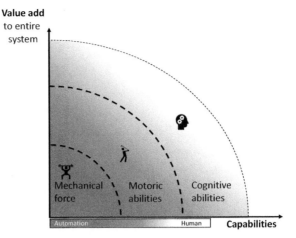

Thus, upheavals and their effect on the "human production factor" are neither new nor comfortable! However, in the past—i.e., before the information age—the substitution of human work by machines has mainly focused on physically and motor challenging activities. This meant that the compilation, analysis, and evaluation of information, which ultimately leads to knowledge, was largely reserved for human individuals or the societal collective. With the increasing sophistication of automats—3D printing comes to mind, for example—and the use of information processing machines such as Robot Process Automation (RPA; see Sect. 6.4.1 for more details) with impressive performance in the field of pattern recognition ("weak AI"), the limit is being pushed even further. Figure 9.2 illustrates this context of value-added versus specific capabilities.

Clearly, this has consequences on society: more and more people tend to go for cognitive jobs based on academic education rather than practical jobs based on apprenticeship. This can be illustrated with the example of Germany in the years 2009–2019: while the entire population increased slightly by 1.7% (CAGR 0.2%), the number of students increased by 37% (CAGR 3%), whereas the number of apprenticeships on the demand side decreased by 5% (CAGR −0.5%) under stable (CAGR −0.06%) supply (see Fig. 9.3) (BMBF 2020).

In the context of the entire population, the tertiary (academic) education contributes to less than 1/3 (30%), some 53% are with secondary (apprenticeship) education, and 17% without professional qualification (BMBF 2020). Very clearly, the educational standards are country dependent as consequences of their development stage and educational system. Whereas on a European level, on average 29% of the population received tertiary education [spread between as low as 17.1% (Italy) and 37.7% (Switzerland) (Eurostat 2019)], in the USA 66.2% basically twice as many high school graduates are enrolled in universities of colleges (US Bureau of Labor Statistics 2020).

Taking a broader view and the analysis shown, current challenges and resolution approaches can be concluded:

Students (millions)   Apprenticeships (millions)

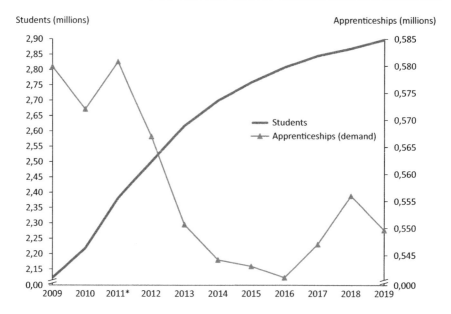

Fig. 9.3 Trend in students and apprenticeships development in Germany [own analysis based on data from (BMBF 2020)]

1. The likelihood that emerging AI technologies will evolve toward increasing sophistication—and with that replacing human routine jobs—is extremely high.
2. In many societies, even in so-called developed countries, only a minority enjoyed higher education standards that enable sustainable, high-demanding cognitive jobs in an age of AI.
3. AI development seems to emerge in a setting similar to the "Tragedy of the Commons": if anyone can do whatever is possible to exploit the technology, this will inevitably lead to a destruction of current societal structures (and jobs). Currently, it seems that everyone is running as fast as possible, though with different approaches, e.g.:
   (a) In the USA, the short-terminism on profit maximization of (a few successful) private corporations based on a neo-liberal democratic system, but the society as such does not benefit from it. The only (indirect) social effect is through voluntary philanthropy of a few mega-rich.
   (b) In China, maximizing the benefit (of the leading party) of the society to strengthen the dictatorship-like leading regime. The importance of AI can be assessed by looking into the excessive valuation of the AI startup in China[5]:

---

[5]The world's highest rated startup "Unicorn" with a valuation of $140 billion is ByteDance (with famous subsidiary TikTok, which led in September 2020 to heavy interventions from the US administration to block the services in the USA if not a significant governance share will be passed over to a US company. https://de.statista.com/infografik/7475/die-10-am-hoechsten-bewerteten-

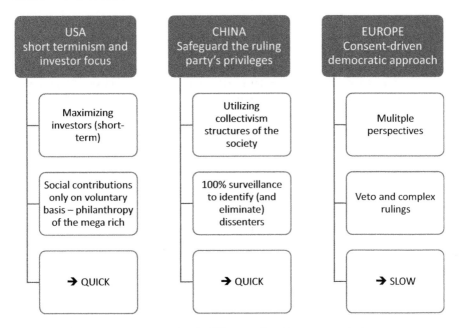

Fig. 9.4 AI implementation approaches in different regions (own presentation)

(c) In Europe, based on consensus and democratic structures, to foster a digital agenda, which inherently suffers from decision delays within the political process, though with the advantage of multiple perspectives. With the experiences from the "General Data Protection Rule" [GDPR (EU 2018)], Europe has demonstrated a leadership position in data access and usage. Although this merely requires significant restrictions of potential technical usage, this initiative sets a worldwide unparalleled standard that respects the ethical and digital dignity of individuals and the society. This leading position in that field may be a nucleus to reach out to further regions as it provides a framework of trust (Fig. 9.4).

4. The lead time of increasing the education level does not correspond to the rapid advancements in AI.
5. (Governmental) programs on advancement in digitization (including AI) and fostering (higher) education both are required, but neither are enough.
6. A fundamental shift in mindset is required for.
   (a) Scientists to sensitize politicians on the spillover effects of AI exploitation, similar as responsible scientists have done in the 1940s and 1950s with the nuclear potential and threats such as the atomic and hydrogen bomb.

---

einhoerner/ (access 04.09.2020) Apparently, Oracle Inc. is to acquire such share in TikTok (Status: Sept. 2020).

(b) Political and economic decision-makers to resist exploiting technology potential for their own benefit without reflecting the spillover effects on societies.

(c) Consumer to restrain from carelessness and apply prudent judgment on (purchasing) decisions similar to what an increasing number of consumers practice in organic food consumption.

7. Key assets in the "open" digital world such as open access software is a cornerstone of the digital evolution. As proven by many occasions throughout the last few decades, proprietary approaches deem to block innovation. As an example, since its introduction in 1991, the operating system LINUX (Netmarketshare 2020) has emerged as platform for millions of (business) servers and desktop computers, and provided the nucleus ("kernel") for the open source mobile operation system Android, which was launched in 2007 that has replaced and outpaced the up-to-then dominating Nokia's proprietary Symbian OS and Microsoft's Mobile Windows). While these achievements are impressive in the open software development, that is characterized by many of intrinsically motivated developers who are driving for better solutions and their own mastery. The ultimate access to the heart (the "kernel") of these technologies lies with some individuals—with the so-called Benevolent Dictators for Life (who deemed to be intrinsically motivated)—such as the initiator of Linux, Linus Thorvald, taking a coordinating role in the further development of the kernel. Astonishingly enough, this loose structure seems to work out quite well). Otherwise, fragmentations on a large scale would be the consequence. For AI algorithms and approaches, a commonly accepted framework could be built up—similar to the data protection framework in the GDPR—to provide fair access to resources and to offer security of investment (i.e., a sound foundation for the individual investments based on fair and stable access to basic intellectual property). Europe may play a leading role here.

9.5   Finish Line Quiz

9.01	What are the key factors to make AI fit?	
	1	Algorithms, data.
	2	Algorithms, processes.
	3	Algorithms, data, processes.
	4	Data, processes.
9.02	What AI approach can be taken in case of missing (data)infrastructure?	
	1	Data-driven vs. process-driven.
	2	Process-driven approach.
	3	Big data-driven approach.
	4	Deep learning approaches.

(continued)

9.03	Why is empathy required in introducing AI solutions?	
	1	Understanding the values of individuals involved is important.
	2	Empathy is not required at all; it is a decision based on technological facts.
	3	It enables to generate trust and to find ethical acceptable solutions.
	4	Answer 1 and 3.
9.04	What ethical opportunity was derived from the implementation of the AI solution within the example of the biochemical producer?	
	1	Higher efficiency generated opened up new decision opportunities.
	2	Generating added value from efficiency gains instead of purely monetizing (in the short term) on those gains.
	3	Use of the efficiency advantage for giving back to the society.
	4	All of the above.
9.05	Higher education is key to cope with increasing requirements on employability in the AI era. What is the difference between the EU (~% of the population receiving tertiary education) and the USA (~% high school graduates enrolling in universities) in that regard?	
	1	EU 30%/USA 60%
	2	EU 30%/USA 30%
	3	EU 60%/USA 30%
	4	EU 60%/USA 60%
9.06	What are the differences in AI implementation approaches per region?	
	1	USA-short-terminism China-investor focus Europe-consent driven
	2	USA-short-terminism China-safeguarding ruling party's privileges Europe-democratic process
	3	USA-short-terminism China-consent driven Europe-investor focus
	4	USA-democratic approach China-investor focus Europe-consent driven
9.07	What is the resulting AI implementation speed per region?	
	1	USA-quick, China-quick, EU-slow
	2	USA-quick, China-slow, EU-slow
	3	USA-quick, China-quick, EU-quick
	4	USA-quick, China-slow, EU-quick

Correct answers can be found in www.vieweg-beratung.de/downloads

References

BMBF. (2020). *Bildung und KulturSchnellmeldungsergebnisse der Hochschulstatistikzu Studierenden und Studienanfänger/-innen – vorläufige Ergebnisse.* Retrieved September 11, 2020, from https://www.bmbf.de/files/BBB%202020%20final%20ohne%20Vorwort_

Sperrfrist%2006-05-2020%2010.15%20Uhr_.pdf, https://www-genesis.destatis.de/genesis/online, Schnellmeldungsergebnisse der Hochschulstatistik zu Studierenden und Studienanfänger/-innen, Vorläufige Ergebnisse, Wintersemester 2019/2020, Seite 11.

EU. (2018). *Complete guide to GDPR compliance*. Retrieved September 22, 2020, from www.GDPR.EU.

EU. (2019). *A European Green Deal. Striving to be the first climate-neutral continent*. Retrieved September 9, 2020, from https://ec.europa.eu/info/strategy/priorities-2019-2024/european-green-deal_en.

Eurostat 2018 in Bpb. (2019). *Bevölkerung nach Bildungsstand*. Retrieved September 11, 2020, from https://www.bpb.de/nachschlagen/zahlen-und-fakten/europa/135810/bevoelkerung-nach-bildungsstand.

Krempl, S. (2020). *Norwegen – Fast die Hälfte der neuen Autos fährt elektrisch*. Heise-Newsticker. Retrieved September 11, 2020, from https://www.heise.de/newsticker/meldung/Norwegen-Fast-die-Haelfte-der-neuen-Autos-faehrt-elektrisch-4628039.html.

Netmarketshare. (2020). *Linus market share*. Retrieved September 22, 2020, from https://netmarketshare.com/linux-market-share?options=%7B%22filter%22%3A%7B%22%24and%22%3A%5B%7B%22deviceType%22%3A%7B%22%24in%22%3A%5B%22Desktop%2Flaptop%22%5D%7D%7D%5D%7D%2C%22dateLabel%22%3A%22Trend%22%2C%22attributes%22%3A%22share%22%2C%22group%22%3A%22platform%22%2C%22sort%22%3A%7B%22share%22%3A-1%7D%2C%22plotKeys%22%3A%5B%7B%22platform%22%3A%22Linux%22%7D%5D%2C%22id%22%3A%22linux%22%2C%22dateInterval%22%3A%22Monthly%22%2C%22dateStart%22%3A%222019-09%22%2C%22dateEnd%22%3A%222020-08%22%2C%22segments%22%3A%22-1000%22%7D.

Perez, C. (2002). *Technological revolutions and financial capital*.

Roser, M. (2013). *Employment in agriculture*. Published online at OurWorldInData.org. Retrieved September 10, 2020, from 'https://ourworldindata.org/employment-in-agriculture'.

Tsvasman, L., & Schild, F. (2019). *AI-Thinking: Dialog eines Vordenkers und eines Praktikers über die Bedeutung künstlicher Intelligenz*. Ergon, Herausgeber.

U.S. Bureau of Labor Statistics. (2020). *College enrollment and work activity of recent high school and college graduates summary*. Retrieved September 11, 2020, from https://www.bls.gov/news.release/hsgec.nr0.htm.

UN. (2020). *Sustainable development goals*. Retrieved August 2, 2020, from https://www.un.org/sustainabledevelopment/sustainable-development-goals/.

Will, M. (2018). *Zahlen, bitte! Die Apollo-Mission mit 32 Kilo Bit – einmal Mond und zurück*. Retrieved October 2, 2020, from https://www.heise.de/newsticker/meldung/Zahlen-bitte-Die-Apollo-Mission-mit-32-Kilo-Bit-einmal-Mond-und-zurueck-4108382.html?hg=2&hgi=12&hgf=false.

Yes, AI Can: The Artificial Intelligence Gold Rush Between Optimistic HR Software Providers, Skeptical HR Managers, and Corporate Ethical Virtues

10

Matthias Groß

Learning Objectives

1. Identify the general potential and shortcomings for AI technologies in the context of HRM.
2. Utilizing the task technology fit theory, learn about eleven HRM-related functions that can be supported and automated by use of AI technology.
3. Analyze the status of utilization of AI technology—depending on the degree of digitization.
4. Analyze the legal boundaries in utilizing AI technologies for HRM-related functions in jurisdictions under tight data protection regulations such as Germany with the GDPR (DSGVO).
5. Elaborate on the skill set required for HR managers working in an AI-supported environment.
6. Reflect the ethical aspects of AI usage in HRM based on the corporate ethic virtues model.

10.1 Practical and Scientific Relevance of AI in HRM

The gold rush of artificial intelligence (AI) has begun and has captured the imagination of many HR managers. What would happen if application robots were to identify the true high potentials from thousands of candidates in milliseconds (see the examples in Sect. 7.5)? Or if algorithms were able to recognize the intention of the most important high performers to resign at an early stage? And that 24/7 without signs of fatigue, sick leave, or careless mistakes. These and similar dreams (and partially realities) really cost companies something, as the results of the market research institute Tractica impressively demonstrate. While in 2016, worldwide sales of 3.2 billion US dollars were recorded with enterprise applications in the field of AI,

M. Groß (✉)
Technische Hochschule Mittelhessen, Campus Giessen, Gießen, Germany
e-mail: matthias.gross@w.thm.de

© The Author(s), under exclusive license to Springer Nature Switzerland AG 2021
S. H. Vieweg (ed.), *AI for the Good*, Management for Professionals,
https://doi.org/10.1007/978-3-030-66913-3_10

this figure had already risen to 7.3 billion US dollars by 2018. In 2020, sales of around 17.3 billion US dollars are expected, and for 2025, the forecast for the market potential of AI is as high as 90 billion US dollars (Tractica 2018). Despite this dynamic market development and the knowledge of AI potential, HR managers are still very cautious even today (see the empirical results in 10.3.2).

While software providers advertise the superhuman AI potential in all HRM areas and HR managers dream of far-reaching AI solutions at future conferences, theory and practice often diverge widely. In everyday corporate life, most HR managers—especially those of German companies—already regard the creation of an AI-affine environment as a major challenge and are rather skeptical about the implementation of AI applications. A lack of technological competence and numerous legal hurdles then cause this future perspective to disappear completely, although there is widespread agreement that AI can take over repetitive HRM tasks, and thus give HR managers more freedom to deal with strategic issues. For example, digital language assistants (chatbots) can "work through" frequently asked questions about vacation entitlements and speech processing algorithms (text mining) can carry out the preselection of cover letters. With its recruiting software "IBM Watson Recruiting," the software provider IBM offers, among other things, the possibility to compare data from incoming applicant documents with the analysis of historical company data. Furthermore, AI tools in the context of recruitment should be able to help to make better decisions in candidate selection by objectifying cognitive biases (e.g., primacy or recency bias) or personal sympathies. In this context, the software company Precire offers an AI solution that uses voice data within a telephone interview to draw conclusions about a candidate's personality, which in turn is intended to increase the candidate's job requirement fit (Dahm and Dregger 2019); further examples were shown in Sect. 7.5.

But beauty is only skin deep. In concrete terms, from a practical business point of view, it can be said, following Thorsten Dirks (currently a member of the Deutsche Lufthansa Board of Management): "If you digitize a shitty process, then you have a shitty digital process." The use of AI is therefore only recommended if the existing analog HR processes are efficient, value creating, in line with the strategy, legal, and non-discriminatory. A much-cited example of the dangers of the digitalization mania of analog HRM tasks is the AI-based application robot developed by the US online mail order company Amazon in 2014 (see Sect. 6.6). This discriminates against women and people with non-white skin color, which is why it has already been retired. But why did the software discriminate against these groups of people, when the software is supposed to be much more objective than human judgment? Very simple: The application robot examined the received applications with a view to an advertised job according to predefined criteria. The underlying training data from the company's history preferred white male candidates—and so did the application robot. This example of discrimination shows that AI applications are not good or bad per se, but always an image of the people (including their settings) who program the applications. From an ethical and data protection perspective, the question for HR managers is therefore how AI applications can be used legally and legitimately. In order to support HR managers in creating an AI-affine environment, this chapter deals with ethical and privacy implications and explores measures to increase the perceived usefulness and usability of HRM-related AI applications.

The ethical and data protection-compliant use of AI applications can not only relieve HR managers of routine tasks, but also strengthen their strategic position within the company. According to the advertising promises of software providers, there are hardly any limits to the use of AI solutions in HRM systems beyond recruitment. Among other things, it is postulated that with the help of predictive analytics software, numerous factors influencing the development of different future scenarios can be taken into account in personnel requirements planning, thus making an important contribution to the optimization of personnel budgeting. In the context of personnel development, it is praised that demand planning can be optimized using AI by assigning suitable training to required skills using a self-learning system based on existing skills and training catalogs (Groß and Dorozalla 2020). AI should also be able to improve the recognition of high performers and to enhance the identification of employees who are suitable for a management career. And, of course, it is now considered good manners to mention in a contribution to AI solutions in HRM that AI can identify so-called likely leaver profiles (i.e., employees who intend to resign) and thus enable early preventive interventions with top performers. While these examples in numerous consultant blog posts and HR vendor webinars romanticize the brave new world of strategic HRM, the reality in most (at least German) companies looks completely different. The majority of those responsible for HRM—primarily in small and medium-sized enterprises (SMEs)—are already "struggling" with the creation of extended reports on key personnel figures, not to mention the strategic use of HR analytics (i.e., the statistical analysis of HRM-related data for evidence-based decision-making). While other business areas (e.g., marketing) already use self-detecting analytics by means of machine learning and decision automation based on it (e.g., for individualized online advertising), HRM often lags behind. Analogous data worlds, isolated IT solutions, a lack of technological competence, and ducking behind legal restrictions often leave HR managers helpless. In order to sensitize HR managers to the potential of AI, the primary goal of this chapter is to systematize the integration possibilities of artificial and human intelligence along HRM systems. In concrete terms, it is intended to offer starting points for the strategic use of AI, which also outline the necessary technological requirements in their basic features.

The fact that the HR department is usually lagging behind in the use of AI compared to other areas of the company is mainly because many HR managers fear that they do not have the necessary technological skills. They are also concerned that they could degenerate into an extended arm of the controlling department in the context of evidence-driven corporate management, or even become completely replaceable. However, waiting in embryonic position until they have rationalized their own way is not a desirable option at this point; instead, the competencies of HR managers should be put to the test. Whereas until now they have been primarily responsible for personnel administration, staff motivation and development, and process management, in the future, HR managers will be increasingly called upon to make strategic value contributions with the help of digital applications. This chapter highlights the specific skills that HR managers of the future will need in order not to be replaced by codes and algorithms.

While in practice skeptical HR managers and optimistic software vendors face each other, there is hardly any empirically proven knowledge in science about the use of AI applications in the HR sector. However, the general interest in the topic of AI seems to be growing from a scientific point of view, which is illustrated by a doubling of publications (from 470,998 to 948,901) on the scientific database EBSCO Discovery Service in the period from 2015 to 2020. On closer inspection, however, it can be seen that these publications are predominantly of a theoretical and conceptual nature and provide only limited empirical evidence for HR managers. The first serious empirical studies in the area of HRM focus primarily on the acceptance by AI users (e.g., Dahm and Dregger 2019; Grotenhermen et al. 2020), but there is no reliable evidence regarding the current penetration at least in German companies. Furthermore, there are hardly any conclusive findings regarding the creation of conducive framework conditions for AI applications in HRM. In addition, the number of consultant and software vendor studies is increasing, which approve the high potential of AI solutions in all areas of a company, but largely ignore concrete areas of application in HRM and their effectiveness in achieving success. All in all, it can be stated that the research discourse has only just begun. From a scientific point of view, the main goal of this chapter is to synthesize the knowledge from existing theoretical contributions or empirical studies on AI application areas in the field of HRM and to compare it with the results of my own empirical study on the status quo in German companies. Based on the task technology fit theory, a conceptual framework for the influencing factors and success effects of AI solutions in HRM will be developed. In summary, the following overarching research question arises for this chapter:

> What added value can be generated by the use of AI solutions in human resource management?

In order to answer this research question, the key questions shown in Fig. 10.1 (own presentation) are examined in this chapter:

To answer the key questions in Fig. 10.1, the present contribution is structured as follows: After the introduction in Sects. 10.1 and 10.2 describes the conceptual understanding, basic functionalities, and potential added values of AI. Using this theoretical basis, Sect. 10.3 specifies a conceptual framework for the effectiveness of HRM-related AI applications, considering the task technology fit theory. Based on this framework and current literature, Sect. 10.3.1 shows concrete AI application areas in HRM. In Sect. 10.3.2, a theory–practice comparison of the described fields of application in German enterprises is carried out by means of my own empirical data. Sect. 10.4 derives from the results of Sect. 10.3 a framework that is conducive to AI-based HRM. The chapter is rounded off by the illumination of the required competencies of the HR manager of the future in Sects. 10.5 and 10.6 concludes with an outlook for future research and derives scientific implications.

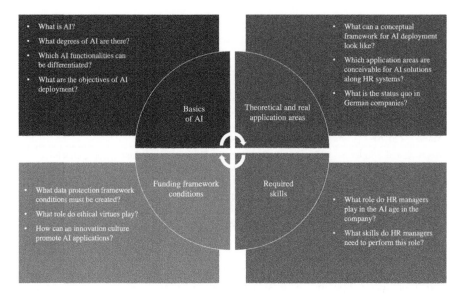

Fig. 10.1 Guiding questions (own presentation)

10.2 AI Concept and Functionalities

The term artificial intelligence electrifies. But what is AI anyway? While the attribute *artificial* usually arouses negative associations or even fears in the sense of non-natural processes, the noun *intelligence* has always fascinated us. Despite numerous publications on the AI hype, there is no coherent definition. Instead, most authors use individual conceptual understandings. Basically, as already shown in Sect. 6.5, AI is a subdiscipline of computer science that aims to equip machines with capabilities that resemble intelligent (human) behavior (Kaplan and Haenlein 2019). Following Richter et al. (2019), Table 10.1 lists selected frequently cited definitions chronologically.

Etymologically, the term AI goes back to the US-American computer scientist John McCarthy, who in 1955 invited researchers from various disciplines to a workshop entitled "Dartmouth Summer Research Project on Artificial Intelligence." Since then, a multitude of different definitions have found their way into the research discourse. The common denominator of these definitions is that this is a scientific field of research in which human intelligence is to be imitated by means of a computer. Narrow definitions focus primarily on structural or behavioral analogies to natural intelligence, i.e., an intelligent technology is structured and/or behaves like a natural intelligent system (cf. Thurstone 1999). Broader definitions focus on functional or capability-based analogies to natural intelligence, i.e., technology performs certain functions and/or has certain capabilities of natural intelligent systems (cf. Heinrich and Stühler 2018). In this chapter, the broad understanding

Table 10.1 Selected AI definitions (own presentation)

McCarthy et al. (1955)	The science and engineering of making intelligent machines, especially intelligent computer programs.
Rich (1986)	Artificial intelligence is the study of how to make computers do things at which, at the moment, people are better.
Thurstone (1999)	To build artifacts—computer programs or robots—that can fulfill human-made goals in a rational and human-like and thus comprehensible way.
Mainzer (2016)	Simulation of intelligent human thinking.
Heinrich and Stühler (2018)	AI generally describes the ability of a machine to independently interpret, solve, and learn from complex problems.
Hagstrom and Maranzan (2019)	Artificial intelligence (AI) refers to the theory and development of computer systems able to perform tasks that normally require human intelligence, such as visual perception, speech recognition, decision-making, and translation between languages.

of the term is followed in order to derive AI functionalities and underlying technological processes. Specifically, this contribution refers to the often-cited definition of Rich (1986). In HRM, AI describes the field of research how to make computers do things where the HR managers are (currently) better. This understanding of the term considers the special strength of human intelligence that humans are able to adapt dynamically to changing conditions by learning (adaptivity). Due to this ability to learn, humans are currently superior to computers, but this is likely to change in the future.

What degrees of AI can be distinguished? The degree of artificial intelligence can be evaluated according to different criteria. In scientific research, the differentiation according to the (1) degree of strength and (2) decision-making competence has proven to be common. (1) Artificial intelligence is basically divided into strong and weak AI. While weak artificial intelligence already reaches or surpasses human intelligence in defined sub-areas, strong artificial intelligence would be at least on the same level as the human brain in all areas. In the scientific and philosophical discussion, some systems are referred to as weak artificial intelligence, which only appear to be intelligent, but behind which there is no artificial intelligence in the strict sense. In the majority of cases, these are purely rule-based systems. Weak artificial intelligence is already used in many areas of everyday life. Some examples are character or text recognition, image recognition, speech recognition, individual control of advertising, or automated translation. A strong artificial intelligence, by contrast, no longer acts only reactively, but also on its own initiative, intelligently and flexibly. As of today, it has not yet been possible to develop strong artificial intelligence. And the discussion about whether the development of such intelligence is even possible continues. Despite all speculation and uncertainty, there is already a fundamental consensus among most researchers and scientists that strong intelligence must have the following characteristics to be considered as such: logical reasoning ability, decision-making ability even in the face of uncertainty, planning and learning ability, ability to communicate in natural language, and combining all

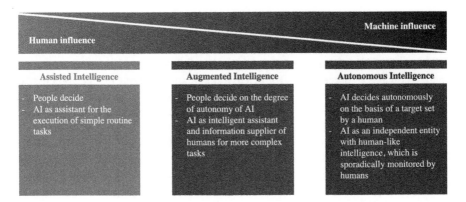

Assisted Intelligence	Augmented Intelligence	Autonomous Intelligence
- People decide - AI as assistant for the execution of simple routine tasks	- People decide on the degree of autonomy of AI - AI as intelligent assistant and information supplier of humans for more complex tasks	- AI decides autonomously on the basis of a target set by a human - AI as an independent entity with human-like intelligence, which is sporadically monitored by humans

Fig. 10.2 Decision-making powers of man and machine in assisted intelligence, augmented intelligence, and autonomous intelligence [own representation based on (Grotenhermen et al. 2020)]

abilities to achieve an overall goal. However, the question of whether strong AI can attain a consciousness of its own and what role empathy, self-knowledge, memory, and wisdom play in connection with the abovementioned qualities remains open. With regard to the strength of AI, the focus of this chapter is accordingly on weak AI.

(2) The progress in the learning ability of computers requires a deeper examination of the decision-making powers between man and machine. In the literature, a distinction is often made between three degrees of AI (Grotenhermen et al. 2020): assisted intelligence, augmented intelligence, and autonomous intelligence (see Fig. 10.2). Assisted intelligence describes the automation of simple tasks to save costs and time. Augmented intelligence describes the hand-in-hand work of human and artificial intelligence, where AI learns from human inputs and the human being benefits from a better decision basis. Autonomous intelligence represents the most advanced level of AI. Here, the machine makes decisions autonomously; the human being has—if at all—a monitoring function. Due to numerous legal restrictions (e.g., Article 22 DSGVO, the German realization of the GDPR), which demand the final decision of the human being, as well as ethical reservations, completely autonomous systems in the sense of autonomous intelligence are currently only conditionally conceivable in Germany. The use of AI in Germany is therefore primarily about the teamwork of man and machine. Assisted and augmented types of intelligence are therefore of particular interest. Assisted intelligence applications can relieve HR managers of routine tasks, freeing them up for strategic tasks, while augmented intelligence solutions are an important building block on the path to evidence-based HRM. Figure 10.2 summarizes the different decision-making powers of man and machine.

Which functionalities make AI a vicarious agent or intelligent assistant of HR managers? In order to specify the functionalities, I will refer in the following to the statements of Strohmeier and Piazza (2015), who have already conceptually dealt with the use of AI in personnel management. Based on a broad understanding of the term, which focuses on functional or skill-oriented analogies to human intelligence, (1) knowledge, (2) thinking, and (3) language represent elementary cognitive abilities that can be represented by different AI technologies. (1) Knowledge is distinguished into three facets: knowledge generation, knowledge representation, and knowledge processing. Knowledge generation refers to the process of identifying new, potentially useful, and valid information in data (e.g., pattern recognition). A wide range of applications is available for this purpose [e.g., classification, association, segmentation, and prediction techniques (Wu et al. 2008)]. Knowledge representation serves the formal representation of knowledge in a computer. Technical methods of knowledge representation (e.g., semantic networks and ontologies) are used, for example, in machine translation programs, in the construction of expert systems, and in database query programs (Tanwar et al. 2010). Knowledge processing makes use of knowledge represented in a computer to produce new knowledge. In this context, the scientific methods of abduction, deduction, and induction are applied (Reichertz 2003). (2) Thinking is defined as the search for solutions (of optimization problems). For the reproduction of thinking processes the A* search algorithm, the mountaineering algorithms, the particle swarm optimization, as well as genetic algorithms are proposed [e.g., (Kahraman et al. 2011; Strohmeier and Piazza 2015)]. (3) Language is divided into text and speech processing. Text processing techniques aim at supporting tasks (e.g., topic extraction) related to written language in an automated way. For this purpose, a number of word processing techniques are available (e.g., named-entity recognition; Popovski et al. 2020). Speech processing techniques focus on tasks related to spoken language. Special attention is given to automatic speech recognition and speech synthesis (e.g., hidden Markov model; Mustafa et al. 2019). The functionalities outlined in this paragraph form the technological framework for the specification of the application fields of AI in HRM in Sect. 10.3.

What goals are usually associated with the use of AI? According to Wilson and Daughtery (2018), five different objectives are pursued in the context of business process optimization: (1) flexibility, (2) speed, (3) scalability, (4) decision optimization, and (5) customization. In the course of digital transformation, HR processes must be aligned with these five objectives. In Sect. 10.3, these are incorporated into the conceptual framework as dependent variables (see Fig. 10.3).

10.3   AI in HRM

AI will fundamentally change the way people work. This transformation is taking place on two levels: first- and second-order change (Roedenbeck 2020). First-order change refers to the use of AI by the target group of HRM—the workforce. Thus, HRM has to equip executives or employees with the technological competencies required for the use of AI along the value chain—this applies to both recruitment and personnel development. In addition, when planning medium- and long-term personnel requirements, HR managers must keep in mind the rationalization potential of AI, which essentially arises in routine tasks. In this respect, first-order change can

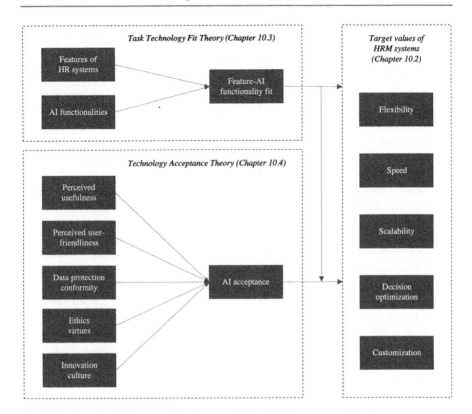

Fig. 10.3 Conceptual framework for the use of AI in HRM (own presentation)

also affect personnel layoffs. At this point, it can be stated that it is not so much complete occupational fields that will disappear, but rather that areas of competence will shift—which brings personnel development back into focus (Stock-Homburg and Groß 2019).

Second-order change refers to human resource management itself. For example, many processes that are currently "manual" in nature could be executed or supported by AI. According to the relevant literature, the use of AI could not only unfold high potential for efficiency and effectiveness, but also achieve a gain in quality (Roedenbeck 2020). With regard to the quality gain, several meta-studies induce that the decision quality of algorithms is generally higher than that of expert judgements (e.g., in promotion decisions or performance evaluations; Biemann and Weckmüller 2016; Strohmeier 2020). In practice, this empirical finding tends to be counterbalanced by a rather low level of acceptance of AI solutions by users or HR managers, especially in relevant personnel decisions (e.g., selection and remuneration; Dahm and Dregger 2019; Grotenhermen et al. 2020). In order to resolve this contradiction, this chapter will first outline areas of application for the use of AI in HRM on the basis of the task technology fit theory and then analyze the status quo in German companies using its own empirical data.

Based on Sect. 10.2, especially the described functionalities of AI, this chapter explores application areas of AI in HRM. The theoretical framework for the following explanations is the task technology fit theory. The theory developed by Goodhue and Thompson (1995) states that a better fit between task characteristics and system properties leads to higher performance. Based on this assumption, it is necessary to examine areas of application regarding the best possible fit of HRM features and AI functionalities. While the AI functionalities as well as potential targets have already been specified in Sect. 10.2, the next step is to operationalize the task characteristics of human resource management systems. In this context, the categorization of Stock-Homburg and Groß (2019), which differentiates HRM systems into employee flow and reward systems, will be used. The employee flow systems map the life cycle of employees in a company and accordingly include personnel requirements planning, recruitment, development, and release. For ethical reasons, we refrain from illuminating the AI deployment options in the context of personnel release. The reward systems include the structured assessment of employees and the creation of performance-related incentives for managers and employees. With reference to Groß and Dorozalla (2020), employee self-service is considered as a characteristic of personnel administration in addition to the employee flow and reward systems. The 11 selected task characteristics from the HRM systems shown above are described in detail in Sect. 10.3.1 and are linked to the AI functionalities (see Sect. 10.2) in an overview in Fig. 10.2. Based on this, Sect. 10.3.2 compares theory and practice for German companies.

Due to the multitude of HRM activities and AI functionalities, there is an almost infinite number of conceivable task technology combinations. The associated exploration task goes far beyond the scope of this chapter, which is why a conscious selection is made in the following. Following Strohmeier and Piazza (2015), two selection criteria will be applied: First, both the broad spectrum of AI functionalities and the broad spectrum of task characteristics of HRM will be covered as far as possible. Secondly, "mature" fields of application (i.e., those AI applications that are already used in practice at least occasionally) should be preferred to "futuristic" scenarios with uncertain practical feasibility. As shown in Fig. 10.3, it is assumed that a higher feature-AI functionality fit leads to an increase in flexibility, speed, scalability, decision optimization, and customization of HRM activities.

10.3.1 Application Areas of AI Along the HRM Systems

In the area of personnel requirements planning, the focus is on the development of predictive systems. Relevant forecasts mainly relate to (1) gross or net requirements, (2) absences from work, and (3) intentions to terminate employment. Predictive systems can be programmed on the basis of artificial neural networks (ANN) (Roedenbeck 2020). ANN are information-processing systems consisting of a certain number of information-processing units (neurons) containing mathematical functions and connected by directed and weighted links (Pérez-Campdesuñer et al. 2018). ANN represent a category of knowledge generation that is capable of solving clustering, classification, estimation, and prediction tasks (Strohmeier and Piazza 2015), which is why these neural networks are predestined for the prediction of gross or net demand, absenteeism, and termination intentions (see Fig. 10.4). While the programming logic is identical for the three applications mentioned above, the required input factors as well as the analysis objects to be considered differ.

1. For the *forecast of medium-term personnel requirements*, the recruitment figures, incoming orders, fluctuation rates, and staff turnover rates of recent years can be used as an internal data basis. These can be supplemented by external data (e.g., unemployment rate, industry indicators) to increase the predictive power. The same parameters are used as output data, but only those of the current period are under review. If the neural network is trained with these data, the personnel requirements for different time intervals or scenarios can be derived (Roedenbeck 2020). So that the forecasts do not get lost in detail on individual functions, a grouping in job families is useful. By considering job families that are critical to success, transfer and synergy potential can also be identified (Libuda and Fleischmann 2018).

2. In addition to medium-term gross and net personnel requirements planning, operational resource planning plays an important role. The *forecast of absenteeism* can significantly facilitate short-term planning work, which is why numerous studies on predictor variables have been conducted in the scientific community. In summary, social, individual, and organizational factors show a high predictive power. These include leadership behavior, company support, stress at work, personal work attitude, team cohesion, and corporate culture (Kangas et al. 2017). Furthermore, it is postulated that demographic characteristics provide information about health-related absences. Leao et al. (2017), for example, use a data sample of 18,450 employees to show that gender, age, educational background, industry, and type of employment (full-time vs. part-time) are reliable predictors of absenteeism. Furthermore, it has been empirically proven that the absenteeism behavior of employees in the past can be used to predict future absenteeism (Ivancevich 1985). For example, sick leave around weekends and holidays can be used to predict future absenteeism in relation to comparable calendar events. In addition, weather data and special events (e.g., carnival) can be used as relevant prognosis indicators for absenteeism. All these outlined predictor variables can be used as input variables for the absenteeism prognosis when programming an ANN. The output variables can be modeled as a classification task: "yes" or "no" forms the classes with respect to absenteeism at a certain point in time. For ethical or data protection reasons, the forecasts made at the individual level should be condensed to the departmental or divisional level. In this context, it is conceivable to extend the predictive AI by prescriptive skills. For example, forecasted absenteeism could be reported directly to temporary employment agencies in the form of demand notifications, or newly incoming vacation requests could be put to the test (Groß and Dorozalla 2020).

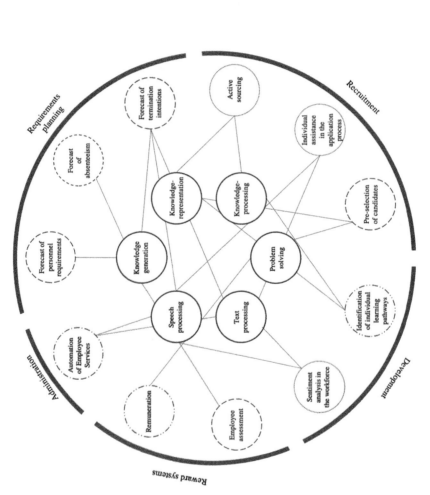

Fig. 10.4 Matching of AI functionalities and selected HRM tasks (own presentation)

3. The *forecast of termination intentions* has always been one of the favorite fantasies of HR managers. Although legally and ethically controversial, such an early warning system could make HR work much easier and realize visible or invisible cost savings. Specifically, HR managers could develop targeted interventions to counteract the dismissal of top performers. Accordingly, numerous studies have dealt with the identification of predictor variables for employee turnover. The most important categories include—as with absenteeism prediction—variables at the organizational and individual level. At the organizational level, it is especially the satisfaction with the management, the opportunity for individual development, the informative communication of the management, the fairness in personnel assessment, the sense of justice in payment, and an appreciative corporate culture that counteracts the intention to dismiss (Chang et al. 2013). On an individual job level, the so-called job characteristics according to Hackman and Oldman (autonomy, feedback, variety of requirements, importance of tasks, holistic approach) are of particular importance. It is assumed that these job characteristics result in significant psychological states (e.g., self-efficacy, sense of meaning, commitment), which in turn affect the intention to quit (Slattery et al. 2010). In addition, socio-demographic factors are also relevant in this context. For example, the study by Pérez-Campdesuñer and colleagues (Pérez-Campdesuñer et al. 2018) shows that average income, educational level, and age have a significant influence on the intention to terminate a contract. The organizational, individual, and demographic factors shown serve as input variables for the ANN to be programmed. In analogy to the forecast of absenteeism, the output is shown in binary. Naturally, the analysis of the intention to quit only makes sense on an individual level. While the application maturity seems to be already proven from a technical point of view (Ekawati 2019), ethical and data protection issues currently prevent the use of this predictive AI solution in Germany. Therefore, it seems worthwhile to consider an aggregated termination forecast for the relevant business areas in order to be able to react flexibly to the upcoming waves of terminations.
   In the area of recruitment, further fields of application for AI are opening up. For example, the (4) active sourcing, (5) application, and (6) selection process can be supported.
4. In the *(digital) active sourcing process*, companies are often faced with the challenge that the terminology used by the company and the applicants is different. On web-based job portals, for example, different terms are often used to describe qualifications, skills, or positions. Classic full-text search engines that search a specific area or the entire Internet for documents or resources based on specific words or phrases and output them in a listing often reach their limits when matching providers and applicants due to heterogeneous terminology. A semantic knowledge network can provide a remedy in this context. Semantic knowledge networks represent content as a network of terms, logical term relationships, and diverse term designations and are to be assigned to knowledge representation as a subfield of AI Arena et al. (2018);

(see also Fig. 10.4). With this functionality digitized knowledge can be exchanged across applications and platforms. For example, in contrast to a classical full-text search, a semantic knowledge network is able to link the terms "production manager" in a job advertisement and "line manager" in a professional network as matching search result. Semantic search algorithms, however, must first acquire the background knowledge of job titles, functions, and competence descriptions, i.e., they must be trained. Often semantic networks are implemented as ANN and linked with a curiosity learning function to track down candidates internally and externally (Roedenbeck 2020). Curiosity networks identify the desired competencies of a job advertisement and compare them with the CVs of employees and candidates in the applicant pool to generate proposals. Further developed systems also include external CV databases (e.g., professional networks such as XING in Germany or LinkedIn). The partial automation of the search task by means of semantic knowledge networks in combination with machine learning processes can significantly accelerate the finding of suitable candidates (Kulkarni and Che 2019).

5. AI also offers efficiency potential during the application process in the form of *assistance services*. In particular text- and/or language-based dialog systems (chat bots) are used. These can answer questions from applicants 24/7 and assist them in real time during the application process. While simple chatbots use a database of information and ready-made answers in the sense of a full-text search to answer simple questions of applicants, semi-autonomous chatbots based on machine learning can also provide intelligent answers to complex questions and act as virtual personal assistants (Kowald and Bruns 2019). In the following, the application possibilities of AI-based chatbots along the application process will be outlined:

   (a) If a prospective candidate visits the career site of a company, the correspondence can be taken over by the chatbot. The chatbot answers questions about advertised positions, the application process, or the corporate culture.

   (b) If an interested candidate decides to apply, the chatbot collects the submitted documents and checks their completeness.

   (c) Based on the submitted documents as well as a short interview by the chatbot, an initial assessment of the person-job-fit can already be made (see also genetic algorithms for preselection in the following paragraph). Depending on the results, the documents will be forwarded to the responsible department, an alternative (better fitting) position will be offered if available, or admission to the applicant pool will be suggested.

   (d) Once the application is completed, the chatbot will keep the applicant informed of the application status by means of a tracking code.

   (e) At the end of the application process, the chatbot records the satisfaction of the applicants by means of a structured feedback protocol. The use of virtual personal assistants not only reduces the administrative expenditure for the personnel responsible persons but also increases in particular the reaction speed on the part of the enterprises. This speed of reaction represents a significant competitive advantage in the changing labor market (from an employer's to an employee's market). In addition, the chatbot with the corresponding training data is also able to support foreign-language applicants during the application process.

6. As indicated in the previous paragraph, AI can be used to *preselect applicants*. For the evaluation of text-based applications, the use of genetic algorithms, whose nomenclature is borrowed from evolutionary biology (Strohmeier and Piazza 2015), among other things, lends itself. Genetic algorithms, which can be assigned to statistical optimization methods, generate sample solutions according to certain objective functions and problem-specific constraints in order to optimize the "survival of the fit test" (Chehouri et al. 2017). The target definitions or restrictions can vary depending on the intended use. In the following, the semantic and typological matching procedures are described as examples. In the semantic matching process, semantic networks are used in analogy to the digital personnel search in order to realize an automated comparison between the input of the applicants (e.g., information in the CV) and the stored wishes of the HR managers (e.g., competence profiles of the job advertisements). Depending on the match, each applicant receives a cumulative "fitness value" that serves as a basis for selection (Lee et al. 2018). It is important to note that traditional preselection systems can be subject to a programmed bias due to a (too) strong focus on demographic variables (see Amazon example in Sect. 10.1). However, this "recruitment bias" can be relativized or neutralized by the additional use of typological matching procedures. The typological matching procedure involves the assignment of applicants to personality types. All qualifications, abilities, and characteristics desirable for the respective job are summarized in a personality type, which is the basis for matching. Established interest and personality tests are often used to collect the necessary information from applicants (e.g., Myers-Briggs type indicator; Randall et al. 2017). The question of which matching method to use depends largely on the type of competence to be used for selection. Thus, semantic matching procedures seem to be superior in the assessment of hard skills, whereas typological matching procedures are predestined to assess soft skills. For both procedures, they can enable a faster selection of applicants. In addition, AI should help the selection process to become more transparent and provide a non-discriminatory selection of personnel (Cohen 2019). However, it must be clear that AI can only be used in a supporting way. The final decision must be made by the HR manager.

There is also potential for AI applications in the area of *personnel development*. For example, the focus is on (7) identification of individual learning paths and (8) sentiment analysis within the company.

7. To ensure competitiveness in a volatile environment, HR managers must *continuously develop* their managers and employees while taking personal and corporate objectives into account. However, the manual assignment of suitable further training to required competencies is extremely time-consuming. Here again, matching algorithms can help by generating suggestions for personal

learning paths on the basis of competence and training catalogs (Upadhyay and Khandelwal 2019). In order to train this self-learning recommendation system, relevant competencies and existing/planned further education offers are transferred into word clouds and plotted against each other in a vector space, so that similarity rates are generated (Zhao et al. 2019). As a result, matrices with all possible combinations of competences and training opportunities with corresponding similarity rates are obtained, which are the input for the matching. Based on the best matching and individual topic preferences identified through the interaction of employees with the recommendation system (Pinkwart and Rüdian 2020), personal learning paths can now be suggested. Such a self-learning recommendation system not only increases the accuracy of the fit of competence requirements to training offers, but also minimizes the use of resources compared to manual assignment.

8. Naturally, HR managers are interested in knowing how certain HRM activities (e.g., training measures) affect the *mood within the workforce*. However, it is almost impossible to gain a comprehensive and profound picture of the mood by personal means. The use of employee surveys is also limited (keywords: effort and wear and tear effects). Text mining, which describes a bundle of algorithms for the discovery of meaning structures from weakly structured text data (Besimi et al. 2019), can help in this context. Particularly relevant for HRM is the so-called sentiment analysis, which can be used to automatically extract "positive," "neutral," and "negative" feelings from text documents (e.g., posts on a social intranet or comments on an employer rating portal). From a technical point of view, sentiment analysis is divided into two components: text preprocessing and text classification. Text preprocessing refers to the decomposition of the text into individual terms (tokenization), the linguistic categorization of these terms (tagging), their reduction to the root form (lemmatization), and their transformation into a vector that reflects the relative frequency of all identified terms (vector space model) (Strohmeier and Piazza 2015). The text classification takes up the vector models by algorithms that evaluate their content (see Villarroel Ordenes et al. 2017). A significant added value of text-based mood analysis is the ability to analyze large amounts of text in real time and to react quickly to negative trends. Employee fears could also be identified and addressed at an early stage (e.g., fear of contagion during the COVID-19 crisis).

Reward systems include (9) employee assessment and (10) remuneration (Stock-Homburg and Groß 2019).

9. When *evaluating* employees, there is usually the problem that HR managers must rely on the judgment of the respective direct superiors of the employees. However, numerous studies suggest that manager evaluations are subject to various evaluation errors (e.g., primacy and recency effects) if the judges are not sufficiently psychologically trained (Stock-Homburg and Groß 2019). Although so-called 360-degree feedbacks help to objectify the subjective judgment of superiors, this multiperspective procedure is very time-consuming and can therefore only be implemented at longer intervals (e.g., annually). At this

point, AI can make an important contribution in the form of neural networks for pattern recognition. The algorithmic analysis of large amounts of data makes it possible not only to detect performance fluctuations in real time, but also to identify individual performance patterns. In concrete terms, ANN can determine weighted indicators from various data sources (e.g., the number and duration of customer appointments or number of work from home days), which influence the individual performance of employees. This information can then be used to develop personal recommendations for the employees. It is important to note that AI should not be used at this point as a monitoring tool for individual employee performance, but rather as a personal "performance coach" to sensitize employees to their behavioral and performance patterns. In addition, the systematic evaluation of metadata from various sources at the company level opens up new possibilities for personnel assessment. For example, aggregated sensor data from wearables, communication data from the social intranet, or movement data from mobile devices offer new insights into the social structure (see in detail (Bernstein and Waber 2019)]. Pattern recognition algorithms enable companies to analyze in real time how closely departments are networked with each other, which employee groups are most effective or innovative, and where the informal opinion leaders in the company can be found (Groß and Dorozalla 2020). These insights into the social structure provide important information on corporate performance.

10. The *remuneration* can be divided into three types: fixed remuneration, variable remuneration, and (non-monetary) additional benefits. In times of the so-called war for talents, HR managers are faced with the challenge of putting together the most attractive remuneration packages possible in order to attract and retain qualified employees. The development of individually optimized compensation proposals is a combinatorial optimization problem that can be solved, for example, by means of an evolutionary algorithm (cf. comments on point 6). The relevant search space for solutions is formed by combinations of the three mentioned compensation variants that are legally and fiscally permissible, whereby the non-monetary compensation components enjoy special relevance. By analyzing various employee data (e.g., tax class, previous selection of non-monetary compensation components, or focus on reducing statutory charges), an individually optimized compensation proposal can be created. Specifically, genetic algorithms automatically suggest a compensation based on employees' preferences, which can also reduce taxes for employers and employees (Dorozalla and Jeddeloh 2019; Groß and Dorozalla 2020).

11. In addition to the AI-based management of executives and employees, the digitalization of the *administration of employees* plays an important role in HR transformation. In recent years, digital personnel files have found their way into companies in this context. The digital personnel file is an electronic document management system that simplifies the administration of HRM-related documents and digitizes standardized HRM processes. Changes to personnel master data (e.g., change of address) or uploads of documents (e.g., vacation requests) can be made not only by the HR managers but also by the

employees themselves (employee self-service), which leads to a significant time saving for the HR departments. AI is not necessarily due to the triviality of these tasks (Roedenbeck 2020). However, intelligent personal language assistants are suitable for advising and supporting employees in employee self-service (Strohmeier and Piazza 2015). Analogous to the language assistants "Siri" (Apple) or "Alexa" (Amazon), employees can request information (e.g., remaining vacation days) or use assistance services (e.g., forwarding to the input website for tax class changes). The advantage of these assistants based on speech recognition for HR managers is that numerous sophisticated speech processing systems already exist. The implementation effort is therefore primarily focused on the creation of internal knowledge databases, which assign suitable answers or work orders to the recognized statements (Roedenbeck 2020).

The explanations of this chapter illustrate that the fields of application of AI in HRM are manifold and go far beyond the field of recruitment. Figure 10.4 links the shown AI functionalities from Sect. 1.3 with the described HRM tasks from this chapter.

10.3.2 Status Quo of HRM-Related AI Applications in German Companies

Based on the previously outlined application areas of AI in HRM, a non-representative survey of the status quo in German companies was conducted. For this purpose, 118 companies of different sizes and branches were interviewed[1]. The sample consisted of 60% service companies, 32% manufacturing companies, and 8% public institutions. With regard to company size (number of employees), the distribution was as follows: 32% with less than 100 employees, 22% with 101 to 500 employees, 21% with 501 to 2000 employees, and 25% with more than 2000 employees.

First of all, the results are presented and interpreted in terms of selected conditions that are conducive to the implementation of AI in HRM, before specific areas of application along the HRM systems are examined. With regard to the question of whether there is an official AI representative in the company, only 33% of the respondents answered "yes," corresponding to 67% "no." A similar pattern of answers was found in the question of whether companies have already developed an explicit AI strategy. Here, 38% answered "yes," corresponding to 62% "no." Furthermore, the vast majority of the companies surveyed (83%) have not yet

---

[1]At the time of submission of this manuscript, the survey had not yet been completed, so that not all of the final generated data points could be considered in the evaluation of this chapter. The results presented here are therefore to be considered preliminary.

concluded a company agreement on the use of AI. These results indicate that the implementation of AI in the majority of the surveyed companies has had a rather evolutionary character to date and does not follow a systematically managed transformation process. This conclusion confirms the current literature on the status quo of AI in German companies. The study "Artificial Intelligence in Corporate Practice" published in March 2020 by the Fraunhofer IAO shows that although AI as a future topic is generally highly regarded by top management, only a few companies have set a structural course (Bauer et al. 2020). Both the data collected for this chapter and the results of the Fraunhofer IAO show that the size of a company has a significant influence on the strategic importance of AI topics. In particular, small and medium-sized enterprises (SMEs, up to 500 employees) are lagging behind, while large companies are playing a leading role. The results shown are referred to in Sect. 10.4 on the design of beneficial framework conditions.

The status quo analysis along the HRM systems makes it clear that AI has not yet arrived in the HRM of German companies. Specifically, ten of the eleven fields of application outlined in Sect. 10.3.1 were examined (see Fig. 10.5)[2]. The query was based on a four-level maturity model:

- Level 0: The respective HRM process is not digitally supported.
- Level 1: The respective HRM process is supported by Office applications.
- Level 2: The respective HRM process is supported by a personnel information system.
- Level 3: The respective HRM process is supported by AI-based applications.

In order to generate comparable data, respondents were asked to indicate the highest level in each case if their company uses several of the applications mentioned to support a HRM process. For example, it is conceivable that a company uses Microsoft Office applications to create job advertisements (level 1), which in turn serve as input files for a candidate search algorithm. In this case, the company would be assigned to level 3.

The results impressively show that AI-based applications have so far hardly played a significant role in the HRM sector. While the maximum value for level 3 across all HR processes is 5% (preselection process), not a single company uses AI for sentiment analysis and remuneration. On average, only 2.9% of the companies surveyed use AI-based applications in HRM. A more in-depth analysis reveals significant differences in terms of company size. In the group of small and medium-sized companies with fewer than 500 employees, only 0.6% of the companies have used AI applications to date, compared to 5% and 6% in the two larger classes of companies, respectively. While the slight penetration of AI in the HRM sector seemed to be quite expected, the relatively high proportion of

---

[2]The query for the forecast of termination intentions was deliberately omitted, as this application is in a gray area both legally and ethically.

Fig. 10.5 Study results on the status quo of AI in HRM (own presentation)

companies that do not support their HR processes digitally at all is surprising. The percentage of companies that can be assigned to level 0 ranges from 3% (application process) to 69% (sentiment analysis). This result is relevant in that it can be assumed that level 0 has no or very little data that could serve as input data for AI applications. A further finding of the study is that the companies surveyed are predominantly assigned to levels 2 and 3, i.e., that HR processes are primarily supported by classic Microsoft Office applications (e.g., spreadsheet programs) and/or HR information systems. This finding is significant, since the HRM information systems in particular represent an important database for AI applications. The results presented here make current studies on AI applications in personnel practice seem plausible. In the already quoted study of the Fraunhofer IAO, the participants of the study were asked to assess the importance of AI applications for selected business areas. Not surprisingly, it was found that the HRM sector occupied the tenth of eleven ranks—i.e., compared to marketing, sales, or logistics, it hardly receives any attention in the AI debate in companies (Bauer et al. 2020). A similar picture is emerging for Switzerland. A qualitative study of 26 HR practitioners (mainly from large companies) showed that HR processes are currently primarily supported by "old technology" (e.g., online employee surveys). AI-based solutions, on the other hand, are hardly ever used, despite the potential attested to by the study participants (Weibel et al. 2019). These findings form the basis for the design of conducive framework conditions for AI applications in HRM in Sect. 10.4. Figure 10.5 provides an overview of the results on the status quo of AI in concrete application areas.

10.4   Promotional Framework for AI Applications in HRM

Considering the empirical findings from Sect. 10.3.2, the following outlines the framework conditions that are conducive to increasing the acceptance of AI applications in HRM. The theoretical basis for this is the technology acceptance model (TAM). TAM, developed by Davis and colleagues (Davis et al. 1989), is a widely used instrument for the analysis of technology use in the field of information systems. In its original form, the model postulates that the intention to use a technology depends on two variables: (1) perceived usefulness and (2) perceived ease of use. Perceived usefulness measures the extent to which a person feels that an application improves his or her own performance. Perceived ease of use, in turn, measures a person's perception of the effort required to learn how to use the new technology. The described effect structure is considered robust in research and has been confirmed in numerous studies (Wu and Lederer 2009). Over time, TAM has been further developed and various input variables have been added. For the present chapter, the following additional variables are considered: (3) data protection conformity, (4) ethical virtues, and (5) innovation culture. In the following, it is assumed that these five factors increase the acceptance of AI applications in general and within the HRM sector in particular (see also Fig. 10.3).

1. For HR managers to perceive AI applications as useful, AI must make HR work more effective or efficient. In order to make AI potential quickly visible, it is advisable to first focus on applications at the assisted intelligence level, whereby routine tasks can be processed independently or taken over completely (e.g., AI-based language assistant for employee self-services). The next step is to convince HR managers of the usefulness of augmented intelligence applications. For this purpose, the company-wide development of a modular AI architecture seems to make sense. With the help of a portfolio of reusable blocks (e.g., genetic algorithms for optimization problems), AI could be scaled into HRM via "used cases" from other company areas. In this context, an internal AI innovation hub could be effective, in which representatives of different divisions of the company could experiment with AI application possibilities together and exchange ideas with IT specialists. In this way, HR managers would have the opportunity to appreciate the potential of advanced AI applications and benefit from concrete examples from other divisions. Basically, in view of the empirical results of the study carried out, it is recommended that companies bundle their AI goals or AI activities within the framework of a meaningful AI strategy. This AI strategy provides the essential framework conditions against the background of the dynamic developments in technology. In order to increase the perceived usefulness (in all business areas), the AI strategy should be designed as a learning strategy and developed (further) in a participatory way. Taking the company-wide AI strategy into account, HR managers can set priorities for HRM-related AI projects. The following key questions can be taken into account: Which application offers the greatest time saving potential? Which decisions could be better made with AI support? How can the workforce benefit from AI?

2. It is obvious that HR managers do not (cannot) program AI applications themselves but have to have them programmed. To increase the perceived user-friendliness, HR managers should be involved in the development of HRM-related AI applications from the very beginning. The focus should always be on the end users (either the HR managers themselves or the workforce). From user experience research, three main aspects can be derived that should be considered when designing human–machine interaction (Pappas et al. 2019): visual design, information architecture, and interaction design. Visual design refers to the aesthetics, i.e., the colors, images, and symbols of the user interface. Studies show that the aesthetic design of the user interface positively influences the user experience (Chu 2016). In this context, it makes sense to use the corporate design (e.g., colors and logo) and to consider the aesthetic perception of the end user during development. The information architecture describes the structuring of data and information. It should be designed in such a way that users can find information as intuitively as possible. With regard to the perceived user-friendliness, this primarily involves the intelligent design of navigation concepts for input and output data. In order to increase user-friendliness, the AI system should allow HR managers to independently modify the database (input). On the output side, clearly arranged and individually configurable dashboards should support HR managers in their decision-making. The interaction design focuses on

all interactions between users and AI. The human–machine interface is of high importance for the user experience and therefore also for the perceived usability. Since HR managers are in most cases not technology experts, the interaction with the AI should be as intuitive as possible to create a positive overall experience (Tolino and Mariani 2018). For example, user-friendly menu windows are preferable to a purely syntax-based display. Likewise, the AI outputs should be visualized to a high degree.

3. Maintaining compliance with data protection regulations and at the same time developing useful AI applications for HRM is probably the greatest challenge German companies face in order to increase acceptance. A binding legal framework for the use of personal data has been in place since the General Data Protection Regulation (GDPR) came into force in Germany in May 2018 (Datenschutz-Grundverordnung "DSGVO"). Personal data includes all information relating to an identified or identifiable natural person. A person becomes identifiable not only by name, identification number, or location data, but already by one or more characteristics that express his or her physical, psychological, genetic, psychological, economic, cultural, or social identity. At this point, it becomes clear that in this country a large number of the input variables for AI systems are to be classified as personal data (cf. Sect. 10.3.1), which is why the DSGVO plays an important role in programming. According to the DSGVO, companies must take three major restrictions into account when developing personalized AI applications [see (Huff and Götz 2020) for details]. The first hurdle is the "prohibition principle with reservation of permission," according to which a legally standardized reason for permission must be presented for the legality of data collection, data processing, and data use. Classically, the consent of the employees is used as an effective means (workaround) for the legal rule cited. However, the granting of consent is only voluntary in the legal sense if the person concerned is not disadvantaged even in the event of refusal. The special relationship of dependence between employee and employer has to be especially appreciated, which is why in the end only "irrelevant" data analyses are possible. The situation is different if a company can demonstrate a legitimate interest in processing data without endangering employees' interests worthy of protection. At this point, it is recommended that company with works council conclude a company agreement in the sense of a basis for permission, although it should be mentioned that the scope of permission must not exceed the legal requirements. Nevertheless, it can be assumed that a company agreement could lead to an increase in acceptance of AI applications in the company through its signal effect. The second hurdle results from Article 22 DSGVO. This states that a person has the right not to be subjected to a decision based solely on automated processing— including profiling—which has legal effect vis-à-vis him or her or which significantly affects him or her in a similar way. Thus, autonomous intelligence applications (see Fig. 10.2) are not DSGVO compliant. HR managers must therefore ensure that AI applications are only ever used as a decision-making aid (augmented intelligence; e.g., there must be no purely mechanical preselection of applicants). The third hurdle for HRM-related AI applications lies in the

DSGVO principles for data processing. A major restriction results from the so-called purpose limitation, i.e., that the collection of data without a specific purpose, as is often the case with AI applications in other areas of a company, is not permitted. At this point, the solution lies in the purposefulness of AI applications. HR managers must therefore first define a clear set of questions to which a specific knowledge goal is linked. Furthermore, the data minimization principle is of high relevance. This principle states that data collection and processing must be limited to what is appropriate and necessary for the purpose. Accordingly, it is recommended that the reference to persons or the level of aggregation of the data and analysis results be geared to the processing purposes (Huff and Götz 2020). In this context, it should be noted that when purchasing programming services for AI applications—especially from non-European suppliers—it must be ensured that the DSGVO is considered as the legal framework. In principle, it can be assumed that DSGVO-compliant development of AI applications leads to an increase in trust and thus acceptance can be increased.

4. The development of ethical virtues is a fundamental factor in promoting acceptance, because not everything that is legal also meets ethical expectations (see Sect. 10.1). An independent research discourse on the topic of ethics of algorithms has already established itself in the current ethics literature (see, among others, Floridi et al. 2018). The basis for the discussion of ethical virtues in the entrepreneurial context is often the corporate ethic virtues model, which was developed by Kaptein in 2008. This approach states that both economically active individuals and business organizations should possess certain virtues in order to be able to act morally. These seven virtues will be discussed below in relation to the acceptance of AI applications in HRM:

   (a) *Clarity* refers to the extent to which ethical expectations regarding AI applications are made concrete and understandable. Many companies—especially large enterprises—have defined their own AI ethics catalogs, which they make available not only to their employees but also to the general public (e.g., Google or Deutsche Telekom). In this context, well-sounding terms such as fairness, privacy, responsibility, transparency, trust, security, or science are often used. In addition to the ethics catalogs defined by companies themselves, various institutions, facilities, and associations are developing guidelines with concrete standards (e.g., Hambach Declaration on Artificial Intelligence 2019). The guidelines of the "Ethics Council HR Tech," for example, provide solid orientation for HRM. At this point, we recommend that HR managers participate in the development of ethical AI standards to ensure that they are not just empty words for external marketing.

   (b) *Congruency* of executives and top managers describes the degree to which managers, who in most cases define the business purpose and underlying specifications of AI applications, act as role models. If the behavior of the management is in line with the normative expectations of the company, the message to the employees is strengthened to also fulfill these expectations (Kaptein 2008). In concrete terms, this could mean that top management discloses which AI applications they themselves use to manage the company and how ethical standards are adhered to in doing so.

(c) *Feasibility* refers to the framework created by the company to enable managers and employees to comply with AI-related standards. In particular, AI projects must be adequately budgeted in terms of time and money in order to meet ethical standards and at the same time achieve value-added results. In principle, it is advisable to set up an AI task force that includes not only technical specialists and divisional representatives but also members of the works council and trusted representatives.

(d) *Supportability* is the extent to which a company helps its employees identify with the company's ethics. In this context, HRM can make a significant contribution by providing training on the use of AI and the associated ethical standards.

(e) *Transparency* refers to the degree to which the consequences of one's own behavior are visible in the company. Empirical studies emphasize the great importance of transparency not only because of its far-reaching special potential to uncover unethical behavior (Tyler and Blader 2005; Vieweg 2020), but above all because of its beneficial effect on the acceptance of AI (Grotenhermen et al. 2020). With regard to AI applications, therefore, not only the processing of input and output variables should be explained (see also DSGVO for details), but also a look at the AI "black box" should be made possible. In this way, managers and employees have the opportunity to raise and discuss ethical questions.

(f) A lively ethical debate (*discussability*) is the basis for learning from the (near) mistakes and ethical dilemmas of others. The open exchange of information with already experienced AI departments opens up the opportunity for HRM to consider ethical questions right at the beginning of AI projects.

(g) *Sanctionability* describes the extent to which employees believe that misconduct is punished, and ethical behavior is rewarded. Since the lack of sanctionability undermines the effectiveness of standards, it is important to sanction intentional misconduct in the use of AI under labor law. However, this measure should be the last step; rather, prevention through education should be the main focus.

In summary, it can be stated that companies are well advised to develop as many of the ethical practices as possible in order to increase the acceptance of AI applications and to establish a permanent AI-affine culture. HR managers can benefit twofold from the development of ethical virtues in the context of AI. On the one hand, they can raise their own profile by taking on a moderating role in the development process, and on the other hand, they can use the virtues as an ethical framework for building trust.

5. "Culture eats strategy for breakfast"; this quotation from management thinker Peter Drucker (2007) impressively emphasizes the great importance of corporate culture in transformation processes. Based on existing research on the effects of an innovation culture on success (Ramella 2017; Stock et al. 2013), it is obvious that it also plays a key role in increasing acceptance of AI applications. According to Schein (1990), corporate culture can be divided into three levels: values, norms, and artifacts. Values describe in an ideological way which characteristics, qualities, behaviors, or actions are considered desirable. In addition to ethical values such as fairness, transparency, and trust, the values of openness to new experiences and the willingness to experiment are of great importance in the context of AI. Companies need employees who continuously question the status quo, develop innovative ideas, test them, and implement them step by step. To convey these expectations to managers and employees, standards are established. Standards are explicit formulations of values with a concrete reference to appropriate behavior. As formal expressions of the underlying values they are perceived more consciously and are less abstract than cultural values. For example, the value of the willingness to experiment with new technologies can be specified as a norm in personnel selection or employee assessment. In contrast to these two abstract cultural levels, artifacts are phenotypic characteristics of the underlying values and norms (e.g., stories, rituals, events, physical constructions, and graphic representations). Innovation-oriented artifacts represent the most concrete level for employees, as they facilitate the interpretation of the company's innovation efforts. At the artifact level, companies can, for example, use hackathons (i.e., collaborative software development events) to send an important innovation signal for AI application development.

10.5 Competence Profile of a HR Manager in the AI Age

Based on the previous remarks, this chapter will outline a competence profile for HR managers in the AI age. In addition, initial considerations are made on how these future competencies can be developed. The literature research in this context makes it clear that no generally valid model exists. Rather, numerous (rather unscientific) collections of different competencies can be identified. However, an arbitrary list is not very promising for the development of a competence profile (i.e., a structured picture of different competence areas; Groß et al. 2019). In order to derive a competence profile, the future role of HR management in companies will first be examined in order to identify key competence areas. The conceptual basis for this is the HR role model according to Ulrich (1996; see Fig. 10.6).

Based on the two dimensions (1) strategic versus operational focus and (2) process versus people orientation, the HR role model distinguishes four roles that HRM can take on in a company. Since the future topic of AI has a strategic focus and has both a process-related and a people-related dimension, HRM in the AI age should primarily take on the roles of strategic partner and change agent. Strategic partner means that HRM is not about HRM, but about business. In other words, HR managers should

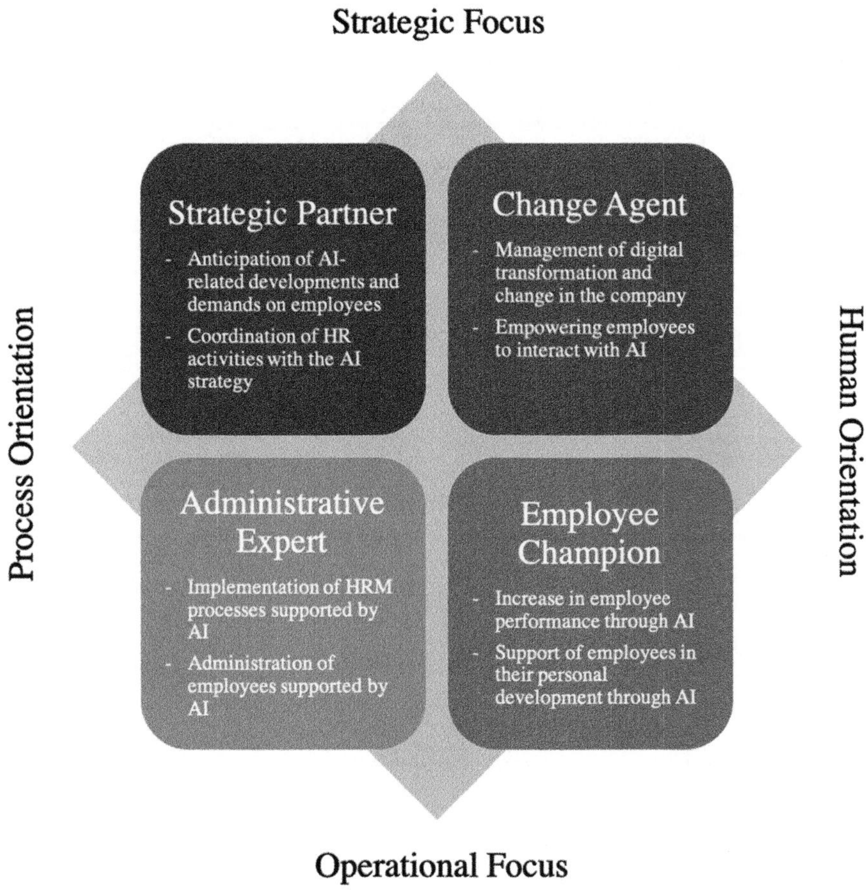

Strategic Focus

Strategic Partner

- Anticipation of AI-related developments and demands on employees
- Coordination of HR activities with the AI strategy

Change Agent

- Management of digital transformation and change in the company
- Empowering employees to interact with AI

Administrative Expert

- Implementation of HRM processes supported by AI
- Administration of employees supported by AI

Employee Champion

- Increase in employee performance through AI
- Support of employees in their personal development through AI

Process Orientation

Human Orientation

Operational Focus

Fig. 10.6 Roles of HRM in the AI Age (own presentation based on [Ulrich 1996])

measure their success not by how many employees they hire or train, but by how strongly HRM activities contribute to business success (e.g., through HR analytics). This includes anticipating future AI trends and aligning the HR strategy with these developments. Being a change agent means that HR managers shape digital transformation in close cooperation with top management and the IT department. This includes setting the organizational course, accompanying the change process, and preparing employees for dealing with AI. In order to meet the requirements of these two roles, the competence profile is operationalized using the dynamic capability theory. According to this theory, the key to the survival of companies in complex and dynamic environments is the permanent recombination of resources to generate innovation (Teece et al. 2016). Three competencies are highlighted: sensing (ability to identify new market, customer, or technology opportunities), seizing (ability to seize opportunities), and reconfiguring (ability to reconfigure the resource base). If this concept is applied to an individual competency profile for HR managers, three

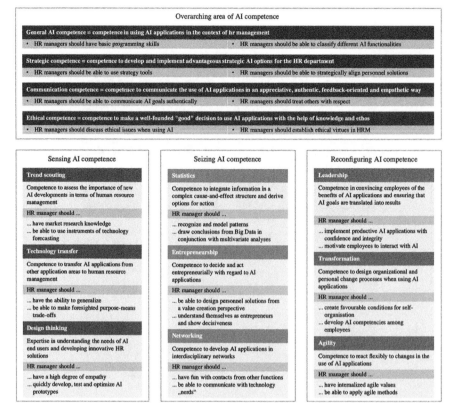

Fig. 10.7 Competence profile of HR managers in the AI age (own presentation)

areas of competence (sensing, seizing, and reconfiguring) and an overarching area can be identified (see Fig. 10.7).

With regard to the competence profile developed, it should be noted that not all HR managers need to have the highest possible level of proficiency in each of the competence areas described; rather, the model presents an ideal picture of different competencies that are more or less relevant depending on the design of the AI environment. Moreover, the examples of operationalization given are not exhaustive, but serve only as illustrations. At this point, it should be added that in addition to the generalist competencies for the strategic roles, special competencies are also required for the remaining operational roles of administrative expert and employee champion (see Fig. 10.6). It should also be pointed out in this context that strategic and operational HRM tasks should be performed from an integrative perspective by several people with different competence profiles. Thus, for the role of administrative expert (i.e., the execution of administrative HRM processes, e.g., contract drafting and payroll accounting), legal and tax expertise is particularly important. The main tasks of the employee champion are to promote the commitment, performance, and competence development of employees. At this point, the knowledge of problems and concerns of the employees is of particular relevance in order to consider the needs of the employees as well as the company's guidelines and to act as a mediator if necessary. In addition to communicative skills, these tasks primarily require profound knowledge of psychology and sociology.

10.6   Scientific Implications and Outlook

The use of AI applications in HRM will increase in the future. In the context of this chapter, eleven AI applications along HRM systems were outlined on the basis of the task technology fit theory (see Sect. 10.3.1). With regard to the research question on the added value of AI in HRM, the potential fields of application go far beyond personnel recruitment. Due to the large number of HRM activities and AI functionalities, however, far more than the task technology combinations discussed in this chapter are conceivable. For example, AI can serve as a personal learning assistant in personnel development, in which the technology takes into account the respective learning needs (e.g., learning speed) when designing individually tailored learning content. However, despite the promising technical possibilities, the comparison of theory and practice with the status quo of AI in HRM shows that German HR managers are very reluctant to act (see Sect. 10.3.2). Scientific studies will be required in the future to identify further conducive conditions for AI applications in HRM (see Sect. 10.4). For example, a representative quantitative study would not only allow the status quo in companies of various sectors and sizes to be determined, but also weighting of factors that are conducive to AI deployment (e.g., by multiple regression). Likewise, the success effects of AI applications in relation to the target variables of HRM should be examined by means of causal analyses (e.g., structural equation model; see Fig. 10.3). Specifically, it should be analyzed to what extent AI applications are more powerful than existing HRM solutions (e.g., support by HRM information systems). In addition, qualitative studies (e.g., expert interviews with HR managers) could reveal restrictions of German companies that have not been considered so far and provide further clues for the design of AI transformation. Focus group analyses in interdisciplinary settings offer the opportunity to identify interfaces of AI applications and already existing IT solutions (e.g., ERP system). In addition, field-experimental methods open up the possibility to investigate the effect of AI applications on the end users in real life. The all-decisive factor in determining whether AI applications are accepted in HRM is the human being. An important element in this context is the competence profile of the HR manager in the AI age developed in this article (see Sect. 10.5), which needs to be validated in future studies. The development of the outlined competences (see Fig. 10.7) closes the circle, because here AI can act as an assistant (see point 7 in Sect. 10.3.1). In addition, HR managers can use both internal (e.g., marketing) and external (e.g., AI startups) job sharing. In conclusion, the future of HRM lies in the intelligent combination of human and artificial intelligence. In order to gain the desired freedom for strategic tasks, HR managers should successively delegate tasks to AI, considering ethical, data protection, and value-adding issues—until a balance has been found between the human being and the thinking machine.

10.7   Finish Line Quiz

10.01		In which key HRM functions can AI support?
	1	Forecast, recruiting, development, remuneration, employee self-services.
	2	Reward system, administration, recruitment, requirements planning, development.
	3	Speech and text processing, knowledge generation, knowledge representation, knowledge processing, problem solving.
	4	Learning pathway identification, sentiment analysis in the workforce, active sourcing, performance evaluation, absenteeism prediction.
10.02		Which combination is correct for AI-based preselection of candidates?
	1	Semantic matching procedures seem to be superior for both hard skills and soft skills.
	2	Typological matching procedures seem to be superior in hard skills, semantic matching procedures in soft skills.
	3	Semantic matching procedures seem to be superior in hard skills, typological matching procedures in soft skills.
	4	Typological matching procedures seem to be superior for both hard skills and soft skills.
10.03		What is another advantage of chatbots in HRM functions beyond cost efficiencies?
	1	To optimize second- and third-level support by providing better data to the HR experts.
	2	Chatbots are not usable in HR functions.
	3	Reduced risk to lose an interesting candidate.
	4	Chatbots do not pay off; they are on the long run more expensive than human HR staff.
10.04		Recent (non-representative) research unveils that at least in small/medium-sized enterprises (SME) in Germany, …
	1	AI support is already used today on basically all different HR functions.
	2	The management is aware of AI advantages, though there is hardly any practical implementation.
	3	Utilization of AI technologies is primarily expected in HR management.
	4	There is no competitive advantage that could be generated with AI-based HRM.
10.05		What are specific ethical and legal aspects to be considered in utilizing AI-based automated processes in HRM?
	1	Assisted intelligence may not be allowed in jurisdictions under the European GDPR rules.
	2	Assisted intelligence may be allowed in jurisdictions under the European GDPR rules like in the Germany the DSGVO.
	3	As long as the AI part is just autonomous intelligence, it may be allowed in jurisdictions under the European GDPR rules like in Germany with the DSGVO.
	4	Fully automated HRM processes such as recruiting using AI technologies may not be allowed in jurisdictions under the European GDPR rules.

(continued)

10.06	It is recommended that companies with a works council in jurisdictions with high data protection standards (such as the EU with GDPR and Germany in particular)...	
	1	... do not enter into company agreements with the workers' council on the AI-based automated collection, processing, analysis, and storage of data, as only irrelevant data can be reflected following the law
	2	... do enter into company agreements with the workers' council on the AI-based automated collection, processing, analysis, and storage of all employee-related data ("big bath" approach).
	3	... do enter into company agreements with the workers' council in the sense of a basic permission without stretching its scope beyond the legal minimum.
	4	... do not enter into company agreements with the workers' council as it would be illegal.
10.07	What are the expectations on changes for the HR role in an AI environment?	
	1	No change of HR skills, as HR managers typically would not program the AI algorithms anyway.
	2	No change of HR skills, as HR managers' activities on focus (strategic vs. operational) and orientation (human vs. process) remain unchanged.
	3	Only in the area of "change agent" as well as "administrative expert" HR managers are expected to foster the use of AI.
	4	In all areas such as "strategic partner" and "employee champion" HR managers are expected to foster the use of AI.
10.08	What unique basic skills are required for HR managers to have in an AI environment?	
	1	HR managers should treat others with respect.
	2	HR managers should have basic programming skills.
	3	HR managers should establish ethical virtues in human resources.
	4	Competence to design organizational and personal change processes.
10.09	What is a special skill set required for HR managers to have in an AI environment?	
	1	Seizing: Represent end users' needs in innovating HR solutions; sensing: Flexibility; reconfiguration: Interdisciplinary networks.
	2	Reconfiguration: Interdisciplinary networks; sensing: Represent end users' needs in innovating HR solutions; sizing: Flexibility.
	3	Reconfiguration: Convincing employees; sensing: Represent end users' needs in innovating HR solutions; seizing: Flexibility.
	4	Sensing: Represent end users' needs in innovating HR solutions; seizing: Interdisciplinary networks; reconfiguration: Flexibility.
10.10	What are suggested next steps to foster AI in HRM?	
	1	Buildup of competencies internally as well as through job sharing with AI startups.
	2	Wait until adequate technology integration (e.g., of AI in ERP systems) becomes available.
	3	Disinvest from "human" HRM altogether, because all HR managers will be substituted by self-service-based AI applications anyway.
	4	Perform a representative qualitative study to identify the real merits of AI in HRM.

Correct answers can be found in www.vieweg-beratung.de/downloads

References

Arena, D., Tsolakis, A. C., Zikos, S., Krinidis, S., Ziogou, C., Ioannidis, D., Voutetakis, S., Tzovaras, D., & Kiritsis, D. (2018). Human resource optimisation through semantically enriched data. *International Journal of Production Research, 56*(8), 2855–2877.

Bauer, W., Ganz, W., Hämmerle, M., & Renner, T. (2020). *Künstliche Intelligenz in der Unternehmenspraxis. Studie zu Auswirkungen auf Dienstleistungen und Produktion.* Fraunhofer-Institut für Arbeitswirtschaft und Organisation IAO. URL: https://www.digital.iao.fraunhofer.de/de/publikationen/KIinderUnternehmenspraxis.html

Bernstein, E., & Waber, B. (2019). The truth about open offices. *Harvard Business Review, 97*(6), 82–91.

Besimi, A., Dika, Z., Shehu, V., & Selimi, M. (2019). Applied text-mining algorithms for Stock Price prediction based on financial news articles. *Managing Global Transitions: International Research Journal, 17*(4), 335–351.

Biemann, T., & Weckmüller, H. (2016). Mensch gegen Maschine: Wie gut sind Algorithmen im HR? *Personal Quaterly, 4,* 44–47.

Chang, W.-J. A., Wang, Y.-S., & Huang, T.-C. (2013). Work design-related antecedents of turnover intention: A multilevel approach. *Human Resource Management, 52*(1), 1–26.

Chehouri, A., Younes, R., Khoder, J., Perron, J., & Ilinca, A. (2017). A selection process for genetic algorithm using clustering analysis. *Algorithms, 10*(4), 123–138.

Chu, S. (2016). Design factors affect user experience for different cultural populations. *Journal of Educational Issues, 2*(2), 307–319.

Cohen, T. (2019). How to leverage artificial intelligence to meet your diversity goals. *Strategic HR Review,* 1–6.

Dahm, M., & Dregger, A. (2019). Der Einsatz von künstlicher Intelligenz im HR: Die Wirkung und Förderung der Akzeptanz von KI-basierten Recruiting-Tools bei potenziellen Nutzern. In: Hermeier, B., Heupel, T., & Fichtner-Rosada, S., *Arbeitswelten der Zukunft.* Springer Professional „Wirtschaft und Recht".

Davis, F., Bagozzi, P., & Warshaw, P. (1989). User acceptance of computer technology – a comparison of two theoretical models. *Management Science, 35*(8), 982–1003.

Dorozalla, F., & Jeddeloh, M. (2019). Hey Boss, ich brauch' mehr Geld. *Personalmagazin, 6,* 64–67.

Drucker, P. F. (2007). *Alles über Management.* Heidelberg: Redline Wirtschaftsverlag.

Ekawati, A. D. (2019). Predictive analytics in employee churn: A systematic literature review. *Journal of Management Information and Decision Sciences, 4,* 387–398.

Floridi, L., Cowls, J., Beltrametti, M., Chatila, R., Chazerand, P., Dignum, V., Luetge, C., Madelin, R., Pagallo, U., Rossi, F., Schafer, B., Valcke, P., & Vayena, E. (2018). AI4People—An ethical framework for a good AI society: Opportunities, risks, principles, and recommendations. *Minds and Machines, 28,* 689–707.

Goodhue, D. L., & Thompson, R. L. (1995). Task-technology fit and individual performance. *MIS Quarterly, 19*(2), 213–236.

Groß, M., & Dorozalla, F. (2020). Das digitale Erwachen – HR-Reifegradmodell der digitalen Transformation. *Personalführung, 3,* 26–33.

Groß, M., Dorozalla, F., & Rödiger, K. (2019). Auswahlinstrumente auf dem Prüfstand. Rekrutierung agiler Mitarbeiter. *Personalführung, 6,* 36–43.

Grotenhermen, J.-G., Oldeweme, A., Bruckes, M., & Uhlending, L. (2020). Künstliche Intelligenz im Personalwesen: Studie zur Akzeptanz von Entscheidungen intelligenter Systeme. *Zeitschrift Führung + Organisation, 1,* 4–9.

Hagstrom, S. L., & Maranzan, K. A. (2019). Bridging the gap between technological advance and professional psychology training: A way forward. *Canadian Psychology, 60*(4), 281–289.

Heinrich, C., & Stühler, G. (2018). Die Digitale Wertschöpfungskette: Künstliche Intelligenz im Einkauf und Supply Chain Management. In C. Gärtner & C. Heinrich (Eds.), *Fallstudien zur*

Digitalen Transformation: Case Studies für die Lehre und praktische Anwendung (pp. 77–88). Wiesbaden: Springer Gabler.

Huff, J., & Götz, T. (2020). Was datengestütztes Personalmanagement kann und darf? *Personalmagazin, 1*, 48–52.

Ivancevich, J. M. (1985). Predicting absenteeism from prior absence and work attitudes. *Academy of Management Journal, 28*(1), 219–228.

Kahraman, C., Kaya, I., & Çevikcan, E. (2011). Intelligence decision Systems in Enterprise Information Management. *Journal of Enterprise Information Management, 24*(4), 360–379.

Kangas, M., Muotka, J., Huhtala, M., Mäkikangas, A., & Feldt, T. (2017). Is the ethical culture of the organization associated with sickness absence? A multilevel analysis in a public sector organization. *Journal of Business Ethics, 140*(1), 131–145.

Kaplan, A., & Haenlein, M. (2019). Siri, Siri, in my hand: Who's the fairest in the land? On the interpretations, illustrations, and implications of artificial intelligence. *Business Horizons, 62*(1), 15–25.

Kaptein, M. (2008). Developing and testing a measure for the ethical culture of organizations: The corporate ethical virtues model. *Journal of Organizational Behavior, 29*(7), 923–947.

Kowald, C., & Bruns, B. (2019). New learning scenarios with Chatbots: Conversational learning with Jix: From digital tutors to serious interactive fiction games. *International Journal of Advanced Corporate Learning, 12*(2), 54–62.

Kulkarni, S. B., & Che, X. (2019). Intelligent software tools for recruiting. *Journal of International Technology & Information Management, 28*(2), 2–16.

Leao, A. L. M., Barbosa-Branco, A., Turchi, M. D., Steenstra, I. A., & Cole, D. C. (2017). Sickness absence among municipal Workers in a Brazilian Municipality: A secondary data analysis. *BMC Research Notes, 10*, 1–9.

Lee, D., Kim, M., Na, I., & Hwang, S. O. (2018). Artificial intelligence based career matching. *Journal of Intelligent & Fuzzy Systems, 35*(6), 6061–6070.

Libuda, I., & Fleischmann, F. (2018). Personalplanung und people analytics. Simulation der zukünftigen Personalstruktur. *Personalführung, 5*, 29–35.

Mainzer, K. (2016). *Künstliche Intelligenz – Wann übernehmen die Maschinen? Technik im Fokus.* Berlin, Heidelberg: Springer.

McCarthy, B., Minsky, M. L., Rochester, N., & Shannon, C. E. (1955). *A proposal for the Dartmouth summer research project on artificial intelligence.*

Mustafa, M. K., Allen, T., & Appiah, K. (2019). A comparative review of dynamic neural networks and hidden Markov model methods for Mobile on-device speech recognition. *Neural Computing & Applications, 31*(2), 891–899.

Pappas, I. O., Mikalef, P., Giannakos, M. N., & Kourouthanassis, P. E. (2019). Explaining user experience in Mobile gaming applications: An fsQCA approach. *Internet Research, 29*(2), 293.

Pérez-Campdesuñer, R., De-Miguel-Guzmán, M., Sánchez-Rodríguez, A., García-Vidal, G., & Martínez-Vivar, R. (2018). Exploring neural networks in the analysis of variables that affect the employee turnover in the organization. *International Journal of Engineering Business Management, 10*, 1–12.

Pinkwart, N., & Rüdian, S. (2020). Die Vermessung des Lernens. *Personalmagazin, 2*, 30–35.

Popovski, G., Seljak, B. K., & Eftimov, T. (2020). A survey of named-entity recognition methods for food information extraction. *IEEE Access, 8*, 31586–31594.

Ramella, F. (2017). The "Enterprise of Innovation" in hard times: Corporate culture and performance in Italian high-tech companies. *European Planning Studies, 25*(11), 1954–1975.

Randall, K., Isaacson, M., & Ciro, C. (2017). Validity and reliability of the Myers-Briggs personality type indicator: A systematic review and meta-analysis. *Journal of Best Practices in Health Professions Diversity, 10*(1), 1–27.

Reichertz, J. (2003). *Die Abduktion in der qualitativen Sozialforschung.* Opladen: Leske & Budrich.

Rich, E. (1986). Artificial intelligence and the humanities. *Computers and the Humanities, 19*(2), 117–125.

Richter, A., Gačić, T., Kölmel, B., & Waidelich, L. (2019). Künstliche Intelligenz und potenzielle Anwendungsfelder im Marketing. In Deutscher Dialogmarketing Verband e.V (Ed.), *Dialogmarketing Perspektiven 2018/2019*. Wiesbaden: Springer Gabler.

Roedenbeck, M. (2020). Die richtigen Fragen stellen: Wie künstliche Intelligenz die Personalarbeit verändern kann. *Organisationsentwicklung, 1*, 64–69.

Schein, E. H. (1990). Organizational culture. *American Psychologist, 45*(2), 109–119.

Slattery, J., Selvarajan, T., Anderson, J., & Sardessai, R. (2010). Relationship between job characteristics and attitudes: A study of temporary employees. *Journal of Applied Social Psychology, 49*, 1539–1565.

Stock, R., Six, B., & Zacharias, N. (2013). Linking multiple layers of innovation-oriented corporate culture, product program innovativeness, and business performance: A contingency approach. *Journal of the Academy of Marketing Science, 41*(3), 283–299.

Stock-Homburg, R., & Groß, M. (2019). *Personalmanagement. Theorien – Konzepte – Instrumente*. Wiesbaden: Springer.

Strohmeier, S. (2020). Künstliche Intelligenz in HR – eine Gefahr? *Personalmagazin, 3*, 38–39.

Strohmeier, S., & Piazza, F. (2015). Artificial intelligence techniques in human resource management—a conceptual exploration. In C. Kahraman & S. Çevik Onar (Eds.), *Intelligent techniques in engineering management. Intelligent systems reference library* (Vol. 87). Cham: Springer.

Tanwar, P., Prasad, T. V., & Aswal, M. S. (2010). Comparative study of three declarative knowledge representation techniques. *International Journal of Computer Science and Engineering, 2*(7), 2274–2281.

Teece, D., Peteraf, M., & Leih, S. (2016). Dynamic capabilities and organizational agility. *California Management Review, 58*(4), 13–35.

Thurstone, L. L. (1999). *The nature of intelligence*. Hove: Psychology Press.

Tolino, U., & Mariani, I. (2018). Do you think what I think? Strategic ways to design product-human conversation. *Strategic Design Research Journal, 11*(3), 254–262.

Tractica. (2018). *Artificial intelligence for Enterprise applications: Deep learning, machine learning, natural language processing, computer vision, machine reasoning, and strong AI: Global market analysis and forecasts*. URL: https://www.bmwi.de/Redaktion/DE/Publikationen/Studien/perspektiven-kuenstliche-intelligenz-fuer-einzelhandel.pdf?__blob=publicationFile&v=12

Tyler, T. R., & Blader, S. L. (2005). Can business effectively regulate employee conduct? The antecedents of rule following in work settings. *Academy of Management Journal, 48*(6), 1143–1158.

Ulrich, D. (1996). *Human resource champion: The next agenda for adding value and delivering results*. Boston: Harvard Business School Press.

Upadhyay, A. K., & Khandelwal, K. (2019). Artificial intelligence-based training learning from application. *Development and Learning in Organizations: An International Journal, 33*(2), 20–23.

Vieweg, S. (2020). Agiles Management als Wegbereiter gelebter Compliance und besserer Corporate Governance. In M. Pfannstiel & P. J. Steinhoff (Eds.), *Transformationsvorhaben mit dem Enterprise Transformation Cycle meistern*. Wiesbaden: Springer Gabler.

Villarroel Ordenes, F., Ludwig, S., De Ruyter, K., Grewald, D., & Wetzels, M. (2017). Unveiling what is written in the stars: Analyzing explicit, implicit, and discourse patterns of sentiment in social media. *Journal of Consumer Research, 43*(6), 875–894.

Weibel, A., Schafheitle, S., & Ebert, I. (2019). Goldgräberstimmung im Personalmanagement? Wie Datafizierungs-Technologien die Personalsteuerung verändern. (German). *Organisationsentwicklung, 3*, 23–29.

Wilson, H. J., & Daughtery, P. R. (2018). Mensch und Maschine als Team. *Harvard Business Manager, 10*, 54–65.

Wu, J., & Lederer, A. (2009). A meta-analysis of the role of environment-based voluntariness in information technology acceptance. *MIS Quarterly, 33*(2), 419-A-9.

Wu, X., Kumar, V., Quinlan, J. R., Ghosh, J., Yang, Q., Motoda, H., & Steinberg, D. (2008). Top 10 algorithms in data mining. *Knowledge Information Systems, 14*(1), 1–37.

Zhao, L., Chen, L., Liu, Q., Zhang, M., Copland, H., Yuan, X., & Elhoseny, M. (2019). Artificial intelligence-based platform for online teaching management systems. *Journal of Intelligent & Fuzzy Systems, 37*(1), 45–51.

Ethical AI Implementation

11

Stefan H. Vieweg

11.1 Learning Objectives

1. Identify the aim and content of key laws related to AI.
2. Elaborate different initiatives such as the RoboLaw or digital manifesto moving toward an ethical reflection on AI issues.
3. Address key questions affecting human rights in relation to AI implementations.
4. Discuss key questions and concepts for thriving toward ethical AI.
5. Identifying ethical issues in AI and data-driven applications, both in cases of good intent (but not good enough execution) and fraudulent settings.
6. Elaborate on fundamental principles that are advisable to be considered in the implementation of ethical AI.
7. Providing a comprehensive overview on the key building blocks of an ethical AI approach with the "House of Ethical AI."
8. Identify (pragmatic) steps on the implementation roadmap of ethical AI for the good.

11.2 Examples of Initiatives to Thrive an Ethical AI

11.2.1 RoboLaw in the EU

AI is not just "a tool" that supports human decisions. As the technology is prone to come to conclusions and decisions without any human interaction, the question evolves how to treat this "subject."

S. H. Vieweg (✉)
Institute of Compliance and Corporate Governance, RFH - University of Applied Sciences Cologne, Cologne, Germany
e-mail: dr.vieweg@vieweg-beratung.de

© The Author(s), under exclusive license to Springer Nature Switzerland AG 2021   227
S. H. Vieweg (ed.), *AI for the Good*, Management for Professionals,
https://doi.org/10.1007/978-3-030-66913-3_11

Example: AI Bot as Boss at Hitachi
Already back in 2015, Hitachi introduced in their warehouses AI bots that issue work orders and instructions to employees. It is based on the AI analysis of employees' previous problem-solving capabilities in finding more efficient ways – the basic quality management idea of continuous improvement (Kaizen) (Gershgorn 2015).

Depersonalized employment relationships impose a legal challenge. Following current legal understanding, e.g., in Germany of the Federal Data Protection Act ("BDSG") (FDPA 2017).

Can a robot be a superior like humans and how is this to be assessed legally and ethically? The following aspects must be considered: On the one hand, robots are not mere aids; they possess a certain degree of autonomy. On the other hand, they are not an independent legal entity.

Due to their "technically conferred intelligence and their independence," robots cannot be classified as a mere tool of the employer. This is the difference between robots and automatic machines: they not only repeat programmed work sequences, but also have a certain degree of autonomy.

A robot is not a person who can make a "legally binding declaration of intent." Nevertheless, it is more than a "messenger" of the employer. Most likely, the robot could be classified as a negotiator of the employer, acting on behalf of the employer but with his own freedom of decision.

A key area of concern is data protection in connection with relatively self-acting robots. The robots take up enormous amounts of data. But what of this data? Can they store and use?

Example: A Robot's Video Eye
A robot's video eye has to notice that a person is in the danger zone of a production plant and immediately stop the machines. But is the robot also allowed to save the fact that the person being observed is not at his workstation at the moment?

Questions of liability are also difficult to decide: Who bears the damage if an autonomous robot causes property damage or even personal injury—the manufacturer or the owner? (Groß and Gressel 2016).

The European Parliament is the first institution worldwide that wants to create a legal framework for legal and ethical questions concerning artificial intelligence (EU 2017). Robots are not like other products but are subject to the same laws. This problem can be demonstrated using the example of autonomous driving: who is liable in case of accident—the manufacturer, the programmer, the driver? And what kind of ethics is to be applied (e.g., see the "trolley problem" in Sect. 1.4.2 as well).

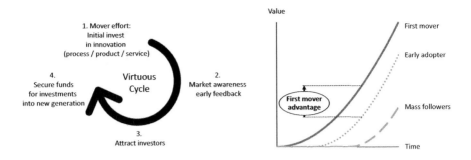

Fig. 11.1 First-mover advantage and the virtuous cycle (own presentation)

Example: Fatal Accident of Uber Autonomous Driving
In 2018, a self-driving Uber Volvo SUV hit and killed a woman riding her bicycle, as the car did not recognize the pedestrian's crosswalk the bicyclist was using. The algorithm did not have the capability of classifying an object as a pedestrian unless that object was near a crosswalk, and the safety driver "didn't keep her eye on road," but she "was streaming the television show 'The Voice'. . . ." (McCausland 2019).

These non-trivial and very complex questions have an essential (to the health and well-being of humans) and cost-intensive impact. For example, is the programmer responsible, who designed and configured the algorithm or provided training datasets for the algorithm responsible (see Sect. 6.6 as well), even if the environment influences the robot? A sensible "risk management approach" may be taken: That is the party liable is the one who can minimize these costs most effectively.

Currently in discussion is the approach of a so-called electronic person or e-person: Basically, this approach suggests treating robots as a corporation with rights and duties that are purely functional for human interests.

Though, ethical issues remain such as the relationship of dependence of a human being (especially a person in need of help) on a robot, because robots cannot have real feelings. The humans the robot is taking care of may not be in a position to differentiate between a real person and a non-human robot. Although typically it is thought of elderly people, small children, or people with mental disabilities, that might actually not be limited to those groups of people, e.g., if addiction of the many of us to so-called social media is considered.

The legal regulation considered by the EU can be seen as an opportunity for Europe (Delvaux 2017). Standards give legal certainty, which lowers economic risks, and thus enables investments into the AI technologies under the compliance provisions set. Here, a competitive advantage can be derived out of virtuous first-mover cycle (see Fig. 11.1).

General principles for the development of robotics and artificial intelligence for civil use include (Delvaux 2017) a call for a EU-wide definition of cyberphysical systems, autonomous systems, intelligent autonomous robots, and their subcategories, and will take into account the following characteristics of intelligent robots:

1. Autonomy is gained through sensors and/or through data exchange with their environment (interconnectivity) and the provision and analysis of their data.
2. The ability to learn by experience and through interaction (optional criterion) shall be given.
3. there is at least a minimum of physical support.
4. there is an ability to adapt their behavior and actions to their environment.
5. no living beings in the biological sense.

Ethical basics for RoboLaw include the assessment regarding the integrity, health, and safety of persons, freedom, integrity and dignity, self-determination and non-discrimination, and protection of personal data. Existing EU legal frameworks should be modernized and, where appropriate, supplemented by ethical requirements that consider the complexity of robotics and its numerous social, medical, and bioethical implications.

A clear, strong, and effective ethical framework for the development, design, manufacture, use, and modification of robots is needed in the form of a charter consisting of a code of conduct for robotic engineers, a code for research ethics committees reviewing robotic protocols, and model licenses for designers and users.

The principle of transparency, according to which it must at all times be possible to state the reasons for any decision taken with the aid of AI that may have a significant impact on the life of one or more persons, considers that it must at all times be possible to convert the calculations of AI systems back into a form that can be understood by humans and that advanced robots should be equipped with a "black box" in which data on each action performed by the machine, including the logical sequences that led to any decisions, are stored.

Ethical frameworks should be based on the principles of benefit, harm prevention, autonomy, and justice, as well as on the principles and values enshrined in Article 2 of the Treaty on THE European Union (EU 2016b) and in the Charter of Fundamental Rights, such as human dignity, equality, justice and fairness, non-discrimination, informed consent, private and family life, and data protection, and on other principles and values underlying Union law, such as non-stigmatization, transparency, autonomy, and individual responsibility and social accountability, and on existing ethical practices and regulatory frameworks. Attention should be paid to robots, which pose a significant threat to confidentiality because they are used in areas that are normally protected and privacy sensitive and because they can generate and transmit personal and sensitive data.

11.2.2 Data Privacy in the EU and the USA

In the EU, the regulation from 2016 (amended 2018) the General Data Protection Regulation (GDPR) (EU 2016a) on the protection of natural persons with regard to the processing of personal data and on the free movement of such data is envisaged. As key principles, the regulation comprises of

1. Right to information: e.g., information about who and why personal data is been processed.
2. Right to access: get access to their own personal data.
3. Right to rectify: request to modify/correct personal data.
4. Withdrawal right/objection right: possibility to withdraw from a previously granted consent to data processing or to object processing for specific purposes, e.g., in a legal dispute.
5. Right to object to automated processing: individuals can, e.g., request a manual review of the personal data, e.g., in case of applying for a loan.
6. Right to be forgotten/right to erase based on applicable laws; after contractual relationships, the individual's data can be requested to be deleted.
7. Data portability right: individuals may ask to be reported back on the collected data to take them, e.g., to other service providers in a machine-readable format.

The GDPR rules matter (Kaminski 2018), as fines in case of infringement are substantial (Wolford 2020): less severe infringements[1] could result in a fine of up to the higher of €10 million or 2% of the total annual worldwide revenue, respectively; in severe cases[2] even up to the higher of €20 million or 4% of the total annual worldwide revenue. Since its start in 2018, until June 2020 275,000 complaints were filed (EC 2019), and until Oct 2020, €250 million of fines for violations in some 400 cases were imposed, the largest against Google (in France and Sweden) of totally €57 m (see Fig. 11.2) in 2019/2020, which is to be compared to approx. USD160.7 bn total revenue, or 0.04% of revenue. As this was due to "Insufficient legal basis for data processing"—a minor case, these fines represent just 2% of the possible range of fine. GDPR fine setting reflects cooperation of the offender.

Going forward, the GDPR may have a further reach into other regions as well. For example in 2019, the EU and Japan reached a mutual EU-Japan Adequacy Decision reflecting "created the largest area of safe and free data flows in the world" (EC 2019).

In Sect. 7.5, the corresponding data privacy act in California, USA (CCPA), was already discussed. Although this initiative originates from California (where many of the Big Tech companies are headquartered, other states are expected swiftly: Nevada, Vermont, Colorado, New York, and Washington (Rosner 2019).

---

[1]Such as affecting organizational, certification, and monitoring issues.

[2]Such as affecting basic principles, conditions of consent, individual's rights related to their own data, and data transfer.

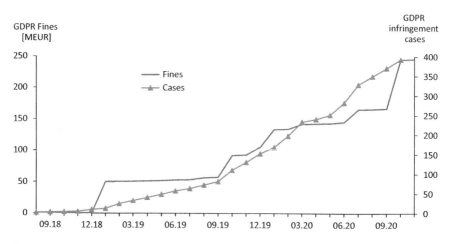

Fig. 11.2 GDPR infringement cases and fines. [own presentation, data based on (enforcementtracker.com 2020)]

In comparison to the GDPR in the EU, the CCPA has a somewhat different approach.

Table 11.1 shows a comparison of the major differences between the approaches. Within the current settings, GDPR rewards cooperation of the offender with reduced fines, whereas with CCPA, 20% of the fines will be used for a special fund (Schwenke 2020) to offset the costs in connection with the CCPA. Overall higher fines in the USA than in the EU are likely to be expected.

11.2.3 Initiatives: Example of AI-Related Postulates from Germany

During the last few years, various initiatives have addressed the issue of data generation, processing, disclosure, and commercial use already. In consequences, digital demands and postulates are available from expert groups that are offered for political decision-makers (Table 11.2).

11.2.4 Initiatives: Example of AI-Related Transparency from the USA

1. *AI Now Institute:* One of AI-related initiatives to establish the "enlightenment" that was addressed in 11.2.3 can be found at the AI Now Institute at New York University. That organization provides interdisciplinary research on understanding the social implications of artificial intelligence with four focus areas: rights and liberties, labor and automation, bias and inclusion, as well as safety and critical infrastructure (AI Now 2020). For example, their annual report of 2019 alone provides a comprehensive set of 494 AI-based concerns and aspects (Crawford et al. 2019).

Table 11.1 Comparison of GDPR and CCPA (own presentation, data based on (Rosner 2019; Schwenke 2020)

Subject	GDPR	CCPA (2018)
Consumer privacy	Fundamental right: data processing illegal unless it complies with at least one out of six lawful cases.	CCPA is not a comprehensive data protection law, but rather serves consumer protection. It is deeme that mutual benefits are derived out of a business relationship that is subject to negotiation.
Scope of businesses subject to regulation	Any company doing business in the EU. Hence, it is not focused on EU citizens only.	Applicable on California residents only. Exempt of smaller companies (w/o data brokers) (1) annual revenue below USD 25 m, or (2) data sets of less than 50,000 consumers (basis: no. of devices) or (3) less than 50% of revenue generated with data selling.
Personal data	Personal and pseudonymous data of individuals (data subjects), and specific "sensitive" data such as ethnic origin, political opinions, religious or philosophical beliefs, trade union membership, genetic data, biometric data, etc.	Broader definition of any data related to a consumer of household, but no distinction of sensitive of pseudonymous data. Tracking data like search history could be included.
Data portability	Right to receive own data in common, machine-readable format or directly to be transferred to another company.	Right to receive own data in common, machine-readable format but no right that such data are directly transferred to another company.
Right to data erasure/to be forgotten	Obligation for data controllers to erase data without undue delay and to inform their data sharing partners accordingly, on request of the consumer.	Deletion right only applies to consumer data collected directly from the consumer, not to any data collected from third-party sources. Broader exceptions, e.g. maintain data for internal lawful use.
Right to opt out of sale of personal information	Broad right for consumers to object any type of commercial use of their personal data.	Specifically prohibits "selling" (in a broader sense) consumer data on their opt-out request.
Consequences of violations	Lump-sum fines per violation: Minor cases: the larger of 2% of annual revenue or €10 m; Major cases: the larger of 4% of annual revenue or €20 m	Individual fine per individual consumer affected by the infringement: USD 2500 per violation and USD 7500 for an intentional violation. As a single incident can affect millions of consumers (residents in California), the resulting fine may greatly exceed the GDPR cap. Furthermore, CCPA allows for USD 100–750 per affected consumer as remedy, presumable

(continued)

Table 11.1 (continued)

Subject	GDPR	CCPA (2018)
		without having to demonstrate actual harm. Hence, that would make class action lawsuits for data breaches much easier to file.

Table 11.2 Comparison of selected different ethical digital initiatives in Germany. (own analysis and presentation based on (Spektrum 2015; Conrad 2019; Datenethikkommission 2019)

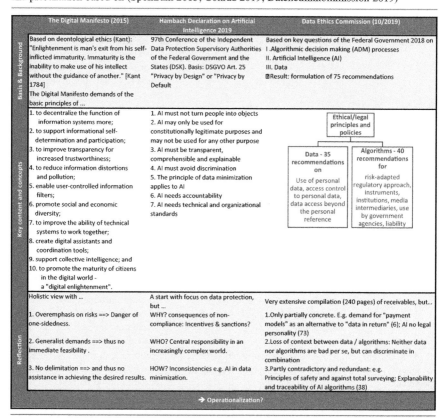

Example AI Data Poisoning and Backdoor Attacks

In the AI Now Reports 2019 two urgent vulnerabilities are elaborated:

1. Data poisoning technique is a method of willingly manipulating AI training data to modify the resulting AI-based decisions. A typical (comparatively innocent) case of spam filter training is mentioned, where by manipulation

(continued)

of the training data, which is used by the spam filter to learn how spam looks, certain spam type will not be detected (as intended by the bad actor).

2. In the "backdoor attack," the attacker uses purposefully set entry points by malicious programmers, so that in later use, manipulation can be conducted by bad actors related to a specific configuration. Reference is made to researchers at NYU. They showed that backdoor attacks on commonly used AI road sign detectors for autonomous vehicles, where a spillover effect on misclassifying US stop signs was seen, were detected on the model that was retrained for Swedish stop signs. Given the rapid trend on model training in the cloud ("Function as a Service"—FaaS), this represents a major vulnerability of the integrity of AI. (Crawford et al. 2019).

3. OpenAI:

According to its own statements, OpenAI has been set up for non-profit reasons with primary fiduciary duty to humanity (OpenAI 2018), so it has ethical standards for AI in their mission statement:

"OpenAI's mission is to ensure that artificial general intelligence (AGI)—by which we mean highly autonomous systems that outperform humans at most economically valuable work—benefits all of humanity. We will attempt to directly build safe and beneficial AGI, but will also consider our mission fulfilled if our work aids others to achieve this outcome."

This organization is supported by PayPal-Tesla-SpaceX founder Elon Musk, and formed an exclusive multiyear partnership with Microsoft in 2019 to build Azure AI supercomputing technologies (Microsoft 2019).

It is left to the reader to assess the non-commercial aspect of this endeavor (Fig. 11.3).

11.3 AI Framing to Safeguard the Good

As shown in the previous section, there are quite some initiatives set up to reflect ethical concerns in digitization in general and AI specifically. Although these initiatives are likely to be helpful, the question arises as to whether these are already sufficient to adequately reflect the effects of AI.

More than ever, the human welfare depends on an interconnection that ensures dignity and prospect of advancement for individuals. Technology like AI can enable exactly that, but only, if the advantaged do not selfishly misuse it for shortsighted purposes at the cost of the vulnerable. The advantaged, having access to capital and knowledge, have a fiduciary duty toward the vulnerable and should act accordingly—as well to foster their own long-term core interests.

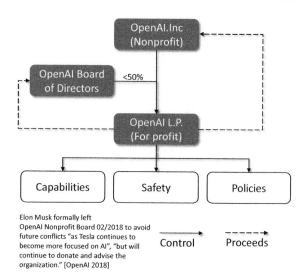

Fig. 11.3 OpenAI corporate structure. (Own presentation based on information from the organzation's website (OpenAI 2018, 2019))

Example UN: Human Rights Council's Resolution on "Digital Technology, Social Protection and Human Rights" Reflecting the report of the UN Special Rapporteur on extreme poverty and human rights, a report submitted in accordance with Human Rights Council resolution 35/19 (Alston 2019), the need for action beyond becomes obvious. In this report, "the grave risk of stumbling, zombie-like, into a digital welfare dystopia is highlighted." In particular, it is argued that Big Tech companies "operate in an almost human rights-free zone, and that this is especially problematic when the private sector is taking a leading role in designing, constructing and even operating significant parts of the digital welfare state." Hence, it is highlighted that it is paramount to urgently define how AI technologies can be utilized to serve the societies to ensure a higher standard of living for the vulnerable and disadvantaged. The current appreciation of efficiency advantages and the addressing of the security and abuse scenarios are however subordinate.

This mandate from the UN Human Rights Council is a clear wake-up call to think more broadly than done so far.

In the following section, the required building blocks for such a holistic approach will be showcased by the metaphor of the House of Ethical AI.

11.4   House of Ethical AI: Shaping the Future with AI

From the previous explanations, significant ethical challenges arise for the age of AI; they directly link back to the fundamentals of business ethics (see Chaps. 3, 4, and Sect. 7.5 as well) and practical considerations addressed in Sect. 9.4. Figure 11.4 summarized the dimension of the issues to be addressed in the form of the House of Ethical AI. Overarching aim in an ethical and comprehensive sense shall be the

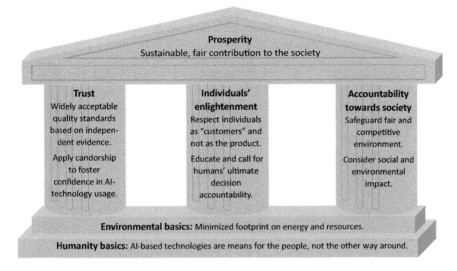

Fig. 11.4 House of Ethical AI (own presentation)

prosperity and wealth creation that can only be achieved with a sustainable approach and fair contribution to the society.

11.4.1 The Foundation of the House of Ethical AI

As a fundamental task it must be ensured that any AI technology respects the basic rights of humanity, as laid down in the UN Declaration of Human Rights (UN 1948). So, the machines need to serve the people, not the other way around. Reflecting Isaac Asimov's famous "Laws of Robotics" (1942, 1.-3. Law, 1983: 0. Law added) (Seiler and Jenkins 2014), obviously these fictitious rules may help as a guardrail.

Asimov's Laws of Robotics
(Seiler and Jenkins 2014):

0. "A robot must not hurt humanity or allow humanity to be harmed by passivity.
1. A robot may not injure a human being or cause harm through inactivity, unless it would violate the zero law.
2. A robot must obey the orders of a human being, unless such orders are contrary to the zeroth or first law.
3. A robot must protect its own existence as long as this protection does not contradict the zeroth, first or second law."

Likewise, the environmental footprint associated with AI technology needs to be minimized. So far, this is very often neglected, as there are no effective incentives to avoid the negative consequences of resource wastefulness, and digitization commonly has an environmental-friendly public image. In Sect. 6.7, the exponential increase in computational resources and therewith environmental and economic costs has been demonstrated. While optimization in particular narrow AI applications is emerging and initiatives to track the "state-of-the-art" ("SOTA")[3] are taken this will not solve the problem, so a fair incentivization is required, which ultimately will have beneficial effects in the pillars "trust" and "enlightenment" as well.

11.4.2 The Pillar of Trust

In order to achieve that humans need to gain confidence in the technology. The good news is that this is absolutely nothing new! It is just a question of how to handle quality. Well-established quality standards provide orientation for decision-making across decision-making as consumers, B2B customers, or public authorities. In particular in critical products and services that can potentially harm individuals like in the food or healthcare industries, these quality standards are enforced by auditing systems with verification and validation that is the basis for consumers' trust.

Such systems can be taken as a starting point to develop an AI framework for trust. It should encounter the two core elements of any AI application: algorithm and data (see Sect. 6.6). Furthermore, the context of its usage needs to be encountered as well: i.e., applying best AI solutions in an repressive or exploitational setting such as pushing users to immaturity in total surveillance (e.g., see Sects. 7.4 and 7.5) contradicts the foundation and the enlightenment pillar of the House of Ethical AI.

While quality proof is visible at the end, it is important to set up a structure in the AI product development and operations that fosters exactly this quality and trust building. The latter is highly mobile: it takes very long to build up and may be destroyed in a single glitch. Hence, the question of leadership prevails. Based on empirical evidence, a clear correlation can be shown between the concept of candorship and better economic performance (Vieweg 2019): For example US companies applying candorship outperformed S&P500 market average by a factor of 1.8, and top quartile's share price development was three times of the bottom quartile (period 2010–2015) (Rittenhouse 2018). Similar results were confirmed for the German market, where DAX30 top quartile's candorship companies outperformed market average by a factor of 1.6, and top quartile's share price

---

[3]For example see the neural network training effort of a well-known ImageNet classification, which could be improved by a factor of 44 compared to the 2012 benchmark (in contrast: the often-cited Moore's Law from the 70th – the trend that computer capabilities double every 18 months – would yield to a factor of 11) (Hernandez and Brown 2020).

development was 2.3 times of the bottom quartile (period 2015–2017) (Vieweg 2019).

Candorship reflects a management approach that is based on values of transparency, authenticity, accountability, honesty, and error culture. This is in harsh contrast to window dressing, green washing, self-delusion, and fogging.[4]

Candorship requires an organizational culture reflecting said values. Proven management methodologies foster decentralization and delegation and at the same time orchestrating the strategy setting and execution. This gives both the flexibility to cope with changing requirements and presenting the efficiency and stability to drive the strategic themes. The leading holistic and open framework is the ScaledAgileFramework (SAFe®) (SAFe 2020) (based on core values of built-in quality and transparency): The "lean-agile" orientation allows rapid learning and adaptation through decentralized decision-making competence within agile teams, and in parallel servant leadership on management level.

11.4.3 The Pillar of Individuals' Enlightenment

Technology has always acted as enabler or facilitator (e.g., see the John Deer examples in Sect. 9.4) which pushed the frontier of possibilities further. Though with AI, there is a new dimension of support, as it is not limited to mechanical or motoric capabilities, but extends to cognitive human capabilities (see Fig. 9.2 in Sect. 9.4): There is a pending risk of addiction to individual using AI support. As illustrated in Sects. 7.4 and 7.5, there is high risk to self-chosen immaturity. Under the false pretenses of "customer centricity," this will lead to consumers' passivity, as this "services" come as an alluring convenience.

Though, ethical AI would respect users as individuals with their own decision competencies and would support them accordingly. This can be illustrated by using the example of pharmaceutical products or prepacked nutritional products: based on regulation requirements, health warnings inform consumers on product ingredients (e.g., on energy, fat, saturates, sugar, salt) and how to use the product rightly and on any collateral effects, e.g., of overconsumption. In the AI context, this requires much more than the disclaimers on data privacy. In particular, this should include decision-relevant information about . . .

1. . . . a particular algorithm's characteristics, the quality to be expected realistically, and its shortcomings
2. . . . the data basis to train the algorithm

---

[4]FOG refers to "fact-deficient obfuscating generalities"; this Ritthouse-influenced abbreviation (fog) from the context of investor relations communication illustrates the problem: disinformation and unclear statements serve to manipulate stakeholders (especially shareholders).

3. ... the processing and the technical environment, e.g., a setting of a trusted hedged environment (probably with less quality) or an open, cloud-based environment accessible to an undefinable group and risk of contamination and attacks
4. ...the environmental footprint
5. ... the interested parties and disclosure or potential conflicts of interest. In this context, the issue of biased information is crucial as it is misleading. So, "disfaked" information in an environment of manipulation through AI-based services should be thought.

Ultimately, the user as individual (human) personality with dignity and accountability needs to take the final decision. Disregarding the technical quality of a system,[5] the final accountability cannot be transferred to a non-human entity, even if judicial constructs like the e-person may be introduced in certain jurisdictions.

To illustrate this basic principle, an extreme example is given where it becomes obvious that technology has its shortcomings and fatalities and serious damages can easily occur.

Example: The Man Who Saved the World (Lebedev 2004)

In 1983, the world was very close to a nuclear world war, with uncalculated consequences: It was a Russian named Petrov[6] who ignored protocols and procedures and withdrew from firing off a nuclear weapon targeting the USA, when all Russian technical systems indicated that there is a threatening first nuclear missile strike with some objects from the USA toward the USSR. Petrov concluded that given the situation between the two superpowers the USA and USSR, a first strike from the USA would not make any sense (or if so, only a massive intervention with hundreds of missiles would) and he assumed that the technical systems provided wrong information: he was right and probably saved the planet—for now.

There are many other examples that prove keeping humans out of final decision loop leads to fatalities. Reference is made to the 2018 and 2019 disasters of Boeing's 737 Max 8 crashes.

Hence, beyond all technical excellence that can be achieved already today and that will emerge in the future, the final accountability needs to be kept to humans (Precht 2019). Why, if there are so many human shortcomings, cognitive biases, and individual motivations? The answer to this question comes back to the fundamental shortcoming of machines: they do not have a desire; they do not have a socialization that would give them the ethical compass of doing right or wrong. And—finally—it would be human persons that have to take the (legal) consequences

---

[5]As an example it is referred to the Uber case in Sect. 11.2.1.

[6]Lebedev, A. (2004): The Man Who Saved the World Finally Recognized. https://web.archive.org/web/20110721000030/http://www.worldcitizens.org/petrov2.html. (access 10.08.2020).

and penalties of wrongdoing. It would not make too much sense to impose a punishment like jail for wrongdoing on a robot.

In parallel, consumers need to be incentivized picking up their decision responsibility, apply prudent judgment (reference is made again to the increasing number of consumers practicing organic food consumption), and restrain from carelessness for convenience.

11.4.4 The Pillar of Accountability Toward Society

AI technologies have the potential to disrupt social cohabitation. Hence, an ethical approach for AI cannot be limited "just" to aspects of individuals such as on data protection or responsibility delegation (e.g., to an e-person). A single-sided perspective on the opportunities of AI technologies such as efficiency increase through automation will brutally fail to consider the societal context in its sphere of influence.

An approach to foster accountability in the context of AI technologies should include assessment measures. Similar to a risk-adjusted perspective well known in traditional asset management or the life cycle assessment ("LCA") according to ISO 14040/14044[7] for the environmental impact, the environmental and social perspective can be captured in a social adjusted valuation. Such a measure of an "AI social linked environmental assessment" ("AISLE") can form a basis to combine the required sustainable perspective. This would need to reflect the socially disadvantaged.

But it is not only an obligation for businesses, *scientists* as well take on a very important role: They need to sensitize politicians on the spillover effects of AI exploitation, as responsible scientists have done in the 1940s and 1950s with the nuclear potential and threats such as the atomic and hydrogen bomb.

> Today's data scientists have the same accountability as had the nuclear scientists some 70 years ago preventing us from the third world war.

Furthermore, taking accountability means clarifying weak structures that the software industry relied on in the past. In the pre-AI age, this was a minor issue as there was technology choice, i.e., operating systems, programs, and the like. In the AI age, more and more dependencies on key joint resources emerge. This can be seen by reflecting the driving AI communities and the provision of key inputs such as specific algorithms (for details, it is referred to Sect. 6.6.1).

Key assets in the "open" digital world such as open access software are a cornerstone of the digital evolution. As proven by many occasions throughout the last few decades, proprietary approaches deem to block innovation. As an example, since its introduction in 1991, the operating system LINUX (Netmarketshare 2020)

---

[7]LCA as defined by ISO is a measure to evaluate the environmental impact of products and services.

has emerged as platform for millions of (business) servers and desktop computers, and provided the nucleus ("kernel") for the open source mobile operation system Android, launched in 2007, which replaced and outpaced the up-to-then dominating Nokia's proprietary operating system "Symbian" and Microsoft's Windows Mobile. While these achievements are impressive in the open software development, that is characterized by many of intrinsically motivated developers who are driving for better solutions and their own mastery. The ultimate access to the heart (the "kernel") of these technologies lies with some individuals—with the so-called benevolent dictators for life ("BDFL") (who deemed to be intrinsically motivated)—such as the initiator of Linux, Linus Thorvald, taking a coordinating role in the further development of the kernel. Astonishingly enough, this loose structure seems to work out quite well so far). Otherwise, fragmentations on a large scale would be the consequence. For AI algorithms and approaches, a commonly accepted framework could be built up—similar to the data protection framework in the GDPR—to provide fair access to resources and to offer security of investment (i.e., a sound foundation for the individual investments based on fair and stable access to basic intellectual property). So, to extend the approach of benevolent dictator for life (BDFL), a truly independent NPO is required with prevention of any acquisitions by companies (as happened to many open platforms like Kaggle or Github, or OpenAI), nor been governed by a single state, and that safeguards the consistency of AI approaches. Hence, Europe may play a leading role here.

Politicians are asked to take their fiduciary duty seriously driving the agenda in the AI age, as the impact of societies will be enormous. According to technology philosopher Precht (2020), the moral intuition of humans is not a predefined and controlled process, but rather a situational and context-dependent one that is closely connected to self-esteem and self-concept. Hence, corrective guardrails are required to cope with the societal and environmental challenges: Precht's view resonates with scientists (see Sect. 7.3) if he sees a massive deterioration of ordinary employment practices. For example in Germany in 2018, there were only 53% of employees who had paid work according to collective agreements. This trend of deterioration of achievements on employment participation will have two negative effects: less people will be able to live on their pensions in the future, and—fueled by automation due to digitization and AI—the rate of unemployment, temporary work, mini-jobs unpaid internships, etc., will increase leading to impoverishment of the middle class. In a "humane society of the future," the unconditional basic income would overcome the current concept of employment-based (and solely economic performance-based) remuneration.

This leads to the necessity for politicians to change the system, otherwise—as technology will dictate (cf. Collingridge dilemma, Sect. 1.5.3)—there may be irreversible social mismatches—at least accelerated by AI, which may even lead to breakup of societies and archaic problem-solving approaches of ancient decades such as unrest, riots, and civil war.

An important first step of taking accountability toward the society includes the avoidance of dependencies from "Big Tech." Despite the alluring offers and lobbying, politicians need to ensure that effective coordinating structures such as fair market conditions on a global level are established. These include (but are not limited to):

1. *Fair taxes:* AI companies to bear a fair share of societal costs (that is commonly called "tax" and typically avoided by them). Currently, in the majority of societies an anachronistic taxation model is in place: assuming that production factors such as (human) work are prevalent, companies only pay taxes if they generate a profit. Though, an international business can easily (and legally, but not ethically) navigate from where profits are generated to where taxes are low: hence, they "optimize" their profits in low-tax jurisdictions, whereas in high-tax countries losses are cumulating (and taxes are avoided). The underlying societal logic (unfortunately outdated in the AI era) is that companies provide opportunities for the citizens to work and based on a fair share of success (say "profit"), the companies shall contribute to the societal infrastructure they are benefiting from. Examples are education (for the employees), public services, roads real estate, and telecommunication infrastructure.

   A fair share of AI contribution to the societal systems needs to include an unavoidable taxation mechanics, e.g., based on similar levels as payroll taxes for human work to be implied for equivalent automation entities (like the e-person as being discussed in the EU).

2. *Fair competition:* Fostering competition and avoiding monopoly or oligopoly market structures that are de facto emerging or existing to a certain extent. This includes the breakup of dominant monopolist as well, similar as breakup of the Bell System in the USA in 1982.

3. *Self-restriction and misuse prevention:* Legal and regulatory settings on an international level are required to minimize the misuse of products and services that ultimately will lead to compromised human rights. There are effective mechanisms and knowledge how to handle it available from the pre-digital age: such structures were set up to ban ABC weapons (atomic/nuclear, biological, chemical) that could be characterized as military and their application could have erased large parts of humanity. The success of such mechanisms is based on two fundamental elements:

   (a) The *clear intent* as laid down in the contracts: For example the Treaty on the Non-Proliferation of Nuclear Weapons ("NPT") (UN NPT 1995).[8]

   (b) *Independent controls* that could trigger off enforcement actions: Example: the International Atomic Energy Agency ("IAEA"): "The International Atomic Energy Agency is the world's central intergovernmental forum for scientific and technical co-operation in the nuclear field. It works for the safe, secure and peaceful uses of nuclear science and technology, contributing to international peace and security and the United Nations' Sustainable Development Goals" (IAEA 2020): This UN organization has a clear and independent mandate.

---

[8]The treaty provided the non-proliferation, disarmament, and peaceful use of nuclear energy.

In the AI era—even in pure civil use cases—there are highly critical situations that urgently need self-restriction: the example is in health care and telemedicine, where no effective controls are in place to avoid misuse and exploitation of individuals.

Example Google Invests in Leading US Telemedicine Services Amwell
Amwell is the one of the largest brokers of telemedicine or telematics services in the USA. Amwell has more than 40,000 service providers (e.g., physicians) including 2000 hospitals that enable c. 80 million US citizens to benefit from virtual medical consultations. In order to "leverage the global presence of Google Cloud," there is a link between the customer accounts of Amwell and Google. (Aerzteblatt 2020) In other words: Google has direct access to VERY sensitive health data of millions of patients. It is claimed that within this partnership, "security and data protection as core principles" are to apply and all services offered would adhere to "strict guidelines on data access and use, including industry regulations on patient health information" (Aerzteblatt 2020).

To reflect this, such statement fulfills the first condition "intent," but it lacks any measure on the second condition "independent controls" (see above). From the past we learnt that despite cheap proclamations data breaches and misuse are common, e.g., "Google's 'Project Nightingale' Gathers Personal Health Data on Millions of Americans" as *The Wall Street Journal* titled (Copeland 2019) when reporting that Google has collected and processed the health data of millions of patients provided by the healthcare organization Ascension, and neither the patients concerned nor the attending physicians gave their consent to the disclosure.

Self-restriction is a nil return, e.g., in the context of Google's acquisition of smart wearables producer Fitbit; in 2019, the opposite may actually be true, following the dpa-report. "At the same time, there was no promise to store data separately, as was once the case when Google took over smarthome specialist Nest" (Welt 2020).

Although careless individuals may initially think that they do not have anything to hide or they are "not interesting" for commercial use, the situation may quickly turn into a massive disadvantage for them next time they apply for a job, a loan etc. when the resulting AI-based profiling will disqualify them due to inadequate living performance parameter...

Disregarding whether the companies apply strict compliance or not, without independent controls prevention of breach of human rights is not effectively possible. Just referring to the law and its procedures ex post is insufficient and unsatisfactory, since the AI impact typically affects large groups of a society.

4. *Societal impact assessment:* Political and economic decision-makers resist exploiting technology potential for their own benefit without reflecting the knock-on effects on societies.

   At a minimum, ethical guardrails are required to ensure that the technology is used to the benefit of societies and businesses in a frame of generally accepted human rights (see the UN Declaration of Human Rights and following human rights conventions, cf. Sect. 4.3) and environmental standards as laid down, e.g., in ISO 14001 ff. or the European EMAS (Eco-Management and Audit Scheme).

5. *Independence and special fiduciary duty:* Public services have a massive disadvantage in many countries, related to AI: AI comprises technologies that require expert knowledge in all key areas: algorithm, data, and its implementation. Typically, AI companies such as Big Tech are in the lead, as they can attract highly skilled people with ease by offering entrepreneurial spirit, interesting working, progression, and remuneration conditions, and—most importantly—a share in a success story. In contrast: if public IT services convey the image of a boring statistical bureau at crummy pay, guess what their recruiting success will be ... So, political decision-maker should take an active role in shaping the framing, instead of surrendering and handing over public affairs to Big Tech and Co.

   It is advisable to reflect best practices where efforts led to a leading organization that drives progress in the name of their fiduciaries. Such examples are independent of individual's capital dominance.

> Antipattern example of lacking fiduciary duty -Finnish patients blackmailed after tens of thousands private psychotherapy notes were hacked: The private psychotherapy services Vastaamo failed to establish decent measures and controls to protect sensitive data of their patients for two years. Back in November 2018, hackers first accessed the patient database, the then CEO concealed the breach from the company's board, and in late October 2020, hackers blackmailed patients threatening the disclosure of their private data. As the company has some 40,000 patients' data on record, this scandal led to a massive crisis forcing Finland's president and prime minister for public statements. (Sipilä 2020)

As can be seen from this example[9] it needs effective and independent measures to implement security in the digital age.

Relying on the cooperation of IT companies is not at all an adequate approach. This can be seen in another potential antipattern:

---

[9]There are many other examples across the world, e.g., it is referred to the investigative platform propublica.org and their 2019 report on "Millions of Americans' Medical Images and Data Are Available on the Internet. Anyone Can Take a Peek." (Gillum et al. 2019)

> Example the German Ministry of Health cooperating with Google: Initially
> this sounds really great: "'Who googles health topics is uncertain and needs
> urgently advice, therefore it is important that one can rely on the information,
> which one finds there,' explained Federal Minister of Health Jens Spahn
> (CDU)" (Aerzteblatt 2020a) to promote the cooperation with Google. The
> Internet giant inserts colored boxes—so-called knowledge panels—"that
> appear next to the search results when searching for 160 diseases and health-
> related topics. These are filled with information" from the Ministry's own
> website gesund.bund.de and a weblink to it. The information reflects
> symptoms and possible treatment.
>
> While this sounds great—initially, the conditions of how Google is entitled
> to use the consumers' data for this specific service remain opaque (not only on
> the costs for this service to the ministry). For example, individuals' search
> requests will not selflessly be rooted by Google to the ministry's website, but
> Google will most likely use them for profiling. Hence, it should not come as a
> surprise if one enters the term "dust allergy," one might find quite soon—
> probably immediately—offers for dust filters, mite-free mattresses, and per-
> haps even for prescription-free medicines against it on the side. . . As this may
> be a minor issue, the criticality was addressed in the Amwell example above.

6. *Social Correctives: Public Awareness to Foster Responsive Governments.*
   In order to reflect the downside of capitalism that focuses on the economic
   progress of the firm, an independent view on the social and environmental aspects
   is more than ever required. Such independent forces can be provided by public
   awareness and responsive government (see 5. above): As soon as a public
   awareness about a harmful development, e.g., on pollution or the tragedy of
   species loss is built, political decision-makers will take corrective actions.
   McAffee sees the combination of the four elements (1). Capitalism, (2). tech
   progress, (3). public awareness, and (4). responsive government as the basis for
   optimism in societal and environmental progress (McAffee 2019).

11.5   Implementation Roadmap for Ethical AI

From the previous chapters, a conclusive roadmap can be generated as cornerstone
for embarking on an ethical acceptable application of AI technologies in the form of
a "fact sheet."

For *businesses* considering introduction or further rollout of AI technologies, the
following considerations should be thought to enable AI for the good (see Fig. 11.5):

1. Ethics: Positioning on the ethical minimal standards such as respecting human
   rights, thrive for self-determination → *Intent.*
2. Governance: establish a leadership approach such as *candorship*, which conveys
   the ethical intent.

Fig. 11.5 Ethical AI implementation roadmap (own presentation)

3. *Quality*: ensure that all driving components of any AI application—algorithm, (training)data, and implementation/processes—are configured in such a way that the intent can be achieved.
4. *Efficiency*: minimize the data and resource consumption, invest in smart algorithms.
5. *Compliance*: ensure that the internationally acceptable legal standards are followed and complied.

For *governments and political decision-makers* it should be paramount to take accountability and to drive the independent framing of the "AI playground" for social fairness, as AI technologies have disruptive potential and scaling effects to masses. A starting point can be found in the identified six focus areas of the pillar of accountability of the House of Ethical AI (see 11.4.4). Therefore, *scientists* need to take a stance to drive for fair and independent knowledge increase as trustable input for the political decision process.

11.6 Finish Line Quiz

11.01	Why are robots not just automatons?	
	1	They are, there is no difference from automatic machines.
	2	They have a certain degree of autonomy.
	3	They are automatons as they are not an independent legal entity.
	4	They are on the same level as humans.
11.02	What is a likely "legal" role of a robot?	
	1	The robot acts as an advisor to a human supervisor.
	2	The robot acts as a messenger of a human supervisor.
	3	The robot acts as a negotiator acting on behalf of a human supervisor.
	4	The robot acts as no degree of freedom in decision-making.

(continued)

11.03	What is a potential approach on regulation of AI systems (RoboLaw), e.g., autonomous driving?	
	1	Shared responsibility: Manufacturer + programmer + driver.
	2	Sole responsibility with the driver.
	3	Sole responsibility with the manufacturer.
	4	Responsibility with the party that can minimize the costs most effectively.
11.04	Which characteristics are to be considered as intelligent robots?	
	1	Autonomy through sensors and/or interconnectivity).
	2	At least a minimum of physical support.
	3	Ability to adapt their behavior and actions to their environment.
	4	All of above.
11.05	What were approximately the cumulated number of infringement cases and fines concerning GDPR in Europe (2018–10/2020)?	
	1	100 cases/€50 million
	2	200 cases/€150 million
	3	300 cases/€250 million
	4	400 cases/€250 million
11.06	What is the key issue with ethical initiatives in Germany shown?	
	1	They do not have any issue.
	2	They are too complex.
	3	They are too unspecific in terms of operationalization.
	4	They are too comprehensive.
11.07	What is one of the focus areas of the AI now institute?	
	1	Providing free market access.
	2	Understanding social implications of AI.
	3	Efficiency improvement on AI algorithms.
	4	Technology sharing.
11.08	Where was the citation "the grave risk of stumbling, zombie-like, into a digital welfare dystopia" taken from?	
	1	From the UN human rights Council's resolution on "digital technology, social protection and human rights.
	2	From the AI now annual report 2019.
	3	From the German digital manifesto of 2015.
	4	From Isaac Asimov's famous book *I, Robot*.
11.09	What is the foundation of the "house of ethical AI"?	
	1	Trust
	2	Humanity
	3	Enlightenment
	4	Accountability
11.10	What are the cornerstones of "self-restriction and misuse prevention" in the "house of ethical AI"?	
	1	Quality and efficiency
	2	Effectiveness and efficiency
	3	Intent and independent control
	4	Fair competition and taxes

Correct answers can be found in www.vieweg-beratung.de/downloads

References

Aerzteblatt. (2020). *Telemedizin: Google hat einen neuen strategischen Partner.* Retrieved November 2, 2020, from https://www.aerzteblatt.de/nachrichten/116079/Telemedizin-Google-hat-einen-neuen-strategischen-Partner.

Aerzteblatt. (2020a). *Gesundheitsinformationen: Spahn startet Kooperation mit Google.* Retrieved November 12, 2020, from https://www.aerzteblatt.de/nachrichten/118196/Gesundheitsinformationen-Spahn-startet-Kooperation-mit-Google.

AI Now. (2020). *AI Now – A research institute examining the social implications of artificial intelligence.* Retrieved November 2, 2020, from https://ainowinstitute.org/.

Alston, Ph. (2019). *Digital technology, social protection and human rights: Report, A/74/493.* Retrieved October 26, 2020, from https://www.ohchr.org/EN/Issues/Poverty/Pages/DigitalTechnology.aspx.

BMJV. (2019). *Gutachten der Datenethikkommission.* Retrieved October 1, 2020, from https://www.bmjv.de/SharedDocs/Downloads/DE/Themen/Fokusthemen/Gutachten_DEK_DE.pdf?__blob=publicationFile&v=2.

Conrad C. (2019). *Die sieben neuen KI-Regeln der Datenschutzkonferenz.* Retrieved October 18, 2019, from https://www.datenschutz-notizen.de/die-sieben-neuen-ki-regeln-der-datenschutzkonferenz-0722439/.

Copeland, R. (2019). *Google's 'project nightingale' gathers personal health data on millions of Americans.* Retrieved November 2, 2020, from https://www.wsj.com/articles/google-s-secret-project-nightingale-gathers-personal-health-data-on-millions-of-americans-11573496790.

Crawford, K., Dobbe, R., Dryer, T, Fried, G., Green, B., Kaziunas, E., Kak, A., Mathur, V., McElroy, E., Sánchez, A. N., Raji, D., Rankin, J. L., Richardson, R., Schultz, J., West, S. M., Whittaker, M. (2019). *AI now 2019 report.* New York: AI Now Institute. Retrieved November 2, 2020, from https://ainowinstitute.org/AI_Now_2019_Report.html.

Delvaux, M. (2017). Europäisches Parlament 2014–2019 BERICHT mit Empfehlungen an die Kommission zu zivilrechtlichen Regelungen im Bereich Robotik (2015/2103(INL)) A8-0005/2017, p. 9.

EC. (2019). *GDPR – the fabric of a success story.* Retrieved November 2, 2020, from https://ec.europa.eu/info/law/law-topic/data-protection/eu-data-protection-rules/gdpr-fabric-success-story_en.

enforcementtracker.com. (2020). Retrieved November 10, 2020, from https://www.enforcementtracker.com/?insights.

EU. (2016a). *Regulation (EU) 2016/679. General data protection regulation.* Retrieved October 2, 2020, from http://data.europa.eu/eli/reg/2016/679/2016-05-04.

EU. (2016b). *Treaty on European Union (Consolidated version 2016).* Retrieved October 2, 2020, from https://eur-lex.europa.eu/legal-content/EN/TXT/?uri=CELEX%3A12016M002

EU. (2017). *Robotic and AI.* https://www.europarl.europa.eu/news/de/press-room/20170210IPR61808/robotik-und-kunstliche-intelligenz-abgeordnete-fur-eu-weite-haftungsregelungen

Federal Data Protection Act. (2017). Federal Data Protection Act of 30 June 2017 (Federal Law Gazette I p. 2097), as last amended by Article 12 of the Act of 20 November 2019 (Federal Law Gazette I, p. 1626).

Gershgorn, D. (2015). *Hitachi hires artificially intelligent bosses for their warehouses.* Retrieved February 15, 2020, from https://www.popsci.com/hitachi-hires-artificial-intelligence-bosses-for-their-warehouses.

Gillum, J., Kao, J., Larson, J. (2019). *Millions of Americans' medical images and data are available on the internet. Anyone can take a peek.* Retrieved November 2, 2020, from https://www.propublica.org/article/millions-of-americans-medical-images-and-data-are-available-on-the-internet.

Groß, N., & Gressel, J. (2016). *Entpersonalisierte Arbeitsverhältnisse als rechtliche Herausforderung, Neue Zeitschrift für Arbeitsrecht 16/2016.*

Hernandez, D., & Brown, T. (2020, May). *AI and efficiency. OpenAI blog 15*. Retrieved November 2, 2020, from https://openai.com/blog/ai-and-efficiency/#rf3.

IAEA. (2020). *Overview IAEA*. Retrieved October 2, 2020, from https://www.iaea.org/about/overview.

Kaminski, K. (2018). *The GDPR's version of algorithmic accountability*, JOTWELL (August 16, 2018) (reviewing Lilian Edwards and Michael Veale, *Slave to the Algorithm? Why a 'right to an explanation' is probably not the remedy you are looking for*, 16 Duke L. & Tech. Rev. 18 (2017), available at SSRN). Retrieved November 2, 2020, from https://cyber.jotwell.com/the-gdprs-version-of-algorithmic-accountability/.

Lebedev, A. (2004). *The man who saved the world finally recognized*. Retrieved August 10, 2020, from https://web.archive.org/web/20110721000030/http://www.worldcitizens.org/petrov2.html.

McAffee, A. (2019). *More from less. The surprising story of how we learned to prosper using fewer resources—And what happens next*. New York: Scribner. Retrieved October 21, 2020, from https://andrewmcafee.org/more-from-less/overivew.

McCausland, P. (2019). *Self-driving Uber car that hit and killed woman did not recognize that pedestrians jaywalk. NBC news*. Retrieved November 2, 2020, from https://www.nbcnews.com/tech/tech-news/self-driving-uber-car-hit-killed-woman-did-not-recognize-n1079281.

Microsoft. (2019). *OpenAI forms exclusive computing partnership with Microsoft to build new Azure AI supercomputing technologies*. Retrieved October 1, 2020, fromhttps://news.microsoft.com/2019/07/22/openai-forms-exclusive-computing-partnership-with-microsoft-to-build-new-azure-ai-supercomputing-technologies/.

Netmarketshare. (2020). *Market share for internet technologies*. Retrieved August 2, 2020, from https://www.netmarketshare.com/?options=%7B%22filter%22%3A%7B%22%24and%22%3A%5B%7B%22deviceType%22%3A%7B%22%24in%22%3A%5B%22Desktop%2Flaptop%22%5D%7D%7D%5D%7D%2C%22dateLabel%22%3A%22Trend%22%2C%22attributes%22%3A%22share%22%2C%22group%22%3A%22browser%22%2C%22sort%22%3A%7B%22share%22%3A-1%7D%2C%22id%22%3A%22browsersDesktop%22%2C%22dateInterval%22%3A%22Monthly%22%2C%22dateStart%22%3A%222019-11%22%2C%22dateEnd%22%3A%222020-10%22%2C%22segments%22%3A%22-1000%22%7D.

OpenAI. (2018). *OpenAI supporters*. Retrieved November 2, 2020, from https://openai.com/blog/openai-supporters/.

OpenAI. (2019). *OpenAI LP*. Retrieved November 2, 2020, from https://openai.com/blog/openai-lp/.

Precht, R. D. (2019). „Nicht alles Neue ist gut." Der Philosoph über die Ähnlichkeiten der Umbrüche vor 200 Jahren und heute, die Denkfehler, die das Silicon Valley mit Marx teilt, und die Gefahren durch Onlineshoppen. In: Handelsblatt 11. Okt. 2019, p. 52f.

Precht, R. D. (2020). *Künstliche Intelligenz und der Sinn des Lebens*. New York: Goldmann.

Rittenhouse, L. J. (2018). *CEO candor and culture survey 2017*. Retrieved February 4, 2019, from www.rittenhouserankings.com/wp-content/uploads/2018/11/2017-Rittenhouse-Rankings-Candor-and-Culture-SurveyTM.pdf.

Rosner, L. J. (2019). *7 key differences between GDPR and CCPA*. Retrieved November 2, 2020, from https://otonomo.io/blog/7-key-differences-between-gdpr-and-ccpa/.

SAFe. (2020). *SAFe 5.0*. Retrieved October 2, 2020, from www.scaledagileframework.com.

Schwenke, Th. (2020). *Neu ab 2020: California consumer privacy act (CCPA) – Neue Pflichten neben der DSGVO?* Retrieved November 2, 2020, from https://datenschutz-generator.de/california-consumer-privacy-act-ccpa-dsgvo/.

Seiler, E., & Jenkins, J.H. (2014). *Frequently asked questions about Isaac Asimov*. Retrieved October 18, 2020, from http://www.asimovonline.com/asimov_FAQ.html#starters2.

Sipilä, J. (2020). *Patients in Finland blackmailed after therapy records were stolen by hackers*. Retrieved October 28, 2020, from https://edition.cnn.com/2020/10/27/tech/finland-therapy-patients-blackmailed-data-breach-intl/index.html.

Spektrum. (2015). *Digitale Demokratie statt Datendiktatur*. Retrieved October 18, 2019, from https://www.spektrum.de/news/wie-algorithmen-und-big-data-unsere-zukunft-bestimmen/1375933.

UN. (1948). *Universal declaration of human rights*. Retrieved August 10, 2020, from https://www.un.org/en/universal-declaration-human-rights/index.html.

UN NPT. (1995). *Treaty on the Non-proliferation of Nuclear Weapons (NPT)*. Retrieved August 2, 2020, from https://www.un.org/disarmament/wmd/nuclear/npt/.

Vieweg, S. (2019). Nachhaltige und effiziente Unternehmensführung durch „Candorship" und „Lean-agile" Organisationsausrichtung. In: Groß, M., Müller-Wiegand, M. Pinnow, D.F. Zukunftsfähige Unternehmensführung. Berlin: SpringerGabler

Welt. (2020). *Google kauft Fitness-Firma Fitbit für zwei Milliarden Dollar*. Retrieved November 2, 2020, from https://www.welt.de/newsticker/dpa_nt/infoline_nt/netzwelt/article202830702/Google-kauft-Fitness-Firma-Fitbit-fuer-zwei-Milliarden-Dollar.html.

Wolford, B. (2020). *What are the GDPR fines?* Retrieved November 2, 2020, from https://gdpr.eu/fines/.

Index

A
AI Now Institute, 232
AI social linked environmental assessment (AISLE), 241
Alexa, 118
Algorithmic decision systems (ADS), 125
Alpha GO, 119
Amoral, 172
Amwell, 244
Analytical hierarchy process (AHP), 85
Artificial general intelligence (AGI), 235
Artificial intelligence (AI), vii, 166
Artificial neural networks (ANN), 84, 200
Ascension, 244
Ashby's Law, 82
Asset managers, 48
Asset owners, 48
Auditing dilemma, 57

B
Back-door attack, 235
Base rate fallacy, 28
BDSG, 228
Benevolent Dictators for Life (BDFL), 242
Big Tech, 9, 69, 236, 245
Bitbucket, 127
Black box, 230
Blockchain technologies (BCT), 107
Boot.AI, 177
Brexit, 62
Brute-force-attacks, 113

C
CAGR, 135
California Consumer Privacy Act (CCPA), 9, 152
Candorship, 238
Capital Asset Pricing Models (CAPM), 24
CCTV, 120, 150
CEDAW, 58
Chapter 11 US Bankruptcy Code, 98
Children's rights convention (CRC), 58
Clearing house, 108
Code of conduct, 230
Cognitive biases, 27–30
Collingridge dilemma, 242
Common good is overexploited, 16
Confirmation bias, 27
Convention against Bribery of Foreign Public Officials, 64
Convention against Torture (CAT), 58
Convivialism, 81
Corona, 3
Correlation, 132
Corruption Perception Index (CPI), 63
Counterfactual explanations, 170
COVID-19, 3
CPED, 58, 59
Cryptographic hash functions (CHF), 108
CSR, 57
Curiosity networks, 204

D
DARPA, 170
Data-driven AI, 179
Data-poisoning, 234
Decentralized Autonomous Organization (DAO), 113
Deep learning (DL), vii, 134
Descriptive ethics, 11
Desiderata, 26
Digital trio, 95
Digitization, 102

Discourse ethics, 17
Disfake, 153, 240
Disruption effects, 97
Distributed ledger technology (DLT), 108, 165
DSGVO, 213
Dynamic capability theory, 217
Dynexity, 102

E
Egocentric bias, 27
eIDAS, 9
Electronic person, 229
Elon Musk, 235
Empathy, 181
Environmental, social, and governance (ESG),
       48
e-person, 229, 240, 243
EU, 229
Explainability, 170
Extrinsic, 35

F
Facial detection, 118, 119
Facial recognition, vii
Factorization, 117
False positive, 28
51% attack, 165
51%-rule, 112
First out-mover, 96
Fitbit, 244
Fragile State Index (FSI), 59
Fridays for Future, 162
Fudge factor, 30
Function as a Service (FaaS), 235
The Fund for Peace, 59
FüPoG, 10

G
GAFA, 32
Gecko.AI, 153
General Data Protection Regulation (GDPR), 9,
       213, 230
Github, 127, 165, 242
GLOBE study, 4
Google, 123, 244
Google AI, 119
Google AI Quantum, 116
Google, Apple, Facebook, Amazon, and
       Microsoft (GAFAM), 9, 121
Google Home, 118
Gordon Gekko, 172

Great Place To Work®, 50
Green Deal, 184
Group-think, 30
Guanxi, 147

H
Halo, 29
Harvard approach, 17
Hash, 111
Hedonistic utilitarianism, 12
HFT, 167
HireVue, 153
Homo oeconomicus, 23, 172
House of Ethical AI, 236
Human intelligence (H-I), 166

I
ICRMW, 58
ICRPD, 58
Impact investment, 48
Inclusive capitalism, 32
Individual core process, 98
Industry 4.0, 102
Initiative New Quality of Work, 88
Innovator's dilemma, 96
Interference, 115
International Atomic Energy Agency (IAEA),
       243
International Convention on the Elimination of
       All Forms of Racial Discrimination
       (ICERD), 58
International Covenant on Civil and Political
       Rights (ICCPR), 57
International Covenant on Economic, Social
       and Cultural Rights (ICESCR), 58
International Monetary Fund (IMF), 63
Internet of Things (IoT), 102
Invisible hand, 31, 69

K
Kaggle, 127, 164, 242
Kaizen, 228
Keras, 128
Kernel, 242
Knowledge panels, 246

L
Labor lease, 47, 48
Lean-agile, 239
Legacy portfolio theory, 172

Life cycle assessment (LCA), 29, 241
Linus Thorvald, 242
Linux, 242

M
Management-by-objective (MBO), 67
Megvii, 119
Merkle root, 111
Mining, 111
Mining clouds, 113
Modern portfolio theory, 172
Monological ethics, 16
Mya, 153

N
Natural language processing (NLP), 107
New Silk Route, 119, 151
Next Society, 78
Noblesse oblige, 65
Nodes, 111
Nonce, 111
Non-Proliferation Treaty (NPT), 243
Normative corporate governance, 50
Normative ethics, 11

O
Obesity, 43
Objectives-key-results (OKR), 67
OECD's outlook on the future of work, 103
Offshorability, 145
OpenAI, 235
Optical character recognition (OCR), 107
Organic meat, 41, 42
Orphan Block, 111
Overconfidence Bias, 27

P
Parity point, 99
Party of trust, 108
Pattern recognition, vii
PDF, 118
Perception threshold, 97
Porter's five forces, 102
Preferential utilitarianism, 12
Prisoners dilemma, 14
Problem of many hands, 172
Process-driven, 179
Professional employer organization (PEO), 48
Project Nightingale, 244
Public key cryptography (PKC), 116

Public key infrastructure (PKI), 116
Pytorch, 128

Q
Quantum computing, 115
Qubits, 115

R
Raison d'être, 50
Realtime, 108
Re-educational camps, 121
Responsible Minerals Initiative (RMI), 72
Risk management approach, 229
Robo advisors, 165
RoboLaw, 227–230
Robot Process Automation (RPA), 104
RSA, 117
Rubicon, 5

S
SAFe®, 239
SAI SA8000, 42
SARS-CoV-2, 3
Search engine optimization (SEO), 57
Semantic Knowledge Nets, 203
Servant leadership, 239
SHA, 109
Shareholder Value, 33
Share of wallet, 44
Sharp Eyes, 121, 150
Siri, 118
Social core process, 98
Social credit, 120
Social media, 123
SpaceX, 235
Speech recognition, vii
Spiral Dynamics, 78, 79
Stakeholders, 39
State of the Art (SOTA), 238
Stewardship, 35
Strawmen, 68
Strong AI, vii, 13, 126
Supercomputer, 114
Sustainable Development Goals (SDG), 183
Syntegration, 86

T
Task core process, 98
Task technology fit theory, 194
Technology acceptance model (TAM), 211

Telematics, 244
Telemedicine, 244
Tensorflow, 128
Tesla, 235
Text mining, 206
Text recognition, vii
Three Laws of Robotics, 164
Tobin's Q, 51
Tragedy of the Commons, 16, 61–62, 186
Triage, 13
Trolley problem, 12, 228
Trust center, 108
T-shaped skills, 166
TÜV Süd, 57

U
Uber, 229
UN Declaration of Human Rights, 57–59, 237
Unicorn, 119
United Nations Convention against Corruption
    (UNCAC), 64
Universal Declaration of Human Rights, 6
Utilitarianism, 12

V
Vale, 57
Value Memes, 78
Vastaamo, 245
Vector space model, 206
Veggie, 5
Veil of ignorance, 18
Volatility, uncertainty, complexity, and
    ambiguity (VUCA), 163

W
Weak AI, vii, 126, 185
Whistle blowing, 46
Wisdom 2.0, 81
World Health Organization (WHO), 63

X
XaaS, 104
XAI, 170
Xingjiang, 121